FOUR MINOR PROPHETS

Obadiah, Jonah,
Habakkuk, and Haggai

Their Message for Today

By
FRANK E. GAEBELEIN

MOODY PRESS

CHICAGO

PREFACE

THIS VOLUME grew out of expository addresses given in churches
and at conferences in various parts of the United States, in
Canada, and also in Germany. The expositions first appeared in
the magazine *Our Hope*, and those on Obadiah and Jonah were
published by Our Hope Press under the title *The Servant and
the Dove*.

I am grateful to Moody Press for bringing together in book
form these four studies, now extensively revised and entitled
Four Minor Prophets: Their Message for Today. Such they are—
Obadiah with his message of judgment, Jonah with his dramatic
story, Habakkuk with his insight into the problem of evil, Haggai
with his stirring exhortations to do God's work. In preparing this
book for publication, I have done much rewriting and added
considerable new material.

No author can write without reflecting his convictions. But
convictions do not absolve him from the responsibility of ac-
quaintance with both sides of disputed points. I am committed
to the complete integrity of the Scriptures, yet I trust I have
been fair to those who hold a different view of them. While I
have discussed important historical and linguistic questions, this
book is not a technical commentary. My main purpose is rather
to bring to today's readers the messages of these four remarkable
prophets and to show their unfading relevance. This aim has led
me to explore the devotional and practical truth which characterizes them and indeed all those prophetic books which, called
by the ancient Jews "The Book of the Twelve," are minor only in
length.

The Old Testament prophets were as much forthtellers of God's message for their own times as they were foretellers of the future. Their mission as forthtellers—preachers of the Word of the living God with its continuing claim upon us all—is an enduring one. Those who center their attention chiefly upon the predictive aspect of prophecy are therefore shutting their eyes to some of Scripture's most searching teaching. A major element in the minor prophets is the lode of godly social concern that runs through their pages and gives them such vivid pertinence to our day. Because for most church members and Bible readers these books remain terra incognita, the ministry of many a pastor would be enriched by preaching from them.

For the help received from the many works consulted I make grateful acknowledgment. I am indebted to Charles Lee Feinberg, Ph. D., Th.D., and Alan A. MacRae, Ph.D., for their advice regarding certain linguistic and archeological details. Both Peter F. Gunther, director of Moody Press, and Charles W. McKinney, formerly its editor-in-chief, gave me much encouragement in the completion of this book. To Wilbur M. Smith, D.D., my thanks are due for sharing some resources of his remarkable library. Finally, I express my appreciation to Mary J. Faircloth, manuscript editor of Moody Press, for all her help in preparing these studies for publication.

FRANK E. GAEBELEIN

CONTENTS

7

HAGGAI

THE PROPHECY OF
OBADIAH

INTRODUCTION

A BRIEF BOOK

The prophecy of Obadiah is the shortest book in the Old Testament. This distinction tends to obscure its value, for many a reader has almost unconsciously inferred that such a tiny prophecy must be unimportant. Consider, for example, these words of a seminary professor: "Brevity is not always the soul of wit, for Obadiah was the briefest of prophets, yet he uttered no sentence which is cherished."* But the folly of such an estimate is plain. Since when has brevity been synonymous with insignificance? Brief messages may sometimes be exceptionally important, as in the case of telegrams or military orders. When vital issues are at stake, words are not wasted.

Moreover, Obadiah is in the Bible. And, as the apostle Paul said, "All scripture is given by inspiration of God, and is profitable for doctrine, for reproof, for correction, for instruction in righteousness: that the man of God may be perfect, throughly furnished unto all good works" (2 Ti 3:16-17). Obadiah is in the Scriptures; its canonicity is unquestionable. Obscure though it is, this little book is "profitable" for certain definite reasons. It is not our part to criticize its brevity or, because of its small compass, to ignore its message. Ours is rather the obligation to search this page of prophecy with a readiness to receive the message it has for us.

*Charles Allen Dinsmore, *The English Bible as Literature*, p. 236. Better is the comment of Isidore: "Among all the prophets, he [Obadiah] is the briefest in number of words; in the grace of mysteries he is their equal" (cited in E. B. Pusey, *The Minor Prophets*, 1:351).

AUTHORSHIP

If the book Obadiah wrote is brief, our knowledge of its
author is even slighter. The Old Testament mentions no fewer
than twelve other men bearing the same name as the prophet.
Indeed, Obadiah was a name common in ancient Israel. None of
these twelve, however, is to be identified with the writer of the
prophecy. The fact is that we know nothing of this prophet
beyond the meaning of his name, which is "servant of Jehovah."
Yet the prophet's obscurity is not without significance. For if a
man is to be remembered for one thing only, what more worthy
ground of remembrance can there be than that he was a servant
of the Lord?

Beginning with Eichhorn in 1824, various critical scholars
(among them Ewald, Wellhausen, Marti, Cornill, and Bewer)
have held that the twenty-one verses of Obadiah are of composite authorship. Indeed, Bewer divided the book among four
different writers living at different times. Such theories, however, are largely conjectural and fall short of certainty. It is better
to accept the book at its face value as a unity consistent with its
highly concentrated message.

THE DATE

From these matters we turn to another introductory consideration, that of the date of the book. There is wide disagreement
regarding the time when it was written. Some scholars date the
book as early as c. 850 B.C.; many place it just after the fall of
Jerusalem in 587 B.C.; and still others date it as late as 312 B.C.
The evidence is such as to rule out anything like a dogmatic
conclusion. As Archer says, "This shortest book in the Old Testament ... bears the distinction of being the most difficult of all
prophets to date."[1]

How the book is dated is linked to the identification of the
situation described in verses 10-14. Obadiah has one main
theme—denunciation of Edom, the country of the descendants
of Esau. In verses 1-9 he tells in vivid words what will happen to
Edom; in 10-14 he explains just why this judgment is coming; in
the closing passage (15-21) he looks forward to continuing retribution upon Edom and to the restoration of Israel in the future

kingdom. Now of these three sections, it is upon the interpretation of the middle one that the dating of the book chiefly hinges. For these verses (10-14) are a circumstantial description of a calamity that befell Jerusalem and in which the Edomites had a part.

History records four occasions in Old Testament times† when Jerusalem was invaded. Of these, two best meet the conditions of Obadiah 10-14. They are the sack of Jerusalem in the reign of Jehoram, and its capture by the Chaldeans in 587 B.C. The capture of Jerusalem by the Chaldeans—a calamity in which the Edomites rejoiced and cooperated with enemies of the Jews (Eze 35:1-15; Ps 137:7)—most nearly fits the picture, though there are scholars who claim that the earlier invasion in the time of Jehoram accords best with the requirements. Variance in identifying the events described in verses 10-14 is not a matter of liberal versus conservative scholarship. Recently *The New Scofield Reference Bible*, J. A. Thompson (in *The New Bible Dictionary*), G. H. Livingston (in *The Wycliffe Bible Commentary*), and C. L. Feinberg (in *The Major Messages of the Minor Prophets, Joel, Amos, and Obadiah*) have taken the reference to be to the fall of Jerusalem in 587 B.C. But G. L. Archer, Jr. (*A Survey of Old Testament Introduction*), H. E. Freeman (in *An Introduction to the Old Testament Prophets*), and M. F. Unger (in *Unger's Bible Dictionary*) identify 10-14 with the invasion of Jerusalem in Jehoram's reign, while A. B. Fowler (in *The Zondervan Pictorial Bible Dictionary*) refers them to the time of Ahaz (2 Ch 28:16-18).

Now suppose that the Chaldean invasion of 587 B.C. is identified with verses 10-14 and the book is dated shortly after that time, say, in 585, or even much later. Then a linguistic problem must be faced. For while the King James Version and Revised

---

†(1) 1 Ki 14:25-26 and 2 Ch 12:1-12 (the capture by Shishak, king of Egypt); (2) 2 Ch 21:16-17 (the sack of the city by the Philistines and Arabians in the reign of Jehoram); (3) 2 Ki 14:8-14 and 2 Ch 25:17-24 (Amaziah's defeat by Jehoash and the subsequent overthrow of the city wall); (4) 2 Ki 25 (the capture of Jerusalem by the Chaldeans in 587 B.C.). To these may be added 2 Ch 28:16-18, if one assumes that "had smitten Judah and carried away captives" necessitates the invasion of Jerusalem (cf. *Zondervan Pictorial Bible Dictionary*, s.v. "Obadiah").

Standard Version translate the main verbs in 12-14 as past
("thou shouldest not have looked . . . : neither shouldest thou
have rejoiced," etc., KJV; "you should not have gloated . . . ; you
should not have rejoiced," etc., RSV), in point of fact these verbs
are really imperatives and may well have a future reference.
Thus the American Standard Version and the Jerusalem Bible
render them as imperatives ("look not . . . rejoice not," etc.,
ASV; "do not gloat. . . . Do not exult," etc., Jer. Bible). It is
evident, therefore, that to date the book after the fall of Jerusalem
to the Chaldeans entails turning what seems actually to be a
prediction of the future into a picture of an event already past.
But, as Robinson says, "there is slight ground for thinking that
the prophet while predicting the future is really describing the
past, or that he speaks of what the Edomites had actually done
as of what they ought not to do!"[2]

On the other hand, it must be acknowledged that, although a
case may be made for identifying the situation described in
Obadiah 10-14 with the events of 2 Chronicles 21:16-17 taken
with verses 8-10 of this chapter, the evidence‡ here seems rather
scanty compared with that of the Chaldeans' capture of Jerusalem and the Edomites' action at that time.

Several other factors should also be considered. They are: (1)
the place of the book among the minor prophets, (2) its relation
to Jeremiah, and (3) its relation to Joel and Amos. In regard to
the position of the book, it is a fact that in the Hebrew canon
Obadiah stands fourth among the minor prophets, showing that
he was regarded as early.

The relation between Obadiah and Jeremiah 49:7-22 is of
particular interest. One has only to compare the two to see their
similarity. While Bewer and others have postulated an older

---

‡"Moreover, the Lᴏʀᴅ stirred up against Jehoram the spirit of the
Philistines, and of the Arabians, that were near the Ethiopians: and they
came up into Judah, and brake into it, and carried away all the substance
that was found in the king's house, and his sons also, and his wives; so that
there was never a son left him, save Jehoahaz, the youngest of his sons"
(2 Ch 21:16-17). "In his [Jehoram's] days the Edomites revolted from
under the dominion of Judah, and made themselves a king. Then Jehoram
went forth . . . and smote the Edomites. . . . So the Edomites revolted
from under the hand of Judah unto this day" (2 Ch 21:8-10).

source on which both Obadiah and Jeremiah drew, many scholars have argued for the priority of Obadiah (e.g., Caspari, Orelli, G. A. Smith, Sampey). But if Jeremiah used material from Obadiah, this rules out a late date for the book, because Jeremiah 49:7-22 apparently antedates Nebuchadnezzar's capture of Jerusalem.

Again, there are similarities § between Obadiah and Joel (dated by many c. 830 B.C.). If Joel drew upon Obadiah, as Orelli declares,|| then it would follow that Amos also did so and that Obadiah might be the earliest of the writing prophets.

Sampey sums up the problem of the date of Obadiah in these words: "Our choice must be between a very early date (c. 845) and a date shortly after 587, with the scales almost evenly balanced."[3] Here the *almost* is significant, for it would seem that, despite strong reasons for a date shortly after 587, the scales may dip slightly toward the earlier date. Prophecies may have more than one fulfillment. And may it not be that Obadiah 10-14, while initially applying to the events of 2 Chronicles 21:16-17, 8-10, had their fuller and final fulfillment in the Chaldeans' capture of Jerusalem? Because the evidence rules out a dogmatic conclusion, let us leave the discussion of the problem of dating Obadiah's book on this questioning note.

THE FORM OF THE BOOK

The extreme brevity of the book is the key to an understanding of its form. Here is a prophet who has an overmastering concern. And he voices it with tremendous emphasis. Judgment on Edom is his theme. "Is not my word like as a fire? saith the LORD; and like a hammer that breaketh the rock in pieces?" (Jer

---

§ E.g., Ob 10—Joel 3:19; Ob 11—Joel 3.3; Ob 15—Joel 1:15; 2:1; 3:4, 7, 14; Ob 18—Joel 3:8. Significant is Joel 2:32, an apparent quotation of Ob 17 (cf. *New Bible Dictionary,* s.v. "Obadiah, Book Of"). Cf. also Ob 14—Amos 9:2; Ob 9-10, 18—Amos 1:11-12; Ob 14—Amos 1:6, 9; Ob 19—Amos 9:12; Ob 20—Amos 9:14 (cf. *Unger's Bible Dictionary,* s.v. "Obadiah, Book Of").

|| "Obadiah's oracle is plainly somewhat older than Joel's prophecies . . . and Obadiah's saying, v. 17, is expressly cited . . . [in Joel 2:32]" (H. K. von Orelli, *The Twelve Minor Prophets,* p. 158).

23:29). This is an apt description of Obadiah's few verses, which fall on the ear like a hammer beating out the strokes of God's fiery judgment upon Edom. R. G. Moulton classifies the book as "a Divine speech of doom,"[4] an apt designation. Others have thought of it as a tract against the sin of pride. Certainly its dimensions are those of a tract, and it has something of the pungent directness needed for this kind of writing. One of the best characterizations of this little book as a whole is that of Hugo of St. Victor:

"Obadiah is simple in language, manifold in meaning; few in words, abundant in thoughts, according to that 'the wise man is known by the fewness of his words.' He directeth his prophecy, according to the letter, against Edom; allegorically he inveighs against the world; morally against the flesh. Bearing an image of the Saviour, he hinteth at His coming through whom the world is destroyed, through whom the flesh is subdued, through whom freedom is restored."[5]

THE OUTLINE OF THE BOOK

In the case of a prophecy of such extreme brevity as Obadiah, analysis by outline presents few problems. Of course, interpreters may differ in details, but the main divisions are plain. First of all, we have nine verses of predicted doom (vv. 1-9). Here Obadiah foresees with startling vividness the judgment to come upon Edom. Next is the section consisting of verses 10-14. In the logic of the book these are explanatory; they set forth clear reasons for the doom which Obadiah denounced against Edom and which history substantiates as having fallen upon that wicked people. Finally, there are the concluding seven verses (15-21). These are future in their main import, looking forward even beyond our own times. In them Obadiah's message broadens to embrace one of the great recurrent themes of Old Testament prophecy, the Day of the Lord. Consistently with his single subject he mentions Edom in this coming day; but he also goes beyond Edom, as he envisions the future Messianic kingdom.

On the basis of the foregoing, we may therefore outline the book in this way:

I. Judgment on Edom predicted (1-9)
II. Why Edom was doomed (10-14)
III. The day of the Lord and the coming kingdom (15-21)
    1. The day itself and Edom in that day (15-16)
    2. The kingdom: The restoration of Israel; final judgment on Edom in the time of the kingdom (17-21)

1

JUDGMENT ON EDOM

JUDGMENT ON EDOM PREDICTED (1-9)

The vision of Obadiah. Thus saith the Lord GOD concerning Edom: We have heard a rumour from the LORD, and an ambassador is sent among the [nations], Arise ye, and let us rise up against her in battle (Ob 1).

With no introduction beyond the four terse words "The vision of Obadiah," the prophet plunges into his message, leaving no doubt about the origin of his vision. The man of God who called himself "the servant of Jehovah" does not hesitate to put at the very threshold of his book the authoritative declaration "Thus saith the Lord GOD concerning Edom." This express statement of divine authority is familiar to every reader of the Bible. It has been estimated that such phrases as "thus saith the Lord," "the Lord spoke," "the word of the Lord came" occur about 2,400 times in the Old Testament, and we find them about 1,300 times in the prophetic books alone. Their multiplicity constitutes one of the strong internal evidences for the divine authority of Scripture. For this statement of Obadiah that his words are really the words of the Lord God is either true or false. But if it, together with the hosts of companion declarations, is false, then the veracity of the Bible is indeed impugned. And yet it will be generally admitted that Scripture is the source of our highest ideals of truth and justice. A strange paradox! The difficulty, however, is removed by accepting the prophet's "Thus saith the Lord GOD" at its face value.

Having authenticated his message, Obadiah loses no time in stating the subject of his prophecy. "The Lord GOD," he says, is speaking "concerning Edom." And in fact his book centers upon the ways and destiny of Edom. But who is Edom? Genesis 36:1 gives us the answer. There we read this title over the ninth of the ten "generations" in Genesis: "Now these are the generations of Easu, who is Edom." Edom, then, is another name for Jacob's older twin, Esau. In the Old Testament Edom also signifies the nation that sprang from Esau. Its usage in this respect is much like that of Jacob's other name, Israel. The word *Edom* means "red," and perhaps comes from the color of his skin at birth, or from the color of the lentil pottage for which Esau sold his birthright to his younger brother, or from the red sandstone cliffs of the country of Edom.

The remainder of this opening verse is full of action, as Obadiah begins to picture the coming doom of the Edomites. Using the editorial "we," doubtless with the implication of God's people speaking, he visualizes tidings dispatched from the Lord and passed to and fro among the nations. (The word *heathen* is used in the King James Version, but here and elsewhere it should generally be rendered "nations.") These tidings are of a strongly inflammatory nature. "Arise ye," the ambassador calls out. "Let us rise up against her [Edom] in battle."

> Behold, I have made thee small among the [nations]: thou art greatly despised. The pride of thine heart hath deceived thee, thou that dwellest in the clefts of the rock, whose habitation is high; that saith in his heart, Who shall bring me down to the ground? (Ob 2-3).

Hard upon this call to action, the Lord begins to speak through Obadiah to the descendants of Esau. In view of what is to follow, it is significant that the divine finger points first to the comparative insignificance of Edom, who, though warlike and powerful, never had a great empire. But more than this is implied, because behind the reference there certainly hovers the whole story of the Edomites' progressive decline under the heavy judgments of the God of Israel, whom they so grossly flouted.

At the third verse we must pause to sketch in some geographical and historical background. After the break with Jacob, the Edomites settled in the region south of the Dead Sea, known in

the Old Testament as Mount Seir. The precise boundaries of
their land are obscure, but in Obadiah's time it was probably not
more than about one hundred by twenty miles in extent. In the
days of the prophets, such as Isaiah, the name "Bozrah" (Is 63:1)
is found in connection with Edom. Bozrah was the most
northern of the cities of Edom. However, it is another place,
Sela, for which Edom is unique among ancient kingdoms.

"Thou that dwellest in the cleft of the rock." The Hebrew word
here translated "rock" is *sela,* the allusion undoubtedly being to
the stronghold of the Edomites at the time of Obadiah. Later on,
when the country was taken over by the Nabateans, Sela was
called Petra, which is the Greek equivalent for "rock."

Probably no city of the ancient world is more shrouded in
mysterious fascination than Petra. Widely known in ancient times,
it was utterly lost to civilization for a period of a thousand years.
The story of its recovery reads like the pages of a romance. In
1812 the Swiss explorer Johann Ludwig Burkhardt discovered it
through a ruse. Knowing that the Arabs of the region would
never allow him to enter the city, he claimed to have vowed the
slaughter of a goat to Aaron. As the traditional tomb of Aaron is
upon a mountaintop near Petra, the Arab guide dared make no
reply to the explorer's strategem, fearing by opposition to incur
the wrath of the first of the high priests.*

It was indeed a marvelous scene that greeted Burkhardt as he
left the winding canyon which affords entrance to the forgotten
metropolis, described in John William Burgon's poem as "a
rose-red city, half as old as time." This canyon, or *siq,* as it is
called by the Arabs, is one of the most remarkable gorges in all
the world. Winding between towering rock walls, gorgeous in
their rainbow tints, it is in some places as narrow as twelve feet
and in no place really wide. A small stream flows along its floor
and, as the traveler proceeds along its labyrinthine turns, he sees
under his feet remnants of the ancient paving; while, looking
up at the walls, he may discern traces of the aqueduct by which

---

* See G. L. Robinson, *The Sarcophagus of an Ancient Civilization,* p. 445.
This definitive work is the source of our description of Petra. Also in
Doughty's classic *Travels in Arabia Deserta* there is an account of a visit
to Petra, pp. 39-44.

the inhabitants piped water into the city. So tortuous is this defile of over a mile in extent that authorities say it could have been defended by twelve men against a whole army.

The view that bursts upon the traveler as he emerges from the *siq* is amazing. For one of the strangest buildings of antiquity meets the eye. There, hewn from the rock, is the tremendous facade of a great temple. In classic proportion, column stands upon column, surmounted by cornices, topped with urns, the whole structure towering one hundred thirty feet high. In its desolate setting amid the splendor of the rosy rock, this mysterious building, known as Al-Khazneh, is one of the wonders of archeology.

But Al-Khazneh is not all of Petra. In a setting a mile long and three-quarters of a mile wide, surrounded by the barren mountains in their vivid coloring, is a profusion of ruins, temples, and tombs, cut, many of them, from the rock.†

There are also the remnants of the great theater carved out of stone and seating in tiers some three thousand spectators. On the surrounding peaks are clearly discernible the ancient "high places," where the vile worship of the Edomites was carried on. Such is Sela, or Petra, today. No one lives there. Silent and forlorn it stands in awful desolation.

Read against this background, the third verse of the prophecy comes alive for the modern reader. "The pride of thine heart hath deceived thee." We should mark well that word *pride*; it is the key to the moral and spiritual message of Obadiah. Later we shall be referring to it in more detail.

"Thou that dwellest in the clefts of the rock." That is exactly what the Edomites did. In fact there is evidence that the earlier inhabitants of Sela were cave dwellers, living in holes in the cliffs. The site abounds in natural caves, of which no less than sixty have been found. No wonder that Obadiah says of this nation, "Whose habitation is high"! No wonder that Edom is reported as saying, "Who shall bring me down to the ground?"

---

†To be sure, most of the temples of Petra were constructed in Roman times after the days of Obadiah. Nevertheless, they point back to this strange city in the prophet's day.

> Though thou exalt thyself as the eagle, and though thou set
> thy nest among the stars, thence will I bring thee down, saith
> the LORD (Ob 4).

Humanly speaking, the Edomites could hardly have had a
more impregnable center for their nation. But they forgot one of
the attributes of the Lord. For did not David say of Him, "If I
ascend up into heaven, thou art there: if I make my bed in hell,
behold, thou art there" (Ps 139:8)? Therefore, the Lord, who
made the cliffs and mountains, denounces their fancied security.
The words "though thou exalt thyself as the eagle" are significant. The eagle is an ancient symbol of deity. Moreover, we
have reason to believe that one of the items of the corrupt
religion of the Edomites was the deification of Esau. Truly, the
Lord was against this people and, as history records, they were
debased from their nest among the stars.

> If thieves came to thee, if robbers by night, (how art thou
> cut off!) would they not have stolen till they had enough? if the
> grape gatherers came to thee, would they not leave some grapes?
> (Ob 5)

Here the prophet is using a striking figure of the completeness
of Edom's doom. He compares the future judgment of this wicked people with the nocturnal descent of robbers upon a
vineyard. Such thieves, he is saying, would finally cease from
their stealing without taking every single grape. At least something would be left. But—the implication is—when the judgment of Jehovah falls upon Edom, there will be a clean sweep.
Nothing will remain; everything will be gone.

> How are the things of Esau searched out! how are his hidden
> things sought up! (Ob 6).

As the fourth verse implies the omnipresence of God, so this
verse points to His omniscience. To use one of the very words that
it contains, it confronts us with a searching thought. The God who
was about to punish Edom is not only ever present but also
all-seeing. He can look into the inner recesses of the human
heart. He knows all the dark places of national as well as individual life.

In his book *Christ in the Communist Prisons,* Richard
Wurmbrand tells of one of the many ways in which he was worn
down while he was imprisoned in Romania. "The beds were
removed from the cell and I had barely an hour's sleep at night,
balanced on a chair. Twice every minute the spy hole in the
door gave a metallic click and the eye of a guard appeared.
Often when I dozed he came in and kicked me awake."[1] That
constant surveillance must have been very hard to endure. But in
all spiritual reality the unseen eye of the living God is ever upon
us all. For the unrepentant sinner that divine gaze points to
judgment. In Romans 2:16 Paul speaks of "the day when God
shall judge the secrets of men by Jesus Christ according to my
gospel." For the believer, however, it is different. God is ever
beholding those who are in Christ. But His eye is upon them for
good. His omniscient gaze follows us in tender love. As David
beautifully puts it, the Lord is saying of His own, "I will counsel
you with my eye upon you" (Ps 32:8, RSV).

> All the men of thy confederacy have brought thee even to the
> border: the men that were at peace with thee have deceived
> thee, and prevailed against thee; they that eat thy bread have
> laid a wound under thee: there is none understanding in him
> (Ob 7).

At this point in his prophecy Obadiah refers to the foreign
policy of Edom. The picture is that of emissaries going out from
the Edomites to their allies ("the men of thy confederacy"). The
emissaries have been received courteously and, according to
Oriental custom, have been escorted back to the border of
Edom. But behind this outward amity ruin is lurking, because
the nations at peace with the Edomites are to rise up against
them. Those who have been their friends and have shared their
hospitality will betray them. The prediction means that God will
use the international policies of Edom to bring about its destruction. It all sounds up to date! Echoing through the words of the
ancient prophet, we hear the lesson that statesmanship apart
from God is futile. More than that, it is positively dangerous.
Neither appeasement of a potential enemy nor great armaments
can bring lasting security. The suspicion and tension engendered

among the nations by the possession of nuclear weapons show that security does not lie in force alone. Only God is to be fully trusted.

> Shall I not in that day, saith the LORD, even destroy the wise men out of Edom, and understanding out of the mount of Esau? (Ob 8).

It is significant that the Edomites were proverbial for their wisdom. Indeed, there are some scholars who think that the book of Job came out of an Edomite background.[2] Whether or not they are right, it is interesting that the mention of Teman in the next verse of Obadiah's prophecy suggests the book of Job, for we recall that one of Job's comforters was Eliphaz, the Temanite.

There are, however, several other features of this verse that deserve comment. Among them is the shift of outlook. Thus far the prophet has been viewing the doom of Edom as an accomplished fact. That it is, however, in actuality still distant is shown by the forward look in this verse and in 9 and 10 as indeed in 15-21. It would almost seem that the prophet's vision has been so alive to his own mind as to lead him to describe the future as past history. We may also observe in passing the distinctive expression translated in this eighth verse by "saith the LORD." Scholars tell us that the Hebrew refers to "the solemn utterance of Jehovah."[3] The connotation implies the idea of judgment.

But let us look from these details to the plain lesson of this verse. Just as the foreign policy of Edom is to work against them, so their wisdom, however famed among the nations of antiquity, will prove of no avail against God's judgments. One would be foolish to scorn the intellectual powers God confers upon man. But human reason can never be a substitute for divine leading. Moreover, pride of intellect is one of the great snares of the soul. The individual or nation that finds in its own wisdom all that is necessary for guidance in life is on the sure path to ruin.

> And thy mighty men, O Teman, shall be dismayed, to the end

that every one of the mount of Esau may be cut off by slaughter (Ob 9).

Looking forward once more, Obadiah brings his first pronouncement of doom to an awful close. Teman, to whom we have already alluded in commenting on the preceding verse, was the grandson of Esau (Gen 36:10-11). Here he is used synonymously with Edom. But notice the completeness of the prophesied destruction of the Edomites. Already it has been hinted at in the vivid figure of the thieves and grapegatherers of verse 5. Now for the first, but not the last, time in Obadiah's prophecy it is clearly stated.

As we leave this first section of the book, it is worthy of comment that there is no reference in Obadiah, or, for that matter, anywhere else in the Bible to the religion of the Edomites. That they had a religion is certain from archeological investigation. In fact, the names of certain of their gods are known. Among these are "Kaush," "Hadad," "Ai," and, very significantly, "Edom" and "Esau." It is possible that the earlier descendants of Esau worshiped Jehovah but soon fell back into idolatry. The region of Petra contains a number of "high places" which show traces of having been used for idolatrous worship of a debased order. A heathen feast survived at Mamre, near Hebron, until the time of Constantine, who suppressed it because of its unspeakable vileness.[4] When one reflects upon the privileges of the Edomites, all this is indescribably sad. They were a people sprung directly from one of the patriarchs. They could have adhered to the true worship of Jehovah. Instead they went far beyond their Israelitish brethren in succumbing to the lure of idolatry. And perhaps their crowning sin in this respect was the worship of their progenitor Esau as being himself a god.

2

WHY EDOM WAS DOOMED

REASONS FOR HER JUDGMENT (10-14)

There is a sense in which this little book is like a lawyer's brief. Judgment has been pronounced, doom predicted, and before he closes the prophet will return to still another forecast of punishment. But now he pauses to prove the case. In a remarkable passage, he reveals clearly and definitely the reasons for the complete destruction of the whole nation of Edom.

> For thy violence against thy brother Jacob shame shall cover thee, and thou shalt be cut off for ever (Ob 10).

The proof begins with a topic sentence in which Obadiah penetrates to the heart of Edom's sin in its manifestation as unbrotherliness. The Edomites are to be "cut off for ever." It is a drastic judgment, irrevocable in its consequences. As a matter of fact, the Bible does not contain many such dooms. What Obadiah predicts against Edom is akin in its completeness to the fate of Sodom and Gomorrah.

Now in order to understand the reason for this dreadful punishment, we need to look back into earlier Old Testament history. Every Bible student knows the story* of Jacob and Esau, the two sons of Isaac and Rebekah. It is a sordid tale of carnality and deceit, and it is difficult to commend Jacob's part in it. Yet with all his trickery Jacob had a consuming desire for spiritual blessing. He valued the birthright at its true worth. Esau, to whom it naturally belonged, was typical of the carnal man. He lived for the pleasure of the moment. And so, when he came in tired from the hunt and smelled the rich food his brother had

---

*Genesis 25:19-34; 27:1-46; 28:6-10; 33:1-17.

prepared, he unhesitatingly sold his birthright for the mess of pottage.

The story goes on to depict Esau's remorse and his belated appreciation of his heritage. But it is too late. The birthright is lost, never to be regained. After this, Esau leaves home and marries heathen wives. In a later scene Jacob, with his wives and children, must pass by Esau's territory. He makes elaborate preparations to be reconciled to his brother, and they meet with no outward clash. But the old grudge remained.

Years pass. Jacob's twelve sons have become a great nation, despite the centuries of servitude in Egypt. Delivered by the mighty hand of God through the passover and the destruction of Pharaoh's hosts in the Red Sea, they are on their way to the promised land. The twentieth chapter of Numbers shows them, at the close of their years of wandering, on the borders of Edom. Moses sends messengers from Kadesh to the king of Edom with this request: "Thus saith thy brother Israel, Thou knowest all the travail that hath befallen us." Here the message recounts the years of suffering in Egypt and God's deliverance, continuing as follows: "Let us pass, I pray thee, through thy country: we will not pass through the fields, or through the vineyards, neither will we drink of the water of the wells: we will go by the king's high way, we will not turn to the right hand nor to the left, until we have passed thy borders" (Num 20:14-17). The request is surely a reasonable one. Moreover, it is introduced by a reference to the brotherly relationship between Israel and Edom.

But what a reception it receives! "And Edom said unto him, Thou shalt not pass by me, lest I come out against thee with the sword" (Num 20:18). Again Moses pleads, saying, "We will go by the high way: and if I and my cattle drink of thy water, then I will pay for it: I will only, without doing anything else, go through on my feet" (v. 19). The plea could hardly have been more modest, nor could it very well have been phrased in more humble terms.

But the second request is answered even more callously than the first, for the passage in Numbers goes on to say of the king of Edom, "And he said, Thou shalt not go through." Not only that, but we read that these implacable enemies of Israel were resolved to enforce their prohibition, because the record says, "And Edom came out against him with much people, and a strong hand" (v. 20). The incident closes with this telling comment: "Thus Edom refused to give Israel passage through his border: wherefore Israel turned away from him" (v. 21).

From that day there continued to be bad blood between Israel and Edom. Under Saul (1 Sa 14:47), there was war between the two nations. This war was carried on by David, who slew a vast number of Edomites in the valley of salt (2 Sa 8:13-14; 1 Ch 18:11-13). For a period after this, Edom was under Israel, but at the time of Jehoram, the Edomites revolted. Though Jehoram defeated them, he was unable to stay their rebellion (2 Ki 8:20-22). A little later, when the Philistines and Arabians attacked Judah and took Jerusalem (2 Ch 21:16-17), the Edomites were there, exulting in the tribulation of their hard-pressed brethren.

> In the day that thou stoodest on the other side, in the day that the strangers carried away captive his forces, and foreigners entered into his gates, and cast lots upon Jerusalem, even thou wast as one of them (Ob 11).

The scene is probably the fall of Jerusalem under Nebuchadnezzar's invasion. Especially striking is the last clause, "even thou wast as one of them." It is almost as if one were to say of some Lebanese during the Árab-Israeli War of 1967 that, because he was standing by and rejoicing while the Jordanians were being driven from Jerusalem—Jordan, he was as one of the Israelis.

> But thou shouldest not have looked on the day of thy brother in the day that he became a stranger; neither shouldest thou have rejoiced over the children of Judah in the day of their destruction; neither shouldest thou have spoken proudly in the day of distress (Ob 12).

Here we revert to something already noted in our discussion of the date of the prophecy; this verse, together with 13 and 14, is not accurately translated in the King James and Revised Standard Versions. Instead of reading "Thou shouldest not have looked," "thou shouldest not have rejoiced," "thou shouldest not have entered," and so on, the verbs throughout should be in imperative: "Look not on the day of thy brother," "rejoice not," "enter not into," and so on. Linguistically the passage is looking *forward* rather than backward, as in the common English rendering. To be sure, many modern commentators choose to overlook this fact and insist that, although the prophet's words look forward, he is nevertheless describing a past event. However, there is excellent authority for taking the words at their face value. They are so interpreted, for example, by Dr. Pusey.[1]

One of the curious books in English literature is Robert Burton's† *Anatomy of Melancholy*. Few more fascinating volumes have ever been written than this book, in which the learned author discusses melancholy, conceived of as one of the four humors of medieval medicine. With amazing erudition, Burton anatomizes, or dissects, the melancholy temperament. Something similar is now packed by Obadiah into very few words. In verses 12-14 he has given us nothing less than the anatomy of a damning sin. Let us follow him step by step. "Look not," he begins, "on the day of thy brother in the day that he became a stranger." So the sin which crowned the hatred of Edom for Israel grew out of wrong looking. Like many another sin it was incited by the lust of the eyes. "Rejoice not over the children of Judah in the day of their destruction." The next step was for Edom to add malice to their transgression. Glorying in the downfall of another is bad enough, but when he is a brother, the evil becomes even darker. "Speak not proudly in the day of their distress." Here Edom proceeds to compound the crime with the root sin of pride, already alluded to in verse 3. The expression in the Hebrew text is vivid. It means "to make thy mouth great."[2] One can almost see the boaster with what men even today call a "big mouth," his lips parted in an evil grin and calling out insults.

> Thou shouldest not have entered into the gate of my people in the day of their calamity; yea, thou shouldest not have looked on their affliction in the day of their calamity, nor have laid hands on their substance in the day of their calamity (Ob 13).

---

†1577–1640.

"Enter not into the gate of my people in the day of their calamity." This is presumption. Not only did Edom transgress by looking on that from which they should have veiled their eyes, not only did they rejoice in the downfall of their brethren and speak proudly, but they went further and added to these sins of the spirit others of a material nature. They stepped boldly into the city in order to hasten the ruin of God's people. "Yea, look not on their affliction in the day of their calamity." As if to catch up with himself, Obadiah refers back to this first count against Edom. The repetition underlines the wickedness of their gloating. "Lay not hands on their substance in the day of their calamity." It was but a step from presumption to this sin of greed, whereby Edom further aggravated their transgression.

> Neither shouldest thou have stood in the crossway, to cut off those of his that did escape; neither shouldest thou have delivered up those of his that did remain in the day of distress (Ob 14).

"And stand not in the crossway to cut off those of his that do escape." All the gloating, malice, pride, and presumption have now borne fruit in a crescendo of wickedness. The Edomites have put into practice that which their boasting mouths proclaimed. They have taken up the sword against their brethren and have joined in cutting off those fleeing from Chaldean fury. This was not the first time Edom committed such a sin. In the days of Jehoram they had done the same thing. Nor was it, as history shows, the last time they were to be guilty of it. Some of the refugees were slain. Others were doubtless taken alive by Edom and delivered over bodily to the enemy. Think of it! They took the Lord's people and gave them up to the invaders. To such lengths did this kindred yet enemy people of Israel go in their aggression against God's chosen nation.

It may be that some reader is saying to himself, "What a depressing little prophecy and what gloomy comments!" Well, sin is a dreadful thing. And before we shrug off this portion of Obadiah, we ought to open our eyes and see that everything the prophet has so far mentioned is found on a vastly greater scale today. Who of us that takes a realistic view of human affairs can fail to admit that gloating, malice, pride, presumption, greed, and persecution are today almost worldwide? In Obadiah's time God was against such things, against them to the extent of judgment so strenuous as to spell national annihilation. The Almighty does not change His moral demands. Sin remains sin in His sight. He who punished Edom still declares, "Vengeance is mine; I will repay, saith the Lord" (Ro 12:19).

The case is complete. Obadiah has concluded his examination of Edom's damning sin. Unsparingly he has dissected it. Step by step he has shown its development. With inexorable logic he has demonstrated the causes of that "perpetual hatred" with which Ezekiel was later to charge Edom (Eze 35:5).

The Edomites never changed. And because they never changed, their history is a warning of the fixity of sin long indulged. Think of the first century when the Lord Jesus came into the world. Upon the throne of Judah sat a dynasty of kings known as the Herods. There was Herod the Great, who, in his mad desire to exterminate the infant Christ, slaughtered the innocents (Mt 2:16). He was an Edomite, or, to use the New Testament form of the word, an Idumean. There was his successor, Herod Antipas, who beheaded John the Baptist and whom the Lord Jesus called "that fox" (Lk 13:32). There was also Herod Agrippa I, who killed James and imprisoned Peter. They, too, were of this bitter people, enemies of God like their remote ancestors of whom Obadiah wrote. Hatred was in the blood of Edom, and only the wrath of God could deal with it.

3

THE DAY OF THE LORD

The Day Itself and Edom in That Day (15-16)

There remain only seven verses of the book. They are of great importance, because into them Obadiah has compressed that portion of his message that is still future. These verses, so brief yet so portentous, bring before us one of the cardinal principles of Old Testament prophecy—namely, the universal prediction growing out of the local circumstances. Again and again the prophets speak in this twofold manner. Their message being rooted in the conditions of their own day, they take their point of departure from that which is local. But, under the control of inspiration or, as Peter puts it in his second epistle, "borne along by the Holy Ghost" (2 Pe 1:21), their vision broadens to world-wide scope and future impact. Of this prophetic principle the close of Obadiah is a notable example. Thus far in his denunciation he has confined himself exclusively to the Edomites. Now he speaks of "all the [nations]," and refers in his few closing verses to "the house of Jacob," "they of the south," "they of the plain," "the Philistines," "the fields of Ephraim and the fields of Samaria," "Benjamin," "Gilead," "the children of Israel," "the Canaanites," "Zarephath," "Sepharad," and "the Kingdom." Yet through all this succession he keeps Edom in focus.

> For the day of the LORD is near upon all the [nations]: as thou hast done, it shall be done unto thee: thy reward shall return upon thine own head (Ob 15).

This verse begins by mentioning one of the central themes of prophecy, "the day of the LORD." Every prophetic student should be familiar with the term. It occurs scores of times in the Old Testament, being mentioned over and over again.* Not only so, but we find it in the New Testament as well.†

But what is this day of the Lord, or "day of Jehovah," as it is also called? A comprehensive definition is as follows: "The day of Jehovah (called, also, 'that day,' and 'the great day') is that lengthened period of time beginning with the return of the Lord in glory, and ending with the purgation of the heavens and the earth by fire preparatory to the new heavens and the new earth."[1] From this definition, which is biblically derived, it is plain that the day of the Lord comprehends Armageddon, the judgment of the nations, the millennium, the resurrection of the wicked dead and their final judgment, and the cleansing of the earth by fire. It is obviously preceded by the signs of the last times, including apostasy and worldwide disruption. More immediately prior to it are the rapture of the church, the manifestation of the Antichrist, and the judgments of Revelation 6–13. That it is a time of universal judgment is plain from the statement that "the day of the LORD is near upon *all* the [nations]." Remote as was Obadiah's situation from this still future period of judgment, he yet saw, with the peculiar telescopic vision so characteristic of inspired prophecy, that the principle of retribution whereby the Edomites would pay for their iniquity is not confined to this one people.

But what gives additional food for thought in the prophet's announcement of "the day of the LORD" is his use of the word *near*. At once the question arises, How can Obadiah, or any other Old Testament prophet, speak of the day of the Lord as "near," when already so many years have passed without its arrival? In dealing with this query some understanding of prophetic usage is necessary. For Obadiah is not alone in calling far-off things near. Other examples are found in the following passages: Isaiah 56:1; Ezekiel 30:3; Zephaniah 1:14.

The very fact that the prophets use such a word as *near* of

---

*See Is 2:12; 10:20; 13:6, 9; Eze 13:5; 30:3; Joel 1:15; 2:1, 11; Amos 5:18; Zep 1:7, 15; Zec 14:1; and many other places.

†See 1 Th 5:4; 2 Th 2:2 (the translation should be "day of the Lord," not "day of Christ"); Jude 6; Rev 6:17; and other passages.

events not yet come to pass in our own day underlines the predictive element in their writings. But we must at the same time bear in mind that Obadiah's use of "near" really did fit Edom. *Their* doom was actually waiting at the door. So we see another instance of the distinction between the local and universal elements of Old Testament prophecy. For the individual nation, the day of the Lord—that is, the day of His judgment—is always "near" or "at hand." History is one long record of the fact that judgment does not hover forever over any nation. There comes a time when, as in the cases of Edom and Assyria, Egypt and Babylon, Philistia and even Judah itself, God brings down His wrath upon those peoples who turn away from Him. In this sense, the day of the Lord is "near" upon the nations of our own time. Yet the day of the Lord has a wider significance. For it has a universal aspect, "upon *all* the [nations]," and it applies not just to Obadiah's day but also to this age in which we are living.

"But," someone asks, "exactly how 'near' are we in this present age to the coming day of the Lord in its universal sense?" There is a peril in that question because of the tendency of some to set dates for the prophetic future. However, while our Lord warns against date setting, at the same time He urges us to watch the signs of the end of the age (Mt 24:32-36, 42-51; Mk 13:28-37; Lk 21:29-36). And it seems clear from the accumulation of prophetic signs, now seen together for the first time in history, that the day of the Lord may be close. Perhaps the best word is *imminent*, for it would appear that little remains unfulfilled in the prophetic schedule of Scripture yet to precede the rapture of the church (I Th 4:13-17); and once the rapture takes place, the day of the Lord will follow according to the divine forecast found in Daniel; Matthew 24; Mark 13; Luke 21; Revelation, and similar prophecies.

Now when we say that a prophetic event is "imminent," just what do we mean? An illustration is useful. With a little care one may balance a heavy book on the edge of a table. There the book stays poised. Let the room remain absolutely quiet and the book may stay there indefinitely. Yet at any moment a slight or a heavy jar may cause it to fall.‡ No one can predict the precise instant of its drop, for its fall is imminent. So it is with the next event in the prophetic schedule; the rapture may come in our day, or it may linger far beyond our time. Not itself the day of the Lord, it is the vestibule of that day. Once it occurs, the time of judgment of which Obadiah and the other prophets so united-ly speak will surely begin.

> As thou hast done, it shall be done unto thee; thy reward shall return upon thine own head (Ob 15*b*).

We pass now to the balance of this important verse. From his fleeting vision of all the nations, the prophet narrows his case down to Edom alone. His phraseology is an excellent example of that species of dramatic irony known as poetic justice. The Edomites will be paid in coin like that which they have given their enemies.

In contemplating this spectacle of signal retribution, we need constantly to remind ourselves that God deals with nations much as He deals with persons. There is a valid analogy between national and personal conduct. When we see someone suffering under the manifest judgment of the Almighty, we may fancy that such things cannot happen to us. Both individuals and nations have a tendency to consider themselves special cases. But the holy God plays no favorites. He who dealt with the sin of Edom is the God who deals with our sin. Our only recourse is Christ, because His death for us and for all men has fully satisfied divine justice.

> For as ye have drunk upon my holy mountain, so shall all the [nations] drink continually, yea, they shall drink, and they shall swallow down, and they shall be as though they had not been (Ob 16).

In a striking figure of speech Obadiah restates the thought of

---

‡This illustration is not meant to imply that the plan of God depends upon any human action or fortuitous circumstance; His impending judgments, though they hover over man, come according to His perfect plan.

the second half of the foregoing verse. The picture is that of a carousal. The Edomites are visualized as indulging in a drunken orgy upon Mount Zion, their cruelty to their brethren being likened to this debauchery.§ As they have thus drunk, the prophet is saying, so shall all the nations do in that future day of judgment. Once again we observe the mingling of the local and universal elements in the prophecy. Because Edom has chosen to drink the cup of hatred and aggression, she will be forced in the future to drain the bitter cup of God's wrath, even unto her destruction. But this is not to be the lot of Edom alone; all the nations upon whom the divine wrath is coming will share it.

It is significant that this figure of the cup is also found in Jeremiah. In the twenty-fifth chapter of that prophecy we find a great passage about "the wine cup of fury": "For thus saith the LORD God of Israel unto me; Take the wine cup of this fury at my hand, and cause all the nations, to whom I send thee, to drink it. And they shall drink, and be moved, and be mad, because of the sword that I will send among them. Then took I the cup at the LORD's hand, and made all the nations to drink, unto whom the LORD had sent me" (Jer 25:15-17). Later on in the same chapter there is a song list of peoples and nations, including Edom (v. 21), that are to partake of this wine cup of fury. Then, following the roll call of the nations, the prophet declares: "Thus saith the LORD of hosts, the God of Israel; Drink ye, and be drunken, and spue, and fall, and rise no more, because of the sword which I will send among you. And it shall be, if they refuse to take the cup at thine hand to drink, then shalt thou say unto them, Thus saith the LORD of hosts; Ye shall certainly drink" (Jer 25:27-28). What Jeremiah saw in his prophetic vision was the war lust of the nations. Who will doubt that we are living in a day when this age-old lust has been revived and the world has been drinking the cup of fury as never before?

---

§Not all commentators agree with this interpretation, which is that of Calvin and others, including G. A. Smith, Orelli and Feinberg. Some think that 16*a* is addressed to the Israelites: e.g., Bewer, Horton and The Jerusalem Bible. But to refer 16*a* to Israel misses the strong note of irony implicit in the passage.

And they shall be as though they had not been (Ob 16*b*).

That is the ultimate result of the judgment to be inflicted during the day of the Lord. The nations so dealt with, having swallowed down the cup of divine wrath, will be wiped out. Obadiah's direct reference to the day of the Lord is very brief. But we miss its undoubted application to the present if we fail to see mingled with its brevity a warning for any nation that persists in evil aggression and God-forgetfulness.

4

THE KINGDOM

But upon Mount Zion shall be deliverance, and there shall be
holiness (Ob 17a).

"But—" God's adversatives are always significant. Up to this
point Obadiah's picture of the day of the Lord has been confined
to its judgment aspect. But this verse, together with much that
follows, shows that the God of judgment is also the God of
deliverance. His wrath is in order to bring ultimate blessing upon
those who are the objects of His favor. Observe that this promise
is definitely located; the coming deliverance will appear "upon
Mount Zion." Moreover, it is covenanted through a specific people, "the house of Jacob." In a prophecy so taken up with the sin
of Edom, the mere mention of the word *Jacob* is arresting. It
proves that, though God's judgment was upon Esau, He still
keeps in mind the covenant He made with Jacob long before
Obadiah's day.

This seventeenth verse introduces Obadiah's prophecy of the
Messianic kingdom. In speaking of that kingdom, he is in one of
the main currents of Old Testament prophecy. All the prophetic
books, whether large or small, have something to say about the
kingdom. Whoever studies the whole body of biblical prophecy
cannot escape the implication that the kingdom is to be set up
on earth, unless he does violence to the plain meaning of the
prophetic word. The tendency to spiritualize these predictions
and identify the Messianic kingdom of the prophets with the
church of the New Testament leads to confusion. One does not
have to be a professional theologian to see this. Some years ago

there appeared in the *Atlantic Monthly* an article[1] by S. J. Whitmee, a missionary friend of Robert Louis Stevenson, who knew the author during his last days in Samoa. The article contains these words of Stevenson, showing that he was among those who see the impossibility of identifying the kingdom promises with the church: "I cannot understand how you theologians and preachers can apply to the Church—or multiplicity of churches—Scripture promises which, in their plain meaning apply to God's chosen people, Israel, and to Paslestine; and which consequently must be still future.... The prophetic books are full of teachings which, if they are interpreted literally, would be inspiring, and a magnificent assurance of a great and glorious future; but which, as they are spiritualized, become farcical—as applied to the Church they are a comedy." And Mr. Whitmee went on to comment: "From his belief in the prophetic books of the Old Testament, the teaching of Christ, and the apocalyptic portions of the New Testament, he [Stevenson] possessed the fullest and clearest conception of the Second Coming of Christ, and the establishment of His Kingdom upon earth of all the men I then knew."

But there is more to this verse than its explicit location of the kingdom. Obadiah goes on to say, "And there shall be holiness." These are weighty words, because they show exactly why human efforts alone will never bring in the kingdom. For an essential element of that promised reign of worldwide peace and righteousness is holiness. And holiness is the one thing no man apart from Christ possesses. Let us not be deluded, no, not even by the idealism of our time. Christless peace conferences will never abolish war. No United Nations will bring in the kingdom without the King. The one essential element of holiness will be lacking. Had Obadiah written nothing but these five words, his prophecy would be immortal.

> And the house of Jacob shall possess their possessions (Ob 17*b*).

This is another of the memorable sentences of Obadiah. Like so much of Scripture in general and prophecy in particular, it is susceptible of expanded meaning. One word sums up the mes-

sage of the sentence. That word is *restoration*. For the study of the prophets, whether major or minor, a fundamental principle is that God leaves nothing unresolved. To use a musical figure, God's harmonies always close on perfect cadences. In modern music a composition may end with an unresolved chord hanging in air, so to speak. Far different are the prophets. With marvelous unanimity they close with God's perfect resolution of the tangled harmonies of human destiny. Nor, to use another figure, are there any loose ends. This is especially true of the future history of Israel. God promised an enduring throne and kingdom to David. Because of idolatry and unbelief, that kingdom has been abrogated. But it has never been annulled.*
No one can fully understand the scope of Old Testament prophecy in relation to Israel unless he realizes that the Jews have a national future in God's plan. That future is a specific one and may be recapitulated by the word *restoration*.

The birth of the State of Israel in 1948 began the setting of the stage for Israel's prophesied restoration. In 1948 there were only about 650,000 Jews in Palestine; in 1969 there were approximately 2,500,000. Moreover, through the Six-Day War of 1967 the Israelis have tripled the area of their country and for the first time in over 2,000 years the whole of Jerusalem is in the hands of Jews. Thus a dramatic step has been taken toward "the eventual occupation of the total area from the river of Egypt unto the great river, the river Euphrates," which God promised in the covenant He made with Abraham (Gen 15:18).[2] Though these events are essential precursors of the final restoration of Israel in the kingdom, they are not that restoration, for the Jews still do not recognize their Messiah. But one day they will enter believingly into full possession of their promised heritage. That will be in the time of the Lord's return when the Messiah, "the Branch,"† He who is "the Lion of the tribe of Judah,"‡ will be upon the throne of David, "and so all Israel shall be saved."§

---

*See on this misunderstood subject Ford C. Ottman, *God's Oath,* a study of prophecy in relation to the covenants.
†Is 4:2; 11:1; Jer 23:5; 33:15.
‡Rev 5:5.
§Ro 11:26.

"The house of Jacob shall possess their possessions." There is much about the spiritual life to be learned from those eight words in their broader application; for just as "the house of Jacob" has a covenanted heritage, so the household of Christian faith has its promised blessings. No people on earth have greater potential possessions than Christian believers. By this is not meant material riches. But in the things that are unseen and therefore enduring, Christians possess incalculable wealth. To them God has promised the supply of every need according to His riches in glory by Christ Jesus and for them He makes everything work together for good. Moreover, Christians have in the Bible the full revelation of God. They have dwelling in their hearts the Holy Spirit to guide them into all truth. But how few of us even begin to enter into this heritage!

The writer is reminded of a homey illustration. Years ago, while spending his vacation in the Catskill Mountains, he frequently passed an attractive white house. It was fairly new; the paint on the white clapboards and green shutters was fresh. But there was one strange feature. The front door, even in midsummer, was always tightly shut, the windows fast closed, and the shades pulled down. Curiosity led to inquiry. And this was the story. A hard-working couple had built the house, which they cherished very much. The wife had a passion for perfect housekeeping. So she made certain that the front door was not used, lest footsteps mar the varnished floors. The shades were pulled down so that the sun would not fade the wall paper. Her husband had to enter by the back door, and both husband and wife spent most of their time in the kitchen to save the rest of their home. But did they really possess this house? Obviously not. They had title to it, but they were not possessing their possession, because they were not entering into its use. We smile at them. But what of our own failure to possess our possessions in Christ? When it comes to some of the choicest treasures of our faith, we simply do not possess our possessions. We repeat the Twenty-third Psalm, for instance, and say to ourselves that it is marvelous to think of the Lord's being our Shepherd. But difficulty and trouble come, and we worry. What we have been doing with God's truth is merely to admire it. We have not possessed it to the extent of putting it to full use by unwavering trust.

> And the house of Jacob shall be a fire, and the house of Joseph a flame, and the house of Esau for stubble, and they shall kindle in them, and devour them; and there shall not be any remaining of the house of Esau; for the LORD hath spoken it (Ob 18).

Once again Obadiah reiterates the doom of Edom. This time, however, he mentions those who are to be instruments for inflicting divine judgment upon these people. Once more also the promised doom is a complete one; as in verse 9, it is to overtake all the house of Esau. The prophet's language is unusually forceful. It would seem almost as though his words reflect the flaming indignation that must have filled his heart. "The house of Jacob," he says, "shall be a fire, and the house of Joseph a flame, and the house of Esau for stubble, and they shall kindle in them, and devour them." The mention of the house of Jacob and the house of Joesph is evidently for the purpose of showing that both Judah and Israel will participate in this coming judgment. Other places in the Old Testament use this expression to describe the entire nation (cf. Ps 77:15). Then, having declared the doom of the Edomites, the prophet seals it with a solemn affirmation that "the LORD hath spoken it."

With this eighteenth verse in mind we pause to review the history of Edom following Obadiah's day. After the capture of Jerusalem by Nebuchadnezzar, the Edomites were dispossessed from their mountain fastness of which Petra was the capital. History tells us that a people called the Nabateans‖ drove them out. Having been ejected from their ancient home, the Edomites went to the south of Judea to a region they had taken from the Jews at the time of the captivity. Here they remained for about four centuries, until Judas Maccabaeus decisively defeated them in 164 B.C.# Not long after that, John Hyrcanus, who exercised authority thirty years (135-105 B.C.), conquered them, placing them under a Jewish governor, and incorporated them into Judaism by forcing

---

‖Descended from Nebaioth, the eldest son of Ishmael, Gen 25:13.
#1 Macc 5:3.

their circumcision and obedience to the law.** New Testament history knows them as Idumeans and, as has already been pointed out, the Herods were of this line.

The last picture of the Edomites in ancient history is a terrible one. To the end their character was unchanged. Josephus tells us that at the siege of Jerusalem under the Emperor Titus in A.D. 70, the Idumeans joined with the Zealots in rebellion against the Romans. Aided by John of Gischala, no less than 20,000 Idumeans entered Jerusalem. But no sooner were they there than they turned against their Jewish kin in a mad career of slaughter. Josephus says that 8,500 perished in the outer temple in a day, so bloodthirsty were the Idumeans. Then, leaving the temple area, they methodically devastated the city, massacring even the priests and stamping on their bodies in order to defile them. After doing this, they fell upon the general populace, murdering right and left and torturing those who escaped immediate death.[3]

With this appalling scene, Edom as a nation passes from the sight of history. To be sure, the Jews of the early centuries of the Christian era kept on using the name Edom as a special designation for Rome. But this does not mean that the Edomites continued their national existence. Henceforth they are lost to the eye of history. Where they are today no one knows. Nationally they have disappeared as completely as the Hittites, Philistines, or Babylonians. Obadiah's forecast of doom has been fulfilled to the letter. So must it always be of every word buttressed, as is this little prophecy, by the authoritative assertion, "The LORD hath spoken it." As Balaam said, so long before Obadiah's time, "God is not a man, that he should lie; neither the son of man, that he should repent: hath he said, and shall he not do it? or hath he spoken, and shall he not make it good?" (Num 23:19).

And they of the south shall possess the mount of Esau; and

** "The destruction threatened in *this* verse (18) is to be the work of the Jews themselves, the house of Jacob and Joseph being the instruments by which Esau is finally to be annihilated. This was wrought by Judas Maccabaeus and John Hyrcanus" (F. Meyrick, *The Bible Commentary*, 6:572).

they of the plain the Philistines: and they shall possess the fields
of Ephraim, and the fields of Samaria: and Benjamin shall
possess Gilead. And the captivity of this host of the children of
Israel shall possess that of the Canaanites, even unto Zarephath;
and the captivity of Jerusalem, which is in Sepharad, shall
possess the cities of the south (Ob 19-20).

The nation of Edom has been dealt with, but their land
remains. As every close student of the Old Testament knows,
God's promises to Israel have much to do with the land. Palestine is now in divided hands, but Scripture leaves no doubt that
such is not its final disposition. As surely as God covenanted
with His earthly people Israel, so certain is the final restoration
of the Jew to Palestine, a restoration of which the State of Israel
is the forerunner.

One might write over these two verses this heading in large
letters: "The Final Reapportionment of the Land." Before looking at details of this reapportionment, an observation is in order.
Like so much of prophecy, these sentences at the close of
Obadiah are seemingly far removed from modern life. Their
remoteness, however, is only apparent. Actually there is a connection with one of the most explosive of present-day problems.
As the Israelis and the Arabs are struggling over Palestine, we
may learn from Obadiah that God has His own solution for this
problem men have failed to solve.

How are these two verses to be taken? Are we to agree with
those who seek their fulfillment in the past? Or, like many others,
are we to give up any attempt to take them as meaning what
they say and simply spiritualize these geographical details into a
vague prediction of the dominion of the church? Or, finally, do
we have here a brief outline of God's ultimate solution of the
Palestinian problem during the millennium? Surely this last alternative is best, for read in this way the verses are consistent
with the course of Old Testament prophecy as a whole.

The dual phrases in verse 19, *they of the south* and *they of the
plain,* signify early divisions of Judah used as far back as the
time of Joshua. By "the south" is meant the land south of

Palestine in the direction of the Negev; by "the plain" is meant the great maritime plain along the western coast of Palestine.††

Verse 20 is full of linguistic difficulty. Scholars disagree about the rendering of the word translated "that of the Canaanites," while "Sepharad" is one of the Old Testament problems. However, the general meaning is fairly clear. In contrast to a restored Judah chiefly in view in verse 19, verse 20 sets before us a restoration of the widely scattered captives of Israel as well as the dispersed of Judah. "That of the Canaanites" is perhaps best taken to mean "that which (belongs to) the Canaanites." As for Sepharad, attempts at identification are at best uncertain.‡‡ Jerome thought it an Assyrian word, meaning "boundary." A rabbinical tradition relates it to Spain and thus the Spanish Jews have been called Sephardic Jews. Some scholars have identified it with "Çparda," of the Behistun inscriptions. Others have referred it to Asia Minor and taken it to mean Sardis, the capital of the Lydian kingdom. "The most likely identification," writes Archer, "connects Sepharad with a district referred to in southwestern Media mentioned in an inscription of King Sargon of Assyria. It is well known that Sargon deported some of the ten tribes to the 'cities of the Medes' (see II Kings 18:11). Therefore, this locality would have been very appropriate to mention in Obadiah's prediction."[4] But the problem cannot be settled finally.

Whatever the true solution of these difficulties, we may be certain that these details are all known to God. He has not forgotten His dispersed people. His covenants with them are enduring. And one day, when the Messiah will occupy the throne of David, the tangled skein of these predictions will be unraveled.

> And saviours shall come up on mount Zion to judge the mount of Esau; and the kingdom shall be the LORD's (Ob 21).

In this closing sentence Obadiah's prophecy reaches its pinna-

---

††See T. T. Perowne, The Cambridge Bible, *Obadiah and Jonah,* p. 36. Notice that Benjamin is given the possessions across Jordan in Gilead.

‡‡"Sepharad is unknown" (The Jerusalem Bible, note at Ob 20).

cle. Without in the least minimizing the local application of the
first clause, we may affirm its strong Messianic character. The
Hebrew word translated "saviours" means "deliverers," and is
used also in the book of Judges. Therefore, in the restricted,
historic sense of his prophecy, Obadiah is looking forward to
such human deliverers as Zerubbabel and Judas Maccabaeus.
But these "saviours" are at best foreshadowings of *the* Saviour,
who was yet to come in Obadiah's day and whose second and
glorious appearing we are now awaiting. As Horton in *The Minor
Prophets* says: "We may take the obscure language as the gleam
of a Divine sunshine in a driving mist. . . . But the great word
the kingdom shall be the Lord's, closing the oracle which began
'the day of the Lord is near,' permits us to feel, if not to see, in
the saying 'saviours shall come up,' something more than a mere
victorious army asserting the supremacy of Israel. This prophet
too, dealing only with an age-long enmity and with a threatened
judgment, is impelled by the prophetic spirit, and sees 'saviours'
climbing mount Zion. It is hardly relevant to ask what he meant;
but what he *saw* was the Saviour of the world, the Saviour who
is Judge, the Saviour of whom it is said by the latest of Biblical
prophets, 'the kingdoms of the world are become the kingdoms
of the Lord and of His Christ.' Scientific exegesis sees nothing of
this sort in these words; but we may venture to say it is there."[5]
Yes, Christ *is* surely envisioned in this final sentence. So Obadiah, terse though his words, adds his triumphant note to the
prophetic chorus heralding the consummation of all things in the
return of Christ our Saviour and our King.

"And the kingdom shall be the LORD's." None of the prophets
has a more exalted close than this. It looks forward to the
words of Revelation: "The sovereignty of the world has come
into the possession of our Lord and his Christ, and He will
reign forever and ever" (Rev 11:15, Williams). Human sovereignty never gets beyond the principle of stewardship. Men are
permitted to rule for a time; but the whole teaching of Scripture, whether prophetic as in Obadiah, historic as elsewhere in
the Old Testament, or doctrinal as in so much of the New
Testament, enforces the lesson that God, though temporarily
granting earthly sovereignty to man, holds him responsible for the

way in which this power is exercised. No man-ruled empire nor any nation of this world will endure forever. All will one day be merged into that eternal kingdom over which the Lord Jesus Christ will reign in solitary glory.

5

THE SIN OF PRIDE IN THE
LIGHT OF TODAY

No thoughtful person can study the book of Obadiah without asking some questions. Foremost among these are several that must have occurred to readers of this exposition. They may be framed like this: "Why is this dark book in the Bible? Why is it that not only in Obadiah but also in Jeremiah, Ezekiel, Lamentations, Psalms, Malachi, and even in Romans, the great epistle of the grace of God, the doom pronounced upon Edom is repeated? What relevance, after all, does this far-off prophecy have for our day?" In the answer to these and similar questions lies the searching message of Obadiah for us in these times.

Edom was guilty of the sin of sins, because Edom was guilty of pride. In her case this sin manifested itself in implacable hatred, which has as its outward symptom a violent form of unbrotherliness. Its inward source, however, was pride. Therefore, the key that unlocks the central moral lesson of the book is found in these words in the third verse: "The pride of thine heart hath deceived thee."

How difficult it is to awaken even Christian people to an understanding of the real nature of pride! As G. Campbell Morgan suggests,[1] one may stand before a congregation and hold their breathless interest by a recountal of dramatic stories of lives ruined by drink and other carnal sins. But try to expound a text such as this from Obadiah, "The pride of thine heart hath deceived thee," and there is a marked difference in attention and response. The reason is the fact that the true nature of pride is so little understood.

Look at it this way. Here are two statements, each of which might fall from the lips of some well-meaning church member.

Referring to another person, someone says, "He is a good man but proud." Such a remark hardly strikes our ears as inappropriate and shocking. We are all too willing to admit that goodness and pride may be companions within the same life. But consider this remark, "He is a good man but a thief." Immediately our moral sensibilities are outraged. "Hold on!" we say. "What do you mean? A man cannot at the same time be good and a thief." Yet in the sight of God pride is fully as bad as stealing, if not worse.

The foregoing shows the extent to which sin has blunted the moral perception of men. Even Christians have a certain obtuseness to God's standard of ethics. The best of us find it all too easy to make unbiblical distinctions between sins and sins. We view with abhorrence the transgressions of the flesh and those having to do with material things, while we regard with a sort of half-tolerance the equally deadly (if not more so) sins of the spirit. But the severest denunciations ever uttered by Christ were directed against the sins of the spirit. No group of sinners in the history of the world has been so excoriated as were the scribes and Pharisees by the Lord Jesus in the great diatribe recorded in Matthew 23.

What, then, is pride? First of all, we do well to recognize it as the sin whereby Satan fell. Isaiah puts this vividly when he writes of the fall of Lucifer (Satan): "How art thou fallen from heaven, O Lucifer, son of the morning! how art thou cut down to the ground, who didst weaken the nations! For thou hast said in thine heart, I will ascend into heaven, I will exalt my throne above the stars of God: I will sit also upon the mount of the congregation, in the sides of the north: I will ascend above the heights of the clouds; I will be like the most High" (Is 14:12-14). Satan's original transgression, therefore, lay in his impious self-assurance that aspired to the solitary greatness and glory of God. If there is any sin deserving to be called the source, or root, sin, it is pride. For it was Satan, ejected from heaven because of pride, who introduced sin into the innocency of Eden.

Pride is of protean character, assuming myriads of forms. It is the sin which cheats God by taking credit due Him alone. It is the sin that, in utter indifference to the Almighty, leaves Him out of the reckoning. It is the sin of modern self-sufficiency. Pride is an insult to the sovereignty of the Almighty God upon whom all men are dependent and in whom all live and move and have their being. And of all the sins, pride is most characteristic of today. Nor is it always known by its biblical name. Sometimes we call it secularism and fail to recognize its deadly nature. But secularism is a form of pride; it says in effect something like this to God: "I can do very well without You, thank You; I'll live my own life in my own way." Such is the modern spirit that is urging us to have confidence in ourselves. Such also is the spirit which led a world-famous statesman to say publicly of the United Nations, "We are the masters of our fate."

Pride, the sin of Esau, is naturally congenial to us. Anyone who tries to teach the Genesis story of Jacob and Esau to young people will realize this. Natural sympathies are with Esau. The outdoorsman, the hunter, he appeals much more readily to youth than Jacob, the supplanter, who had so little outwardly attractive about him. But with all his deceit and faults Jacob had one supreme merit his brother lacked. He valued the blessing; he was alive to spiritual things. He wrestled with the Angel until dawn, and would not let him go until he was blessed. Esau was different. Strong and vigorous, he was yet completely indifferent to God. He was without a sense of spiritual proportion; he lacked appreciation of the higher values, and preferred the immediate satisfaction of appetite to his birthright and blessing. Therefore, the author of Hebrews rightly characterized him as a "profane person" (Heb 12:16). Here the word *profane* is used in the primary sense of that which is "before" or "outside the temple." Esau was "profane" in that he was a wholly secular person, living his life apart from God and all that is sacred. He simply did not care for spiritual things.

Now we shall miss the remarkable relevance of Obadiah's message if we fail to recognize the prevalence of the Esau spirit today. The world is full of men and women who are completely indifferent to God and His Son. Not only are they indifferent, but many of them are also actually hostile to the love of God in reconciling the lost world to Himself through His Son. A list of avowed rejectors of the Lord Jesus Christ would contain many of the most distinguished names of our times. Indicative of this deliberate pride of heart, which in stubborn self-sufficiency will have nothing of God's way of redemption, are these lines by Sara Teasdale:

> I would not have a god come in
> To shield me suddenly from sin,
> And set my house of life to rights;
> Nor angels with bright burning wings
> Ordering my earthly thoughts and things;
> Rather my own frail guttering lights
> Windblown and nearly beaten out;
> Rather the terror of the nights
> And long, sick groping after doubt;
> Rather be lost than let my soul
> Slip vaguely from my own control—
> Of my own spirit let me be
> In sole though feeble mastery.*

As the Christian thinks of the present-day "Esaus" in business and professional life and reflects upon the multitude of profane persons everywhere about him, he has a fellow-feeling with the psalmist who said, "Rivers of waters run down mine eyes, because they keep not thy law" (Ps 119:136). Everywhere there is the spectacle of people quite content to live without God. Whole nations like Russia have gone the way of Edom. And what of others like Germany, Sweden, France—yes, and Britain and America? It is possible for nations to go the way of Esau by default, by just not caring about Him who is the ultimate source of all human achievement. The most dangerous tendency in national life is the self-confidence that leads to pride. The lesson God taught Nebuchadnezzar when he looked out on Babylon and said, "Is not this great Babylon, that I have built ... by the might of my power, and for the honour of my majesty?" (Dan 4:30) is one God has had to drill into men over and over again. For God does the building. Man is but the instrument, and an imperfect one at that, in the hands of the sovereign God.

---

*Reprinted with permission of The Macmillan Company from *Collected Poems* by Sara Teasdale. Copyright 1917 by The Macmillan Company, renewed 1945 by Mamie T. Wholess.

Again, as we continue to apply the contemporary message of Obadiah, we must recognize the fact that all the "Esaus" are not unbelievers. It is possible for Christians also to fall into the sin of pride. One has only to dismiss God from the reckoning, one has but to slip into the habit of neglecting his Bible, one has merely to fail to be alone with God daily in prayer, and he too may fall into the sin of making decisions and living his life on a secular basis without placing God and His will foremost. To all such there comes the convicting word of Isaiah, "Who art thou, that . . . forgettest the Lord thy maker?" (Is 51:12-13).

Surely this little book of Obadiah is a dark page of Scripture. But we should thank God that its message does not stand alone. The rest of Scripture, from Genesis to Revelation, tells us over and over again that there is hope for the Esaus. Yes, there *is* hope, even for those who sin the sin of pride, because the holy Son of God humbled Himself and became obedient to death, even the death of the Cross. On Calvary "he was wounded for our transgressions, he was bruised for our iniquities" (Is 53:5). That means that He took upon Himself the full penalty for human pride. Not only that, but, as Paul so wonderfully shows, every believer is identified with Christ's death. Our pride is conquered when we realize that our sin and the corrupt nature in which it dwells were nailed to the cross with the Lord Jesus. The more fully we grasp the meaning of Calvary, the more pride is abased.

NOTES

INTRODUCTION

1. Gleason L. Archer, Jr., *A Survey of Old Testament Introduction,* p. 287.
2. G. L. Robinson, *The Twelve Minor Prophets,* pp. 63-64.
3. *The New International Standard Bible Encyclopaedia,* s.v. "Obadiah, Book Of."
4. R. G. Moulton, *The Modern Reader's Bible,* p. 1593.
5. Hugo, cited in E. B. Pusey, *The Minor Prophets,* 1:251.

CHAPTER 1

1. Richard Wurmbrand and Charles Foley, *Christ in the Communist Prisons,* p. 34.
2. G. L. Robinson, *The Sarcophagus of an Ancient Civilization,* pp. 415 ff.
3. Principal George C. M. Douglas, *The Six Intermediate Minor Prophets,* pp. 16, 61.
4. Robinson, pp. 404-5.

CHAPTER 2

1. E. B. Pusey, *The Minor Prophets,* 1:361-62.
2. See T. T. Perowne, The Cambridge Bible for Schools and Colleges, *Obadiah and Jonah,* p. 33.

CHAPTER 3

1. C. I. Scofield, *The Scofield Reference Bible,* p. 1349.

CHAPTER 4

1. Robert Louis Stevenson, cited in S. J. Whitmee, "Tusitala," *Atlantic Monthly,* 131:344-53.
2. Cf. Charles C. Ryrie, "Perspective on Palestine," *Christianity Today,* May 23, 1969, pp. 8-10.
3. Flavius Josephus, cited in G. L. Robinson, *The Sarcophagus of an Ancient Civilization,* p. 373.
4. Gleason L. Archer, Jr., *A Survey of Old Testament Introduction,* p. 290.
5. R. F. Horton, ed., The New Century Bible, *The Minor Prophets,* 1:192-93.

CHAPTER 5

1. G. Campbell Morgan, *Living Messages of Books of the Bible,* 1:217-18.

THE PROPHECY OF

JONAH

INTRODUCTION

A MISUNDERSTOOD BOOK

Were one portion of the Bible to be singled out as more misunderstood and disbelieved than any other, the choice might well be Jonah. This little prophecy of four brief chapters has become almost proverbial as an example of the "mythological" or "legendary" element in the Old Testament. Many consider Jonah a touchstone of the modern attitude toward Scripture. How often have they said to those who accept the book as history, "But you don't *really* believe, do you, that the whale swallowed Jonah?"

Now it would not be difficult to fill these introductory pages with examples of varying views of this remarkable little book. Many take it as allegory or parable. Others stress what they believe to be its mythological elements. Still others take an eclectic view of its interpretation. But generally the present tendency is to deny its historicity. According to T. K. Cheyne, "The 'great fish' has a mythological appearance . . . [it] is ultimately Tiämat, the dragon of chaos, represented historically by Nebuchadnezzar, by whom for a time God permitted or 'appointed' Israel to be swallowed up."[1] In his classification of the Old Testament books as to their literary form, C. A. Dinsmore[2] unhesitatingly lists Jonah under "prose fiction"; while J. G. Hill speaks of "the humorist Jonah."[3] In similar vein, The Jerusalem Bible, while praising the spiritual message of the book, calls it a "droll adventure" and says that, "though God is indeed master of nature, the successive prodigies here narrated read like . . . practical jokes played by God on his prophet."[4] Fosdick is more restrained in his language, though he does not hesitate to say in his *Modern Use of the Bible*,[5] "There are some narratives of miracles which I do not believe. . . . The story of Jonah and the great fish may be parable." And James D. Smart in *The Inter-preter's Bible* assumes that to take Jonah as history rules out its true, parabolic meaning.[6]

Obviously, reluctance to accept the historicity of the story of Jonah reflects a prevalent view of Scripture. And although a majority of scholars today regard the book as didactic fiction of some kind, there are other scholars who do not hesitate to affirm and defend its historical character. Exegesis, however, is not done by counting heads, nor is truth the monopoly of the majority. There still remain good reasons for taking the events record-ed in Jonah as true happenings.

But though we differ profoundly from those who deny the historicity of Jonah, certain of their comments about the ethical and spiritual values of this prophet should not be overlooked. Thus the tribute of C. H. Cornill to the book is deservedly well known: "I have read the Book of Jonah at least a hundred times, and I will publicly avow that I cannot even now take up this marvellous book, nay, nor even speak of it, without the tears rising to my eyes, and my heart beating higher. This apparently trivial book is one of the deepest and grandest that was ever written, and I should like to say to everyone who approaches it, 'Take off thy shoes, for the place whereon thou standest is holy ground.' "[7]

It is evident that a sense of balance is needed for any ade-quate understanding of Jonah. Such an understanding should be based on thorough consideration of its background and a careful examination of its message, verse by verse. And those who, merely on a priori grounds and hearsay, rule out the historicity of this portion of Scripture might think about this sentence from the pen of Herbert Spencer: "There is a principle which is a bar to all information, which is proof against all arguments, and which cannot fail to keep a man in everlasting ignorance; this principle is contempt prior to investigation."[8]

AUTHORSHIP

The book is anonymous. Nowhere in it is Jonah declared to be the author. He was, however, an historical character (2 Ki 14:25) and tradition has persistently held that the book is autobiographical. Most critical scholars, however, take the book to have been written by an unknown author centuries after Jonah's time.

Yet the traditional view cannot be ignored. E. B. Pusey, the great Anglican scholar of the nineteenth century, and Regius Professor of Hebrew at Oxford, ably defended Jonah's authorship.[9] Prominent among other advocates of Jonah's authorship, aside from Pusey, are T. T. Perowne, Principal George C. M. Douglas, and E. D. Hart-Davies, whose *Jonah: Prophet and Patriot* is a more recent defense of the book. Among contemporary scholars who take the traditional view seriously are G. L. Robinson, G. L. Archer, Jr.,* S. J. Schultz, and H. L. Ellison.

Now if the book is only a work of fiction, then it may well be of very late date, and Jonah could not possibly be its author. But if the evidence for its historicity is adequate, then the prophet himself may have written it. Indeed, such a view accounts for a good deal. It sheds light, for example, upon the prayer from the fish's belly. It helps us understand the unsparing portrayal of the prophet's character and failures. For it is more likely that this unflattering portrait is the work of a man who, having been taught an unforgettable lesson by a loving God, does not spare himself in setting it down, than that it is an imaginary story attached to the name of a prophet of a former age.

However, those of us who are in favor of the traditional view must be frank to recognize it not as something to be dogmatically asserted but rather as what we consider a probable solution of the question of authorship. After all, so far as direct statement goes, Scripture is silent regarding the identity of the author. Therefore, our conclusions remain only inferences drawn from biblical data.

DATE

If Jonah is regarded as the author, it follows that the book must be dated very early. For as we shall see in considering Jonah the man, he lived in the days of Jeroboam II. Therefore,

---

*Archer's discussion of the authorship and historicity of the book is impressive (cf. *A Survey of Old Testament Introduction*, pp. 296 ff.).

the book may be placed somewhere within the reign of Jeroboam II over Israel, c. 793-753 B.C.[10]

On the other hand, those who reject the historicity of the events set forth in Jonah date the book in the postexilic period. Some (e.g., G. A. Smith and J. A. Bewer) are inclined to place it very late, though not after 300 B.C.

HISTORICITY

Why do so many disbelieve the historical character of Jonah's experiences? Points generally made against their historicity are these: (1) The book is obviously myth or legend. The abundance of the supernatural and the incredible nature of some of the miracles (Jonah and the great fish, the conversion of Nineveh) preclude its being taken seriously as history. (2) The mission of Jonah to Nineveh is unprecedented. (3) The statement that "Nineveh *was* [italics supplied] an exceeding great city" (3:3) implies that Nineveh had long since disappeared. (4) The phrase "of three days' journey" (3:3) grossly exaggerates the city's actual area. (5) The reference to "the king of Nineveh" (3:6) is an unhistorical usage and should be "the king of Assyria." (6) The book contains Aramaisms (late words) incompatible with Jonah's times.

Answers to these points include the following: (1) "The form of the book . . . is that of a simple historical narrative, and was so regarded by both Jews and Christians until a century ago."†[11] Two apocryphal books (Tobit and 3 Maccabees) and the Jewish historian Josephus regard Jonah's call and mission to Nineveh as factual.[12] Furthermore, objection to the concentration of the supernatural in Jonah merely begs the question of God's omnipotence. And study of the biblical supernatural reveals that it is not capricious but linked to important periods and events. Jonah's call and mission are of this nature. (2) Other prophets

---

†Thus H. L. Ellison says, "Those who deny the book's factual truth must bear the onus of explaining how a book so very different from the other prophetic books ever came to be included in the prophetic canon, how it was forgotten that it was symbolic or didactic fiction, and above all how our Lord was incapable of realizing its true nature" (*The Prophets of Israel,* p. 56).

went to foreign nations—Elijah to Sarepta (1 Ki 17:8 ff.), Elisha to Damascus (2 Ki 8:7 ff.; cf. also Ho 5:13).[13] (3) The "Nineveh was" is simply a common narrative usage (see p. 98) and in view of the nature of Hebrew verbs[14] cannot be pressed as proving that the city had perished before Jonah was written. (4) "Of three days' journey" while it "may be intended as a designation of the city's diameter" may be "nothing more than a rough expression to indicate that the city was a large one."[15] Moreover, adjacent populations were probably reckoned with the city (see p. 99). (5) There is Old Testament precedent for the designation "king of Nineveh:" Ahab is called not only "king of Israel" but also "king of Samaria" (1 Ki 21:1); Ben-hadad is referred to in Chronicles as "king of Damascus" (2 Ch 24:23) as well as "king of Syria."[16] (6) "Aramaisms occur in Old Testament books for both early and late periods. . . . The recently discovered texts from Ras Shamra contain Aramaic elements (c. 1400-1500 B.C.)."[17]

But beyond such considerations as these there stands another and a crucial aspect of the historicity of Jonah. It has to do not just with what scholars think of the book but with our Lord's references to Jonah, which are recorded in the New Testament in Matthew 12:38-42; Matthew 16:4; Luke 11:29-32. The fuller reference in Matthew reads as follows: "Then certain of the scribes and of the Pharisees answered, saying, Master, we would see a sign from thee. But he answered and said unto them, An evil and adulterous generation seeketh after a sign; and there shall no sign be given to it, but the sign of the prophet Jonas: for as Jonas was three days and three nights in the [sea monster's] belly; so shall the Son of man be three days and three nights in the heart of the earth. The men of Nineveh shall rise in judgment with this generation, and shall condemn it: because they repented at the preaching of Jonah; and, behold, a greater than Jonah is here. The queen of the south shall rise up in the judgment with this generation, and shall condemn it: for she came from the uttermost parts of the earth to hear the wisdom of Solomon; and, behold, a greater than Solomon is here" (12:38-42).

This passage raises great problems for adherents of the fictional view of Jonah. Its plain meaning is that Jesus was referring to

Jonah's experience as an actual fact. To be sure, there are some who say that Jesus was mistaken in thinking that Jonah had really been in the belly of the great fish. But this is untenable because of its grave Christological implications. Most of those, however, who hold a nonhistorical view of the events in Jonah explain our Lord's reference to the prophet by saying that He was simply using a mythological reference for an illustrative purpose. In other words, He was using the story as a preacher today might mention a figure from literature such as Shakespeare's Hamlet or Melville's Captain Ahab.

While this sounds plausible, it is too facile to stand up under careful scrutiny of Matthew 12:38-42. For in these words our Lord not only mentions Jonah but also the "queen of the south" (the queen of Sheba), Solomon, and the men of Nineveh—historical, all of them. Surely it would have been very unusual for our Lord to link in the same breath the mythological and the historical. Just imagine Him saying something like this: "As [the mythological] Jonah was three days and three nights in the [mythological] fish's belly; so shall the Son of man be three days and three nights in the heart of the earth. The [real] men of Nineveh shall rise in judgment with this [real] generation and shall condemn it: because they [the real men of Nineveh] repented at the preaching of the [mythological] Jonah and, behold, a greater than Jonah is here."‡ Obviously, such a mixture is ridiculous. Not only so but it would also have been strange, were Jonah's experience only mythology, for our Lord to have chosen it as the type of His coming resurrection, the key historical fact without which our faith is futile (1 Co 15:17).

Moreover, the form of our Lord's words seems clearly to imply historical reality. Note the parallel in construction between Matthew 12:40, "For as Jonas was three days and three nights in the whale's belly; so shall the Son of man be three days and three

‡Robinson aptly remarks: "In the same connection he [our Lord] goes on to speak of the Queen of the South . . . and it certainly seems unlikely that he would mingle real and fictitious names in the same context. If the account of the Queen of the South were history, and the story of Jonah were fiction, Jesus might surely have discriminated between them in the interests of intellectual honesty" (*The Twelve Minor Prophets*, p. 88). Cf. also the note on Matthew 12:41 in the *New Scofield Reference Bible*.

nights in the heart of the earth," and John 3:14, "And as Moses lifted up the serpent in the wilderness, even so must the Son of man be lifted up," wherein Christ refers to the historical event of Numbers 21:5-9. Between Luke 11:30 and John 3:14 there is the same parallel. (In the Greek text of Jn 3:14 the words of comparison are *kathōs . . . houtōs* and likewise in Lk 11:30; in Mt 12:40 they are *hōsper . . . houtōs*. However, *hōsper* like *kathōs* means "just as.") No, we cannot escape the fact that the divine Son of God definitely and unequivocally compared Himself with Jonah. It is evident that for Him the marvelous experience of this rebellious prophet was a foreshadowing of His own death and resurrection.

JONAH: THE MAN AND HIS WORK

Uncertainties as to the authorship and date of the prophecy arise, as we have seen, from the absence of direct statements in Scripture relative to these points. However, there is no uncertainty as to the fact that a prophet named Jonah lived. Second Kings 14:25 definitely mentions Jonah, the son of Amittai, as a native of Gath-hepher in the tribe of Zebulon (Jos 19:13). The meaning of Jonah's name ("dove") and that of his father, Amittai ("truthful"), may be significant in view of his commission to be the Lord's messenger. According to Orelli,[18] Gath-hepher is probably to be identified with El Meshed, a place north of Nazareth. Jonah was therefore a Galilean prophet. The reference in 2 Kings shows him foretelling the restoration in the reign of Jeroboam II of the land of the northern kingdom to its former extent. This earlier ministry of Jonah must have brought him a certain amount of notoriety, because he predicted success and widened territory for his people.

Nowhere else in the historical books of the Old Testament is there any other reference to Jonah. He next meets us in the Bible in the prophecy bearing his name. Following that are the three references in the New Testament (Mt 12:38-42; 16:4; and Lk 11:29-32) discussed above. These confer great distinction on him; he is the only one of the minor prophets mentioned by Jesus.

The more one reflects about Jonah, his mission, and his book, the more remarkable it all becomes. No prophet in the Old

Testament is more strongly Jewish. Yet no Old Testament prophet is so exclusively devoted to ministry to the Gentiles. In a time when Israel regarded all other nations as heathen and outside the blessing of Jehovah, Jonah, a most intensely nationalistic Jew, was used for a surpassingly great work among the Gentiles. Again, his book is peculiar in that, though rightly placed among the prophets, it contains less direct prophecy than any other of its companions. In fact, when one isolates the actual words of Jonah's message to Nineveh, he finds that in the Hebrew they are only five in number. Unlike other prophetic books, Jonah is first and foremost a narrative. But as study of it will show, its prophetic message lies not only in what Jonah said to Nineveh, but in what God said and did to Jonah in connection with the divine commission given him. Moreover, these four chapters are noteworthy for a remarkable concentration of the supernatural.

Regardless of differences of opinion as to authorship, there is general agreement that the book of Jonah shows a high degree of literary expertness. Indeed, it is one of the most skillful narratives ever written, as Charles Reade, the author of the classic historical novel, *The Cloister and the Hearth,* declared in his tribute to it: "Jonah is the most beautiful story ever written in so small a compass. It contains 48 verses and 1,328 words. There is a growth of character, a distinct plot worked out without haste or crudity. Only a great artist could have hit on a perfect proportion between dialogue and narrative."[19] This may well stand as an answer to those who attack the book because of lack of detail. It is not the fact that the author does not mention certain things that is so remarkable; it is the fact that into a little book which may be read in five or ten minutes he has packed such a wealth of emotion, historical data, and lofty spiritual truth.

No man can define the mysterious process whereby the Spirit of God inspired the writings of Scripture. We only know that the result of this process is the revelation God desired us to have. And we also recognize from the internal evidence of Scripture itself that the inspired writers were no mere automatons; nothing is more plain than that they differed in literary talent and use of language. For the one book of prophecy that is in itself a story and that has such a worldwide outlook, it is significant that God chose a writer of such preeminent skill.

THE OUTLINE OF THE BOOK

In structure Jonah is an orderly book. Step by step the story moves forward. So much is packed into a few pages that the tendency in outlining it is toward over-elaboration. The story is so living that it seems almost inhuman to indulge in what might slip into over-analysis. Nevertheless, because an outline is a necessary guide for expository study, the following one is suggested:

    I. Jonah's commission (1:1-2)
    II. Jonah's disobedience (1:3)
    III. Jonah's discipline (1:4—2:9)
       A. The storm (1:4-11)
       B. Jonah in the deep (1:12—2:9)
          1. Jonah thrown into the sea (1:12-16)
          2. Jonah swallowed by the fish (1:17)
          3. Jonah's prayer (2:1-9)
    IV. Jonah's deliverance (2:10)
    V. Jonah's recommission (3:1-2)
    VI. Jonah's obedience (3:3-10)
       A. Jonah's compliance (3:3)
       B. Its results (3:4-10)
          1. Jonah's message (3:4)
          2. The repentance of Nineveh (3:5)
          3. The king's repentance and proclamation (3:6-9)
          4. God's "repentance" (3:10)
    VII. Jonah disgruntled (4:1-3)
    VIII. Jonah taught his final lessons (4:4-11)
       A. The gourd, worm, and wind (4:4-8)
       B. God's final words to Jonah (4:9-11)

An alternative to this outline is a fourfold one. It is less complete than the larger analysis, but has the merit of harmony with the chapter divisions. Although in many portions of the

Bible the chapter divisions are illogical, in Jonah this is not the case. On the contrary there is a clear correspondence between the chapters and the story. This correspondence may be set forth like this:

    I. The prophet who was afraid of God's mercy
   II. The prayer
  III. The conversion of a great city
   IV. The wideness of God's mercy

In studying the prophecy verse by verse, our aim will be twofold: first, to clarify the meaning of the text; second, to deal with difficulties as adequately as possible. In either case the deeper purpose will be to provide a background for an understanding of the essential spiritual message.

1

COMMISSIONED BUT DISOBEDIENT

JONAH'S COMMISSION (1:1-2)

Now the word of the LORD came unto Jonah the son of Amittai, saying, Arise, go to Nineveh, that great city, and cry against it; for their wickedness is come up before me (Jon 1:1-2).

The initial "now" is in Hebrew the equivalent of *and.* Other Old Testament books begin with this connective. For example, Exodus, Leviticus, and Numbers use it to show their continuity with what immediately precedes them. With Jonah, however, the continuity may not be with something the prophet had already written but rather a more general historical connection, as in Ruth 1:1. Perowne remarks, "There is a reference in his [Jonah's] own mind to the national records that have gone before, and he consciously takes up the thread of passing history."[1]

In its clear assertion that the Word of the Lord came to the prophet, the opening follows the familiar pattern of other prophetic writings. Little need be said here regarding Jonah's personal background because it has been discussed in the introduction. However, the meaning of his name (dove) and that of his father Amittai (truthful) bears repeating.

Verse 2 records Jonah's original call. No one knows just what the prophet was doing when God spoke to him. But whatever his occupation, we may be sure that the divine word came with urgent clarity. "Arise," Jonah is commanded, "go to Nineveh, that great city, and cry against it." Nothing further is stated as to the exact words Jonah is to utter in Nineveh. But the reason for

67

his commission is given; God expressly tells the prophet of the wickedness of the city, the implication being that this wickedness had reached such proportions as to demand that the Lord do something about it.

But what about the wickedness of Nineveh? The city was one of the most ancient of capitals. It is first mentioned in Genesis 10:11, "Out of that land [the land of Shinar, v. 10] went forth Asshur, and builded Nineveh." Later it became the capital of the Assyrian Empire. Archeology has confirmed what the Bible says about the wickedness of the Assyrians. That they were a blasphemous people is shown by the horrible words of Rabshakeh, the mouthpiece of Sennacherib, in the days of King Hezekiah (2 Ki 18). But their wickedness took the special form of brutality. Assurbanipal, the grandson of Sennacherib, was accustomed to tear off the lips and hands of his victims. Tiglath-pileser flayed captives alive and made great piles of their skulls. Such deeds were no alleged atrocities; the Assyrians themselves have preserved them for posterity in their own histories and bas-reliefs on their monuments. It was, then, to this city, so abominably wicked, that Jonah, the son of Amittai, was to go and deliver the Lord's message.

"Go to Nineveh, that great city, and cry against it." The expression "Cry against it" may also be rendered, "Cry unto it," as the parallel word, "preach unto it," in 3:2 suggests. It was not only that Jonah was commanded to denounce Nineveh; he was also commissioned to preach *to* the city. The exact nature of the message he was to declare to Nineveh is tersely stated in 3:4, and its reception (3:5-9) and Jonah's comment (4:2) show that it entailed a call to repent.

"Their wickedness is come up before me." The thought here is obviously that the accumulation of sin in Nineveh was so great as to demand God's attention. While God is cognizant of all sin, His forbearance is great. We have a hint of this in Romans 2:4-5, where Paul speaks of the ungodly who despise the riches of God's goodness and forbearance and long-suffering. But there comes a day when God has to take action. That day was at hand for Nineveh. It could be avoided only by the wholehearted repentance of the entire city.

How often, in time of calamity, one hears statements like these: "Why doesn't God do something? Why does He let this awful situation continue?" The answer is a simple one. God *is* doing something about the world situation. God is continually in charge, even though His action is veiled from human sight. His hand is at work in the affairs of men. Let us never accuse Him of not doing something, when He who is the Sovereign over all things "works in a mysterious way His wonders to perform."

JONAH'S DISOBEDIENCE (1:3)

> But Jonah rose up to flee unto Tarshish from the presence of the LORD, and went down to Joppa; and he found a ship going to Tarshish: so he paid the fare thereof, and went down into it, to go with them unto Tarshish from the presence of the LORD (Jon 1:3).

For the proper understanding of the book of Jonah much depends upon the view taken of the prophet's motive in disobeying God. Consider the facts. Jonah has received one of the strangest and most difficult commissions given any Old Testament prophet. A zealous Israelite, he has been commissioned not only to prophesy against a foreign capital and call it to repentance; he has also been ordered to go to that capital and proclaim God's message in person. Many other Old Testament prophets denounced heathen cities, but in practically every case they delivered their message while among their own people.* With Jonah it was different; he had to go in person to the place against which he was prophesying and proclaim his message face to face with the heathen.

Now, when this came home to Jonah, he did a rash thing. He arose not to obey God but to do exactly the opposite of what God had commanded. Translate Jonah's action into geographical terms and you see it for what it was. Nineveh was approximately five hundred miles northeast of Palestine. But Jonah got up and

---

*First Ki 17:8 ff.; 2 Ki 8:7 ff.; and Ho 5:13 have been cited as exceptions, but they are hardly parallel to the extraordinary difficulty of Jonah's commission.

went to Joppa, the nearest seaport. There he took a ship for
Tarshish. Most scholars agree in the identification of Tarshish
with ancient Tartessus in Spain. This means that instead of
going five hundred miles northeast to Nineveh, Jonah set out on
a journey of two thousand miles due west. Rather than obey
God he would traverse the length of the Mediterranean Sea!

The phrase "from the presence of the LORD," at the end of
verse 3, has been misunderstood. Some scholars who presuppose
the evolution of the Hebrew religion from the idea of a tribal
deity point to it as evidence for their view. Jonah, they say,
conceived of Jehovah as a mere local, Palestinian God. He
thought that, in running away from Galilee, he would escape
from the God who inhabited that country. Such a view, however, is not convincing. There are plenty of passages in the Old
Testament prior to Jonah's time which show conclusively that
the Jews did not think of Jehovah as merely associated with
their land, but rather as the Lord of all heaven and earth. Psalm
139, traditionally attributed to David, gives a sublime answer to
this notion of a tribal deity. The prophet who weaves into his
prayer in the time of extremity (chap. 2) text after text from the
Psalms may well have known these wonderful words about
God's omnipresence with their haunting questions, "Whither
shall I go from thy Spirit? Or whither shall I flee from thy
presence?" He knew that not even "the wings of the morning"
could take him away from his Lord.

Granted all this, what does the phrase "from the presence of
the Lord" mean in reference to Jonah's flight? Very probably it
refers to his desire to get away from his official ministration as
the Lord's prophet. This is in accord with the statement of the
Targum to the effect that he might not prophesy in the name of
the Lord.[2] Pusey also puts it well when he says, "Jonah fled, not
from God's presence but from standing before Him as His servant
and minister."[3]

The preposition used to describe the direction of Jonah's flight
is significant. Having arisen and determined to flee "from the
presence of the LORD," he went, the text tells us, "*down* to
Joppa.*" Whenever any one, whether ancient prophet or modern
believer, deliberately goes counter to the Lord's call, he takes a

downward step. It may seem from the worldly point of view that departure from God's plan will lead to promotion. Actually, however, it always spells descent. There can be no real elevation of life apart from the will of God. The man who puts aside God's call for any other consideration is on a downward path. Not only so, but he follows this path at the price of great personal labor, suffering, and pain. It costs to disobey God.

We now face the crucial problem of Jonah's motive in fleeing. Why, when the call of Jehovah was so clear and urgent, did he flatly disobey? Various solutions have been proposed. For instance, there are those who say that Jonah was afraid. He realized the greatness of Nineveh and its cruel might. He trembled at the thought of going alone and defenseless into the midst of this center of bestial cruelty. So he ran away.[4] Surely, however, this view fails to do justice to the prophet's character. He showed no fear in the terrible tempest, nor did he quail before his impending doom of being cast into the sea. No, timidity will not account for his flight.

"But," others say, "Jonah was a bigoted Jew. He felt that Jehovah was the private God of Israel alone. The thought of calling a Gentile people to repentance was utterly abhorrent to his strong racial feelings. Therefore, he disobeyed." This suggestion comes nearer the truth; yet it is still faulty. Jonah was indeed a zealous Jew. Nevertheless, his very zeal for the Lord would presume his obedience to such a clear command as had come to him. It is difficult to suppose that, having received such an unmistakable command, he would defy it, when defiance would logically imply his setting himself up as superior in judgment to his Lord.

The third explanation accuses Jonah of exaggerated pride in his prophetic office. Advocates of this view argue that he fully realized not only the divine nature of his call but also its favorable outcome for Nineveh. Being imbued with a great sense of his dignity as a prophet, he simply could not bear to accept a position which demanded that he pronounce judgment upon a people, only to find later on that God would forgive them and judgment would be withheld. But again, the motive is inadequate. A sense of the dignity of the prophetic office is all very well, but it is doubtful whether it would lead to such enormity of rebellion as Jonah showed.

What, then, is the best explanation of the prophet's flight? One phrase, love for his country and people,† solves the problem. Jonah was a zealous Jew, and he was also imbued with the greatness of the prophetic office. As a zealous Jew and a prophet as well, he had a deep concern for his own people. He had only to look at the international situation in his day to see the menace of Assyria. Already this great empire had begun to attack Palestine and to claim sovereignty over it. Assyrian inscriptions themselves record that Adadnirari III, a contemporary of Jeroboam II, imposed tribute upon Israel, and that his grandfather, Shalmaneser III, had warred with Ahab and had received tribute from Jehu.[5]

A modern illustration may help us understand the strain Jonah's commission placed upon him. Suppose some representative Jew during the Hitler regime had received a clear call from God to prophesy to Berlin with a view to the forgiveness of Nazi Germany and its escape from judgment. Surely the fulfillment of such a commission would seem intolerable. Thus it was with Jonah. Realizing that Nineveh was going to fall upon comparatively defenseless Israel, he deliberately repudiated God's commission to call it to repentance. His patriotic concern for Israel was stretched to the breaking point, and his concern won over his fidelity to God. Let us, therefore, be slow in condemning him. His motive was not ignoble. Nevertheless, it shows how even the best of intentions may stand in the way of complete obedience to the Lord. The trouble with Jonah was one that affects many a Christian today; it was simply refusal to do the will of God for fear of the consequences. How much better to follow God in everything, realizing that He knows exactly what He is doing and that the consequences are all in His control. When God calls us to do a thing, worry over the outcome is one of the snares the adversary uses to keep us from obeying.

---

†For a convincing statement of this explanation, see D. E. Hart-Davies, *Jonah: Prophet and Patriot.*

2

THE CONSEQUENCES OF DISOBEYING GOD

JONAH'S DISCIPLINE (1:4—2:9)

So far as Jonah was concerned, his disobedience was final. Once his mind was made up to renounce the commission of Jehovah, he acted with a decision consistent with his choice (v. 3). Nor did God then interpose any obstacle in his way. When the prophet "rose up to flee," God might have turned him back then and there. When he took the further step of going down to Joppa, the divine hand might have interrupted the fateful journey in any one of a thousand different ways. Even when Jonah actually paid his fare and bought his ticket for Tarshish, God might yet have laid hold upon him and placed him back upon the pathway of obedience. But God did nothing of the kind. Once Jonah had decided upon the great sin of disobedience, he found it only too easy to continue in it.

The application is timeless. Though it was the pagan Virgil who wrote the famous phrase *Facilis descensus Averno* ("Easy is the descent to hades"), he spoke the truth. Let us Christians not forget that even the most religious persons may sin with terrible facility, if they once make up their minds to take the first step downward. Sometimes, indeed, God graciously intervenes and stops the sinner short, as He later did with Jonah. But not always does He act thus. The only safe rule of life is to remember that the initial step out of God's will is potentially as deep a plunge into iniquity as a jump from a precipice. The gravitational pull of sin is too powerful for our fallen human nature, and none of us is strong enough to take with impunity even one step toward evil.*

Jonah thought he was through with God. In fleeing from the divine presence, he had sought to resign his commission as a prophet. But God was not through with Jonah. An officer in an army may resign the commission of his president or king, but an ambassador of the Lord is on a different basis. His service is for life, and he may not repudiate it without the danger of incurring God's discipline.

THE STORM

> But the LORD sent out a great wind into the sea, and there was a mighty tempest in the sea, so that the ship was like to be broken. Then the mariners were afraid, and cried every man unto his god, and cast forth the wares that were in the ship into the sea, to lighten it of them. But Jonah was gone down into the sides of the ship; and he lay, and was fast asleep (Jon 1:4-5).

Now we begin to see that in running away from God Jonah was attempting the impossible. "But the LORD," the narrative continues in contrast to the beginning of verse 3, "But Jonah." "But the LORD sent out a great wind into the sea." The Hebrew verb is vivid, having the sense of "hurled." It was no ordinary storm that broke upon the ship, but the very hurricane expression of God's power. One of the treasures of American art is a picture of this storm by Albert Pinkham Ryder, the greatest master of imaginative painting America has had. The scene is a terrible one—mountainous waves, a ghastly light suffusing the lashing sea, the battered ship, the fear-ridden faces of the mariners, the face of the Lord looming through the clouds. Let us not hesitate to grant the plain significance of the impressive words, "But the LORD hurled a great wind into the sea, and there was a mighty tempest." They reveal the first step in God's supernatural pursuit of His disobedient servant. For Jonah, God was the "hound of heaven" so unforgettably portrayed in Francis Thompson's poem with that title.

---

*See S. C. Burn, *The Prophet Jonah*, pp. 56-57, for an interesting development of this practical truth.

"Then the mariners were afraid, and cried every man unto his god." A fine feature of this chapter is the portrait of the mariners, sketched so briefly yet tellingly. From the particular Hebrew word used to denote them to their final grateful vow to the God whom their perilous experience taught them to fear "exceedingly" (v. 16), they are pictured as men who rise to a difficult occasion with uncommon nobility of character. Yes, they were afraid, these ancient "salts."† But their fear was not cowardice. It was rather the natural shrinking of mortals from the overwhelming forces of nature. If the modern seaman feels terror in a hurricane today, despite the thousands of tons of floating steel beneath his feet, what of these sailors in their primitive wooden ship with no motive power but tempest-torn sails and puny oars, yet caught in the grip of a sea whipped to fury by this Jehovah-hurled storm?

"And cried every man unto his god, and cast forth the wares that were in the ship into the sea, to lighten it of them." Over twenty-five hundred years have elapsed since the vessel bearing Jonah was buffeted in that hurricane, yet men today are still behaving as did those sailors. Human nature changes little through the years. Recent wars have revealed the same human traits manifested by those mariners long ago, as in time of extreme peril modern men have turned to some power outside themselves. "Every man [cried] unto his own god." It is one thing to be a Christian in time of desperate danger; it is another thing to be an unbeliever. The Christian cries to his Lord and his God whom he knows personally; the unbeliever to a god whom he does not know. To be sure, there have been conversions on battlefields and among shipwrecked sailors. But it is presumption to think that all in peril will inevitably find God. Such conversions are, however, exceptional.

"But Jonah was gone down into the sides of the ship;‡ and he lay and was fast asleep."Once safely aboard ship, Jonah evident-

---

†Such is the meaning of the Hebrew word for mariners (*mallach*) according to E. B. Pusey, *The Minor Prophets*, 1:375.

‡The Hebrew word used in verse 3 means a decked vessel. The ships of Tarshish were among the largest afloat at that time. See S. C. Burn, *The Prophet Jonah*, p. 55.

ly lost no time in going below deck. There he found a quiet place where he promptly fell asleep. "But how could he do so?" someone asks. "How could he remain asleep in all the din and uproar of the howling storm?" We do not have to resort, as some have done, to the supposition of a seasick prophet to answer the question! We need only remember that in his own mind Jonah was a doomed man. He had solemnly renounced his commission as a prophet. He had deliberately left "the presence of the LORD." Therefore, he could not but consider himself lost. What if the ship sank? He was through with all that had given his life meaning. Out of love for his people he had turned his back on God and now he had, he felt, every right to think that God had turned His back on him. So, with the dull hopelessness of the condemned, he sought refuge in sleep, the only anodyne available to take him for a few hours out of his unhappy state. Many a littler man than Jonah has turned to drink or drugs as a release from the burdens of life. But there is no human expedient that can permanently still a tortured soul. A man cannot remain asleep forever. The awakening to reality is inevitable. The only cure for disobeying God is to repent and get back into the will of God.

> So the shipmaster came to him, and said unto him, What meanest thou, O sleeper? Arise, call upon thy God, if so be that God will think upon us, that we perish not (Jon 1:6).

Attention now shifts from the mariners as a group to the shipmaster, or captain. (The Hebrew word means "chief pilot.") The most extreme measures have failed to ease the plight of vessel and crew. The gods of the heathen sailors have been appealed to without result. Reading between the lines, we see in the action of the captain in awakening Jonah an appreciation of the importance of unanimity in prayer. Heathen though he was, he was not satisfied until every single soul aboard his ship had called upon his god for deliverance. Therefore, he hurried below to arouse Jonah.§

---

§John A. Hutton reminds us that we are not told that Jonah prayed at this time. Somewhat dogmatically, he says, "A man does not pray who is

In the meantime, the sea continued with unabated fury. So we see in the next verse an effort on the part of the crew to solve the mystery of the dreadful storm which has them at its mercy. That it was no ordinary storm they were convinced. They had discussed it and had come to the plain conclusion that some higher power or, as they were soon to realize, the Lord Himself, was pursuing their ship. And, in facing the question why their ship has been marked out for this judgment, they decide that the divine vengeance is directed against some person on board. It was but logical, therefore, and quite in accord with the ancient custom, sanctioned even by biblical usage, for them to cast lots in order to find out the fugitive from heavenly justice.

> And they said everyone to his fellow, Come, and let us cast lots, that we may know for whose cause this evil is upon us. So they cast lots, and the lot fell upon Jonah (Jon 1:7).

According to Proverbs 16:33, "The lot is cast into the lap; but the whole disposing thereof is of the LORD." Also, Acts 1:23-26 tells how Matthias was chosen by lot to take the place of Judas. Are we, then, now to use this method of ascertaining God's will? Hardly, when we remember that Christians in this age have the written Word of God and the Holy Spirit to guide them.‖ Those who have, as Paul beautifully puts it, "the mind of Christ" (1 Co 2:16) need not resort to lots as a means of determining difficult questions. Nevertheless, the sovereign God who knows all things could and did overrule the result of the lots cast by the sailors in such a way as to bring His will to pass.

> Then said they unto him, Tell us, we pray thee, for whose cause this evil is upon us; What is thine occupation? And whence comest thou? What is thy country? And of what people art thou? (Jon 1:8).

---

in a state of sin. Such a man cannot pray. He must first repent. *At that moment Jonah was the only heathen man on board.* Compared with him at that moment, those heathen were believers" (*The Persistent Word of God*, p. 42).

‖It is significant that lots are not mentioned after the descent of the Holy Spirit at Pentecost, Ac 2:1-13; the reference to lots in Ac 1:26 is the last in Scripture. (See T. T. Perowne, The Cambridge Bible for Schools and Colleges, *Obadiah and Jonah*, p. 64.)

Jonah was awake. Instead of being on a ship sailing toward his far-off destination of Tarshish, he found himself aboard a vessel gripped by a furious storm. All about him was the roar of the tempest. As he staggered on deck, he was a marked man. God had allowed the lot to fall upon him. Everyone of the crew from captain down must have looked askance upon the fugitive prophet, realizing that here was the man responsible for their awful predicament. This eighth verse gives a circumstantial report. For its best effectiveness it should be read aloud. The frightened mariners threw question after question at Jonah. The interrogation was a searching one, but the prophet was not slow to respond. He not only awoke in the storm, he also came to his senses spiritually. His answer, which revealed the true Jonah rather than the disobedient runaway, is one of the noble Old Testament confessions of faith.

> And he said unto them, I am an Hebrew; and I fear the
> LORD, the God of heaven, which hath made the sea and the dry
> land (Jon 1:9).

Let us not lose sight of the dramatic scene under which this confession was spoken. The storm was at its terrible height, the winds shrieking and the waves pounding and breaking over the battered ship. Around Jonah was clustered a group of desperate but awed men. Bravely he faced them and far more than answered their questions. They had asked him his occupation and country; he replied with a confession of his God.

What might we have answered under similar circumstances? Or, putting aside the circumstances which were, after all, so wholly exceptional, what would we reply now, were we in time of stress called to account as to our occupation, our origin, and our country? It is easy, when thus challenged, to reply with bare facts and no more. But Jonah went further. In addition to acknowledging himself a Hebrew, he gave a witness then and there for his Lord. He may have been endeavoring to resign his commission, but he could not change his heart, which remained that of a true prophet. So he pointed these mariners to the only Lord God. In doing so he became the human instrument whereby they were ultimately turned to an acknowledgment of the

living God. For it was to God as the creator that Jonah was
witnessing. Nothing could have been more effective than this
appeal to the only one great enough to still that terrible tempest.
The very heart of his confession was the declaration that he
feared the Lord. Only a true Israelite could have said that, for
only God's people knew the meaning of the fear of the Lord.

Worthy of comment are two linguistic details. The first is
Jonah's statement that he was "an Hebrew." Had he called himself "an Israelite," it would have been out of character. According to Dr. Pusey, his designation of himself as "an Hebrew"
was entirely appropriate, because he used the name whereby
Israelites always referred to themselves when speaking to foreigners. Much the same holds for Jonah's calling the Lord "the
God of heaven." It was this title Abraham used in speaking of
God to his Gentile servant (Gen 24:7). So Daniel spoke of Him to
Nebuchadnezzar (Dan 2:37, 44), and in the same terms Cyrus
acknowledged the Lord (2 Ch 36:23).

> Then were the men exceedingly afraid, and said unto him,
> Why hast thou done this? For the men knew that he fled from
> the presence of the LORD, because he had told them (Jon
> 1:10).

The mariners' fear has already been mentioned (v. 5). There,
however, it was the storm that frightened them. Here, they are
"exceedingly afraid," because they have heard Jonah's confession. In conformity with the principle that what is true and
noble tends to reproduce itself,[2] that confession immediately
began to bear fruit in the lives of these sailors. Step by step they
responded to Jonah's true witness to his Lord. Before, they had
been afraid of the storm. Now, they went on to the higher
ground of fearing the Lord, thus recognizing the Creator above
the creature.

The next question, "Why hast thou done this?" must have
been spoken not so much out of inquiry as amazement and
reproach. Having received Jonah's witness to the Lord, these
heathen seamen, who had lived so long in darkness, could not
understand how a prophet who served such a God would dare
disobey Him.

The second sentence of this tenth verse shows the skill with which the narrative is written. To report Jonah's whole confession would have slowed up the story. To leave out any reference to it would have led to obscurity. But the author was a literary craftsman. So he did exactly the right thing by inserting this brief reference to how Jonah had already told the mariners the whole story of his flight.

> Then said they unto him, What shall we do unto thee, that the sea may be calm unto us? For the sea wrought, and was tempestuous (Jon 1:11).

There was no doubt in the mariners' minds that Jonah was the cause of their deadly peril. The lot had fallen upon him, he had witnessed boldly to his country and God, and had confessed his sin. Now they realized that behind the storm was the vengeance of the God of heaven, who had made the sea. They began to understand that the reckoning was between Jonah and the Lord, and that therefore something further must happen to the disobedient prophet. But the thing that brought this insight home to them with blinding urgency was the condition of the sea. Our English version is vivid enough, but the Hebrew is even more powerful. A literal translation would read like this: "The sea was going and whirling."[3] The tempest had now become a maelstrom directed straight at the vessel and the fugitive it harbored.

JONAH IN THE DEEP (1:12–2:9)
Jonah thrown into the sea

> And he said unto them, Take me up, and cast me forth into the sea; so shall the sea be calm unto you: for I know that for my sake this great tempest is upon you (Jon 1:12).

Some have suggested that Jonah might have settled matters by jumping overboard! But for Jonah that was impossible. He really believed in the Lord. He knew perfectly well that his life was not his own. He did disobey God. But he would never have fallen into the sin of self-destruction. Had that been his tendency, he might well have done away with himself in the very beginning instead of embarking for Tarshish. However, he did not hesitate to ask the sailors to be his executioners, realizing that, if God were to see fit to allow them to cast him into the sea, his death would be with divine sanction. Between the lines of this verse a tone of assurance sounds. Jonah knew exactly what would happen to the storm when he was thrown into the raging water, for he understood its cause. Moreover, in his zeal for his people he was quite willing to perish. The picture is that of a resolute man bravely facing a deserved sentence of death.

> Nevertheless the men rowed hard to bring it to the land; but they could not: for the sea wrought, and was tempestuous against them (Jon 1:13).

Here are the mariners at their best. They had every right to do away with Jonah at once. Yet their natural kindness of heart intervened. Pagans though they were, they were not yet willing to go to the lengths of throwing him overboard. The Hebrew text makes their efforts live. "Nevertheless," it reads, "the men *digged* to bring it to the land." One can almost see the desperate sailors bending their backs to the great oars, and, as we say even today, "digging" into their task. Yet admitting all this, let us not fall into the error of misinterpreting the natural benevolence of these kindly sailors. It is quite true, as one writer on Jonah says, that "their effort to save him . . . is a credit to unenlightened humanity." But it is quite false to draw the conclusion, as the same author does, that "the theory of total depravity does not hold as we learn more of the benevolence that exists even among savages. . . . The Hottentots were kindly to one another before their contact with Europeans, and the Zulus and Kaffirs, uncontaminated by their contact with Europeans, have virtues which we might well pray for; cruelty to children and impurity are not found among them."[4]

Such a statement reveals a misunderstanding of total depravity. This Bible doctrine does not mean that every human being is a base villain full only of criminal instincts. It means that corruption extends to every part of fallen man's nature and that there is nothing in man that can commend him to a righteous God. Biblical theology recognizes the worldwide benefits of common grace. God makes His sun to rise upon the evil and the good, and sends rain upon the just and unjust (Mt 5:45). There is goodness among the unsaved, including primitive peoples. Nevertheless, even the best of them are living in sin and darkness, and the benevolence that in their hearts reflects God's common grace is not sufficient to atone for their sins. There is no warrant, therefore, for reading into this portion of the story of Jonah any ground for an attack upon total depravity. The denial of this doctrine leads too readily to the perilous view that man, being naturally good, needs no Saviour. As for the mariners, they had evidently been touched by Jonah's noble confession even more deeply than they themselves could realize at the time.

> Wherefore they cried unto the LORD, and said, We beseech thee, O Lord, we beseech thee, let us not perish for this man's life, and lay not upon us innocent blood: for thou, O LORD, hast done as it pleased thee. So they took up Jonah, and cast him forth into the sea: and the sea ceased from her raging (Jon 1:14-15).

Despite their humane intentions, the sailors soon found their task hopeless. With a prayer upon their lips, therefore, they cast Jonah into the sea. What they prayed is well worth pondering. Pusey calls it "a wonderful, concise, confession of faith."[5] As he points out, they compressed the whole message of man's agency and God's providence into three simple Hebrew words which may be explained in English like this, "As [Thou] willedst [Thou] didst."[6] There, indeed, is an example of submission to God! As soon as those words were uttered and Jonah cast into the waters, "the sea ceased from her raging" (v. 15). The original text may be read, "The sea *stood* from her raging," the word *stood* implying the expectant attitude of a servant ready to obey.

These mariners had heard the word of God through Jonah. In their simple way they had received the truth and believed God. They knew that, along with the prophet, they were under God's eye and in His hands. They were willing even to acknowledge that God had done exactly as He had willed. They had come to the place of full submission to the divine will and purpose. And when they reached that place and acted upon their belief, the storm stood still. It is by no means fanciful to see in all this a picture of every man in the storm of life. The moment we realize that God is in our storms and doing exactly as He wills, then we find peace. Few greater lines have ever been written outside Scripture than Dante's sublime declaration, "In Thy will is our peace."

But what are we to think of the sudden cessation of the storm? The book of Jonah contains within its few pages one of the greatest concentrations of the supernatural in the Bible. Yet it is significant that the majority of them are based upon natural phenomena. Storms are not supernatural, but the text (v. 4) tells us that the Lord hurled this one into the sea in which the ship bearing Jonah to Tarshish was sailing. Nor is it supernatural for storms to cease. But the way this storm stopped was the work of the Lord. It was a case of "stormy wind fulfilling His word" (Ps 148:8), as when centuries later Christ stilled the tempest on the Sea of Galilee (Mt 8:23-27).

> Then the men feared the Lord exceedingly, and offered a sacrifice unto the Lord, and made vows (Jon 1:16).

This verse confirms the view that the mariners were converted. If action is evidence of faith, then it is safe to assume that Jonah's companions aboard ship were turned to the one true God. For the third time it is said that they "feared." Here the nature of their fear seems plain. It is that "fear of the Lord which is the beginning of wisdom." Nor were they half-hearted in this holy emotion, but, as the text tells us, they feared Him "exceedingly."

What follows is additional proof of their spiritual sincerity. They lost no time in offering a sacrifice. Then, on top of that, they "made vows." The word for sacrifice at this point in the Hebrew text is *zebach*. It is a term that may be used of a sacrifice entailing the shedding of blood, but not of one made by burning. In that case, the word might be *ôlāh*. Obviously, in a wooden ship of this ancient type a burnt-offering would have been highly dangerous. Doubtless the mariners took one of the livestock carried as cargo on the ship and offered the animal

to the Lord. They also "made vows." The latter statement points
to their conversion. Almost any man, including the atheist, will
cry to God in peril and will even make promises to be fulfilled
upon deliverance. It is a different thing to make one's vows *after*
deliverance, when the benefit has been received. Those who do
this are obligating themselves to do something for God not as a
bargain but as a voluntary expression of gratitude. Uninstructed
as these mariners were in all Jonah knew about God, their
example nevertheless witnesses to the value of promptness in
thanksgiving. To give thanks to "the Lord, who daily loads us
with benefits" (Ps 68:19) is something we Christians may well
learn more about. Ready to call upon Him in time of need, we
are too slow in thanking Him when He has helped us. Those who
walk in close fellowship with God are seldom remiss in express-
ing their gratitude to Him.

Jonah swallowed by the fish

> Now the LORD had prepared a great fish to swallow up Jonah.
> And Jonah was in the belly of the fish three days and three
> nights (Jon 1:17).

For most people the book of Jonah means just one thing—the
story of the prophet's being swallowed by a whale and then
being cast up alive. Few Old Testament miracles are more
famous than this one; none has been more ridiculed from ancient
times until the present. In the second century Lucian derided it,
while some of Augustine's hearers in the fifth century listened to
it with unbelieving laughter. Even now many equate belief in it
with obscurantism.

Yet responsible exposition of Jonah demands thoughtful and
respectful consideration of the three sentences (1:17; 2:10) that
tell us what happened to the prophet when the sailors threw
him into the raging sea.

To take this miracle seriously does not mean, however, that a
disproportionate amount of attention must be focused upon it or
that what happened must be proved. Jonah is not in the Bible
that we might, as someone has said, "pore over the whale and
forget God." Nor is it there that, as Thomas John Carlisle sug-

gests, we might forget what God was doing inside His disobedient prophet's heart:

> I was so obsessed
> with what was going on
> inside the whale
> that I missed
> seeing the drama
> inside Jonah.[7]

Preoccupation with this spectacular miracle leads to distortion of the perspective in which Scripture places it. Instead of trying to "prove" the reality of Jonah's encounter with the great fish, we who accept its historicity should center our attention upon his encounter with God, of which this miracle is a part but by no means the whole. We believe in God's strange way of dealing with His disobedient prophet not because there are whales or enormous fish that can gulp down a man, but because our Lord referred so explicitly to Jonah's experience and because human incredulity is irrelevant to divine omnipotence. As G. K. Chesterton said, "The incredible thing about miracles is that they happen."[8]

There are two ways of "poring over the whale and forgetting God," or of being more interested in "what was going on inside the whale" than in "seeing the drama inside Jonah." One is by endeavoring to make it all so plausible that the miracle is practically explained away. To do this may come from a covert skepticism that needs to bolster faith by rationalism. The other is by endeavoring to "disprove" the actuality of the event by citing all sorts of mythological and legendary parallels and so using conjecture to support unbelief. In either case, a single feature of this skillful and orderly narrative takes the center of the stage and stops the action instead of advancing it as the author so clearly intended.

It is not, therefore, to evade further discussion# of this celebrated miracle but to preserve a balance in expounding the

---

#The reader will find in the appendix a presentation of some apologetic and illustrative material relating to Jonah and the great fish.

book that we go on, after brief comment on the words "three days and three nights."

"And Jonah was in the belly of the fish three days and three nights" (1:17b). There are some who have difficulty with this statement and also with Matthew 12:40 because our Lord's body was not actually in the grave a full seventy-two hours.** But surely Orelli's comment, which is substantially the position of many present-day authorities,[9] is satisfactory: *"three days and three nights . . .* is not to be punctiliously understood of seventy-two hours; but according to Hebrew idiom, of a space of time reaching backward and forward beyond twenty-four hours."††[10]

**Cf. E. A. Miller, *Was Christ Crucified on Good Friday?* (an argument for placing the crucifixion on Wednesday) and R. M. Allen, *Three Days in the Grave* (an argument for Thursday). R. A. Torrey held the Wednesday theory (cf. his *Difficulties in the Bible,* pp. 104-109).

††For further discussion of the "three days and three nights" see the appendix.

3

PRAYER AND DELIVERANCE

JONAH'S PRAYER

Then Jonah prayed unto the LORD his God out of the fish's belly, and said, I cried by reason of mine affliction unto the LORD, and he heard me; out of the belly of hell cried I, and thou heardest my voice. For thou hadst cast me into the deep, in the midst of the seas; and the floods compassed me about: all thy billows and thy waves passed over me. Then I said, I am cast out of thy sight; yet I will look again toward thy holy temple. The waters compassed me about, even to the soul: the depth closed me round about, the weeds were wrapped about my head. I went down to the bottoms of the mountains; the earth with her bars was about me for ever: yet hast thou brought up my life from corruption, O LORD my God. When my soul fainted within me I remembered the LORD: and my prayer came in unto thee, into thine holy temple. They that observe lying vanities forsake their own mercy. But I will sacrifice unto thee with the voice of thanksgiving; I will pay that that I have vowed. Salvation is of the LORD (Jon 2:1-9).

The entire second chapter of the book, the last verse excepted, deals with Jonah's prayer. As with so much else in this wonderful narrative, it has given rise to divergent opinions. On the one hand, there are those who insist that for the prophet actually to have uttered such a prayer is impossible not only physically but also psychologically. On the other hand, believers in the historicity of Jonah's experience disagree as to the interpretation of the chapter, some even insisting that this prayer was spoken while the prophet was literally in sheol, or hades. But surely they complicate the record by saying that the prophet died within the great fish and later rose from the dead.

87

Now there are several reasons why the latter view fails to
carry conviction. For one thing it is a gratuitous addition to the
supernatural element of the narrative. Our God is the doer of
mighty works. But let us not make the mistake of reading into
the text miracles that are not clearly stated therein. In the next
place, the fact that Jonah says in his prayer, "Out of the belly of
hell* cried I," does not necessarily prove him to have been
physically dead. Even now someone in extreme danger might
speak of himself as in "the jaws of death." Similar phrases occur
in the Psalms, from which Jonah so largely drew the phraseology
of his prayer. In Psalm 18:5, for example, David says, "The cords
of Sheol entangled me, the snares of death confronted me"
(RSV). Again he says in Psalm 30:3, "Thou has brought up my
soul from Sheol, restored me to life from among those gone
down to the Pit" (RSV). But who would insist that this language
should be pressed to the extent of making it an article of belief
that David experienced physical death and resurrection?

To be sure, Jonah is a type of the burial and resurrection of
Christ. Yet that does not demand his physical death any more
than Joseph, another Old Testament type of our Lord, had to die
and be raised again when his brethren cast him into the pit
whence he was drawn by the passing Midianites. Typology does
not mean identity of every detail. As a matter of fact, had Jonah
undergone physical death, this might have invalidated another
great line of typical teaching for which his preservation alive has
a key meaning. For the prophet not only prefigures the Lord
Jesus Christ; he also stands for the Jews. At present they are
thrown into the raging sea of the nations, in the midst of which,
as a nation, they are being preserved *alive*, awaiting their restoration.

The view of some critics that the prayer is psychologically
impossible needs little refutation. Persons rescued from drown-
ing have spoken of the extraordinary activity of the mind in the
seconds before unconsciousness. Jonah was a true prophet. Both

---

*Hebrew, *Sheol*. The New Testament equivalent is the Greek, *hades*.
Sheol is the Old Testament term for the abode of the dead and is used as
a parallel to the grave.

his intellect and heart were saturated with the Word of God. The natural thing would be for him to cry out in scriptural terms exactly as he did. It is the disposition of the spiritual to pray continually during time of great stress.

But having gone thus far, we must hasten to guard against dogmatism as to the time when the prophet prayed. Both Pusey and Perowne think it to have been at the close of his imprisonment within the fish.[1] Others believe that Jonah composed the prayer after being cast up upon the shore. In this case, it would be a reminiscence of his terrible experience, containing, of course, the gist of his cries to God. There is, of course, no valid reason why Jonah could not actually have prayed the prayer recorded in this chapter while he was inside the sea monster. Whatever our view, there is nothing to be gained by insisting, as does one commentator, that Jonah literally "went groping among the deep hidden rocks which run along the coast of Palestine."[2] The fact seems to be that Jonah must have been swallowed by the fish very soon after being cast overboard and that it was within the fish that he "went down to the bottoms of the mountains" (v. 6).

We come now to the exposition of Jonah's prayer. Strange as it may seem, there are those who deny that it is a prayer at all, even though the text plainly says, "And Jonah *prayed* unto the LORD his God." Denial of the prayer character of Jonah's words in this second chapter is based upon the fact that what he said contains not one word of petition. But since when is prayer confined to petition? If Jonah's words are not prayer, then the outpouring of Hannah's heart following the promise of Samuel's birth† was not prayer. In fact, the Hebrew word *palal* in Jonah 2:1 is the same word used of Hannah's utterance. It is the most frequent word for "pray" in the Old Testament, where it occurs over seventy times. Its original sense is significant; according to Young's *Analytical Concordance* it means "to judge self," "to pray habitually."

As we reflect upon the significance of this ancient word, we

---

†First Samuel 2:1-10. Nor, by the same token, was Mary's Magnificat (Lk 1:46-55) prayer!

realize how far short our own prayer life falls. Every child of God has the right of access to the throne of grace through the work of Christ. We may use this privilege for personal petition and also for intercession. But it is sad that we so frequently use it only in these ways. Prayer is broader than petition. God is our Father. He wants us to come to Him as His children. The relationship between a son and his father would be strange indeed were that son to limit his words to his parent to requests either in his own behalf or in behalf of others. In no human family where love prevails is this the case. On the contrary, children often talk lovingly to their fathers without the slightest thought of getting something. All parents know how happy it makes them when their children express their love and appreciation. So with God and His children. There are times when our most acceptable prayer is simply to go into the heavenly Father's presence and tell Him of our love. There are occasions when nothing is more fitting than an outpouring of thanksgiving without one single word of request. This is one of the lessons of Jonah's prayer. Too often we think of this prophet only as a recalcitrant and disgruntled fugitive. We overlook the fact that by far the longest speech recorded from his lips is this beautiful prayer of thanksgiving.

In order to emphasize its unity, we have quoted the whole prayer. Phrase by phrase comment might do violence to its exalted feeling; sincere emotion is difficult to analyze. Let the reader go through this prayer eight or ten times, meditating as he does, and he will be spiritually enriched. He will also note that Jonah prayed scripturally. Wonderfully interwoven into his words are allusion upon allusion to the psalms. They are free rather than exact direct quotations.

It is a great thing when a child of God learns to pray. It is an even greater thing when he comes to the point of praying biblically. The language of Scripture is the language of heaven. Inevitably the most spiritual Christians draw largely upon the Bible for the phraseology with which they approach God. Many of us do this when in need, as we come before God and plead some specific promise. But Jonah's prayer shows us that praise also is most effectually put in Bible words.

> When my soul fainted within me I remembered the Lord:
> and my prayer came in unto thee, into thine holy temple. They
> that observe lying vanities forsake their own mercy (Jon 2:7-8).

The word *palal* not only means "to pray habitually"; it also
signifies "to judge self." And Jonah's prayer contains this element
also. In these verses he speaks penitently.[3] Indeed, the whole
prayer is a self-judgment of his experience in the sight of the
Lord who so graciously delivered him. There is a sense in which
Jonah was an Old Testament prodigal. It took distress to bring
him to himself. Again we recognize our human kinship with
him. For most of us trial is one of the best schools of prayer.
When our souls, like Jonah's, faint within us, then we too
remember the Lord. It is a rule of the spiritual life that a man
truly comes to his senses when he remembers God. The God-
forgetter is really beside himself.

Jonah, however, not only came to himself; he also went further and placed his finger upon the root of his difficulty. In that
self-judgment which is so important an element of prayer, he
said, "They that observe lying vanities forsake their own mercy"
(v. 8). This is more than a general observation. It is an accurate
diagnosis of the prophet's own trouble.‡ Calvin tells us that
"lying vanities" means "all inventions with which men deceive
themselves."[4] These range from crude images of wood, stone,
and metal to the unseen idols which usurp the place of God in
many a heart.

In one of the latest books of the New Testament the apostle
John closes with this strange injunction, addressed primarily to
Christians: "Little children, keep yourselves from idols" (1 Jn
5:21). "But," someone objects, "Christians cannot worship idols."
Yet they can! Christians can worship the same kind of idol Jonah
worshiped. Not only can they do so; they are doing it every day.
Jonah's idol was self-will; he set up in his own heart an exagger-
ated patriotism to which he bowed rather than to the will of the

---

‡Some see in Jonah's reference to "lying vanities" only his harsh, exclusiv-
istic attitude toward the non-Jewish peoples (cf. D. W. B. Robinson, *The
New Bible Commentary*, p. 717). But surely he is also applying the principle of v. 8 to himself, as v. 9 shows.

only true God. So also Christians today may set up self-will in
their hearts. The specific issue may not be the same as in the case
of Jonah, but the sin is identical. How true it is that those who
observe any form of idolatry do so at the expense of forsaking
their own mercy! Though our God is very merciful, there are
some things He cannot tolerate. Among them is the idol-
worshiping Christian. Bowing down in heart to anything or
anyone aside from the Lord Jesus Christ is tantamount to deliberate desertion of Him who is our mercy and our very present
help in time of trouble.

> But I will sacrifice unto Thee with the voice of thanksgiving;
> I will pay that that I have vowed. Salvation is of the LORD
> (Jon 2:9).

There is a striking similarity between the end of this
second chapter and the close of the first chapter. The mariners
had celebrated their deliverance from the storm through offering
sacrifices and making vows unto the Lord. Here Jonah, also
delivered, promised to pay that which he had vowed. As to the
precise nature of his vow, Scripture says nothing. Whatever it
may have been, we may see behind it the promise to obey God
in everything. The very essence of the vow might well have
been a commitment to live up to the high calling of a prophet
by doing God's bidding, no matter how strange it might seem.
Charles A. Blanchard, in his book, *An Old Testament Gospel*,
has an effective passage on this subject of paying to the Lord
that which one has promised.[5] He points out that many Christians miss blessings that might have been theirs because they
have either forgotten or deliberately overlooked their pledges to
God. So the psalmist says, "Vow, and pay unto the LORD your
God" (Ps 76:11).

"Salvation is of the LORD!" cried Jonah. One cannot imagine a
more fitting close to this unique prayer. The word the prophet
used for "salvation" is an intensive form§ of the Hebrew *Yeshua*,
having the sense of "mighty salvation." Linked to the Hebrew

---

§H. K. von Orelli points out that the Hebrew text has the "fuller, more
solemn form" of the word (*The Twelve Minor Prophets*, p. 178).

word for salvation is "the name Joshua, and its Greek rendering, Jesus. Joshua is a contraction of Jehoshua, which means, 'Jehovah is salvation.' "[6]

What a lesson Jonah has learned! He knew at last who alone can give men salvation. Would that every reader of these words might know by experience the truth of the prophet's heartfelt cry. Yes, "Salvation *is* of the Lord." In these five words is the glory of the Christian faith. No man nor any angel from heaven can save a single soul. But the things that are impossible with men are possible with God (cf. Lk 18:27).

It is helpful to study Jonah's character. It is instructive to examine the evidence for the reality of what happened to him. But to admit the historicity of Jonah cannot save anyone. Intellectual conviction can never redeem anyone; only God saves our souls through faith in Jesus Christ. There is no greater privilege for any of us than to be able to say out of personal experience, "'Salvation is of the LORD.'"

JONAH'S DELIVERANCE (2:10)

And the LORD spake unto the fish, and it vomited out Jonah upon the dry land (Jon 2:10).

Important considerations stem from this verse, which seems at first glance so obvious. It states a fact wholly essential to the deeper meaning of the book, because the action of the fish in casting forth Jonah is the inescapable completion of the type. Indeed one may go so far as to say that just as the redemptive work of Christ depends upon His resurrection, so the central message of Jonah pivots on this verse. Without it, Jonah could never have fulfilled his mission and the likeness of the prophet's experience to that of Christ would be incomplete.

The text says that God spoke to the fish. When we contemplate nature and the marvels of instinct in bird, animal, marine, and insect life, we have no cause to smile at this single declaration. To be sure, it is put in anthropomorphic language. But no thoughtful person would deny God's ability in His own way to influence the sea monster He had prepared for such a special purpose. Nor need we concern ourselves with elaborate demonstration as to the portion of the coast on which Jonah was deposited. Common sense suggests that it was doubtless not far from Joppa. This conclusion is based on the verb in the thirteenth verse of the first chapter, which, as Huxtable[7] shows, should be translated "bring back"; for if the mariners rowed hard to bring the ship *back* to the land (1:13), they could not have been very far from their starting point. The reasonable supposition, therefore, is that Jonah was deposited not very far from Joppa.

Is it not always so with those who disobey God and launch out in self-will? When they are brought to a realization of their sin, the first step in restoration is to go back to the place from which they have departed. It is sad when a Christian gets out of fellowship with God. But it is a happy occasion when he recognizes his need, and comes back to Him and takes up the interrupted fellowship once more.

4

RECOMMISSIONED AND OBEDIENT

And the word of the LORD came unto Jonah the second time, saying, Arise, go unto Nineveh, that great city, and preach unto it the preaching that I bid thee (Jon 3:1-2).

In this third chapter the remarkable story of Jonah reaches its peak. Heretofore the emphasis has been upon the prophet's preparation; tremendous as the miracle of Jonah's preservation in the sea monster has been, it is more a preface than a conclusion. Now the veil is drawn aside, and something of the strange purpose of the Almighty in dealing with His prophet is revealed. If the miracle of the fish is great, that of this chapter is greater. For here is the record of nothing less than the greatest mass conversion in history. Though generalities must always be used with caution, we may say that never again has the world seen anything quite like the result of Jonah's preaching in Nineveh.

Remembering, then, that we are coming to the climax of the narrative, we return to the prophet. We have already seen that he was probably deposited by the fish not far from Joppa. Further speculation about the exact location is fruitless, although many have not hesitated to indulge in it. For example, Josephus says that he was cast forth upon the shore of the Euxine Sea.[1] Nor is there any great value in conjecturing how long Jonah waited before receiving his new commission or in picturing what he did while waiting. All this belongs to the realm of fancy, and, while affording exercise in the use of imagination, is hardly more than fiction. It is wise to be cautious about filling in gaps when Scripture is silent.

> And the word of the LORD came unto Jonah the second
> time (Jon 3:1).

Someone has aptly called this account of the prophet's
recommission "the gospel of the second chance." The reference is not to a second chance of salvation after death, because
Scripture holds out no such hope, but to the good news of
another opportunity of fruitful service for God. Seen in this
light, the opening of this chapter is of comfort to every Christian. For who of us has not on occasion been a Jonah in refusing
to obey some clear leading of the Lord?

A closer look at this verse unfolds vistas of God's grace and
speaks eloquently of the prophet's chastened mind and heart.
Jonah might have presumed upon his miraculous deliverance.
Realizing the complete folly of running away from the divine
command, he might have embarked upon a brash repentance
which would have led him to rush to Nineveh then and there
without another word from God. That he did not do so speaks
volumes both for his humility and for the effectiveness of the
divine chastening. Instead he waited upon the Lord and did
nothing until the word came to him again.

So much for the prophet. But what of God's attitude in all
this? Surely it is a grand lesson in grace. That Jonah was in the
first place forgiven was entirely through God's mercy and not
through any merit of his own. Had he been merely forgiven
without another call to speak forth the Word of God as a
divinely commissioned prophet, we could only marvel at the
grace that forgave so freely.[2] But God does not leave His purpose incompleted. When He strives with a man as He did with
Jonah and, we may add, as He does with many of us, then He
carries through His work to its conclusion. Thus He spoke to His
prophet a second time.

> Arise, go unto Nineveh, that great city, and preach unto it
> the preaching that I bid thee (Jon 3:2).

The comparison between this second commission and the first
one (1:2) shows certain differences. The original command seems
more intimate in tone. Not only does the Lord tell Jonah to go to
Nineveh, but He also takes him into His confidence to the extent

of giving a reason why he is to "cry against" the city: "for their
wickedness is come up before me." Here, however, the command
is more brusque. Jonah is simply ordered to go to Nineveh and to
proclaim there the message God gave him. The command is
renewed and if anything requires even more stringent and un-
questioning obedience than the first one.

What a pregnant statement we have in the words "preach
unto it the preaching that I bid thee." Consider the present-day
ministry. Things would be different in church and community
life were every clergyman today to preach unto the "Nineveh" to
which he is called nothing but the preaching God bids him. One
of the failures of the modern ministry is the substitution of the
word of man for the Word of God. The preaching God bids us
preach today is indissolubly linked with the Bible. Woe to a
preacher who departs from that Book, for, though man may listen
to him with praise, an unbiblical message lacks the spiritual
power that brings eternal results.

JONAH'S OBEDIENCE (3:3-10)

JONAH'S COMPLIANCE (3:3)

> So Jonah arose, and went unto Nineveh, according to the
> word of the LORD. Now Nineveh was an exceeding great city of
> three days' journey (Jon 3:3).

The first part of this verse needs comparatively little comment. It is a plain statement of Jonah's obedience and also of
what he should have done when God first spoke to him. A glance
at 1:3 shows almost its exact opposite. There we read, "But
Jonah rose up to flee unto Tarshish from the presence of the
LORD." Observe the conjunction *but*. When a man disobeys God,
this word of opposition is fitting. In contrast, the statement
before us is introduced by "so," pointing to Jonah's compliance.
Observe also that, when "Jonah arose and went unto Nineveh,"
he did so "according to the word of the LORD." But when he
fled, he fled "from the presence of the LORD." Some things are
spiritually impossible. Among them is disobedience of God according to the Word of God; no one can at the same time rebel

against the divine command and remain loyal to the Lord's edicts. Contrariwise, obedience to God places one in the stream of blessing flowing from the Word of the Lord.

The next sentence suggests several things. Some have made much of the tense of the verb. This is the way their argument goes: The text says, "Now Nineveh *was* an exceeding great city." Therefore Nineveh could not have been in existence in Jonah's day. Had it actually been in existence at that time, the text would have read, "Now Nineveh *is* an exceeding great city." Therefore the book was written *after* the fall of Nineveh.

What shall we say about an argument like that? Well, we may say that common sense answers it. As Perowne points out, the clause in question is part of the narrative preparing the way for the next verse. It merely mentions what Nineveh was and the kind of place Jonah found when he went there. Consider a New Testament parallel. In John 5:2 we read, "Now there is at Jerusalem by the sheep market a pool." Some have reasoned from this that Jerusalem must still have been standing when John wrote his gospel. But if that is insisted upon, what of John's statement (11:18) that "Bethany was nigh unto Jerusalem, about fifteen furlongs" and that Jesus "went forth with his disciples over the brook Cedron, where *was* a garden" (18:1)? And what, also, of 19:41, "In the place where he was crucified there was a garden"?[3] Using the same reasoning, one would have to insist that Jerusalem was both in existence and not in existence at the time John wrote the fourth gospel! Obviously Jonah's use of "was" * is quite in keeping with his narrative style. Only by a slavish literalism that scholars who hold Jonah to be fiction would repudiate elsewhere can it be pressed into service as an argument against the historicity of the book. "The statement that *Nineveh was an exceedingly great city*," says D. W. B. Robinson, "need imply no more than that this is how it was when Jonah

---

*As G. Herbert Livingston says, "The Hebrew language has no true past tense, indeed has no tenses at all. The 'perfect' aspect of the verb may at times be translated into an English past tense, but its sense is much broader. The 'perfect' form may also indicate an act (such as the founding of a city) which has been extended into a state of being. Consequently, all that is intended here is: Nineveh existed in Jonah's day as a great city" (*The Wycliffe Bible Commentary*, p. 848).

went there. . . . But it is curious that the people who are normally adept at discovering secondary interpolations in the books of the Old Testament prefer to leave this note as part of the text and to use it as a lever to bring the date of the whole book to some time long past the fall of Nineveh in 612 A.D."[4]

Passing from this detail, we come to the scene of the prophet's ministry. The Nineveh of Jonah's day is portrayed as "an exceeding great city of three days' journey." The expression *exceeding great city* means literally "a great city to God."[5] Now why was this city so great in God's sight? As we shall see in a moment, Nineveh was indeed a major city and possessed a vast architectural magnificence. But it was not this that made it bulk so large before God. As Mitchell says, "Nineveh was really great to God for the human souls concentrated there. In God's sight territorial extent and architectural mass or magnificence are nothing compared to a human soul, and the spiritual influences which go forth from it, or bear upon it. . . . And a city full of these souls, these myriad of unending lives ... only God can comprehend how great is such a city-full."[6]

Turning to the material side of Nineveh's greatness, here are a few facts from archeology. Though the inner wall of Nineveh was only about seven and three-quarter miles in circumference, the total population was sprawled over a wide extent outside this wall. The phrase of three days' journey may be a colloquialism and need not necessarily mean that it took three whole days to walk through Nineveh. Yet D. J. Wiseman says that "the 'three days' journey' probably refers to the whole administrative district of Nineveh, which was about 30-60 miles across (Hatra-Khorsabad-Nimrud)."[7] Perhaps we might visualize this Assyrian capital as being something like one of our modern urban complexes with outlying areas surrounding the inner city.

The ruins of Nineveh are of impressive magnificence. Palace excavations show halls, rooms, and passages, some still faced with alabaster and sculptured with extraordinarily vivid portrayals of wars, hunting, mythology, and so on. The palace of Sennacherib had a grand entrance with bearded bulls on each side of the doorway. Between each pair of bulls was a figure of the ancient hero-giant carrying a weapon in one hand and with the other grasping a struggling lion. Remarkable in the ruins of the palace of Ashurbanipal are bas-reliefs of great artistic competence, depicting the king's lion hunts. So masterly are they that even today it would be hard to surpass the emotions of fear, rage and suffering shown on the animals' faces.

One of the most significant features of ancient Nineveh that archeology has brought to light is the library found by the workmen of Sir A. H. Layard in 1850. This was housed in two chambers in the palace of Ashurbanipal. The library, written upon clay tablets, contains works on philology, astronomy and astrology, religion, law, science, literature, history and commerce. There are also a large number of letters. It is quite apparent from such remains as these that, though Nineveh was the capital of one of the cruelest and most violent of ancient empires, it was at the same time a city of sophisticated culture.†

ITS RESULTS (3:4-10)
Jonah's message (3:4)

> And Jonah began to enter into the city a day's journey, and he cried, and said, Yet forty days, and Nineveh shall be overthrown (Jon 3:4).

Picture Jonah's entrance into this great city. Surely it was one of the most dramatic moments in history. Imagine the prophet, doubtless with the marks of his awful experience stamped upon his countenance. Clothed in the garb of the Hebrew prophet, he begins to enter the teeming metropolis, crying out the shortest of all prophetic messages. Only eight words in the English Bible, it is even more brief in the original text, where it reads as follows: *ôdh arbāʾîm yôm wenîneweh nehpāketh.*‡ As his voice rises

---

†See *The International Standard Bible Encyclopaedia,* s.v. T. G. Pinches, "Nineveh"; A. H. Sayce, "Nineveh, Library Of." Among more recent articles on Nineveh, that by Wiseman in *The New Bible Dictionary* (s.v. "Nineveh") is outstanding.

‡This is not a technical transliteration but an endeavor to give the reader an idea of the prophet's cry.

We need not suppose that Jonah said nothing but these words. However, they were the core, *the* text of his message, and he doubtless proclaimed them again and again as he preached.

above the hum of ancient traffic and business, a strange silence falls upon the inhabitants. One by one they are convicted of their sin, as the divine Word penetrates their hearts like an arrow of judgment. One can almost hear the intonation of the prophet as he calls out the Hebrew phrases. Yes, the message is brief, but let us never forget that it was the word of the Living God that Jonah proclaimed. Moreover, as Pusey aptly puts it, "Simplicity is always impressive."[8] It is significant that the Assyrian of both "forty" and "days" (*arbâ* and *ûmê* is substantially the same as the Hebrew (*arbâim* and *yôm*). The word *overthrown* might also have been known to the Ninevites.[9] The objection, therefore, that Jonah's message could have had no effect upon Nineveh, because it was spoken in an unknown language, is not impressive. It is folly to assume that Hebrew was completely unknown in a city the size of Nineveh. Nor if Jonah used Aramaic would he have been unintelligible. Surely there were many who could have interpreted the prophet's words.

5

THE CONVERSION OF A GREAT CITY

The repentance of Nineveh (3:5)

> So the people of Nineveh believed God, and proclaimed a
> fast, and put on sackcloth, from the greatest of them even to the
> least of them (Jon 3:5).

Jonah had entered but one day's journey into Nineveh proclaiming God's Word, when marvelous things began to happen.
His prophecy laid immediate hold upon his hearers. Like wild
fire the news spread. Thousands must have crowded around the
prophet and passed the word on to those who could not themselves see him. If we are to take the record in this and the
following verses at all seriously, the result of Jonah's entrance
into Nineveh with his divinely given proclamation was the repentance of the entire city. Let us restate the matter in modern
terms in order to realize afresh its implications. It was as if a
messenger of God were to come to a metropolis the size of
Pittsburgh,* proclaiming just one sentence of divine revelation.
He is not scoffed at or committed as a lunatic. On the contrary,
his words strike consternation into the hearts of those who hear
him. En masse the populace receive the messenger, repent, give
up their evil ways, and turn to God. But the comparison is
inadequate, because Nineveh was more than a great city. It was
a world capital. And, as this chapter tells us, the repentance
occasioned by Jonah's words extended from the common people
right up to the king himself.

---

*On the basis of the reference in the last chapter (4:11) to 120,000
"persons that cannot discern between their right hand and their left hand"
(i.e., children below the age of discretion), it may be estimated that
Nineveh had a population of about 600,000.

"But this is supernatural," someone says. Certainly it is supernatural. In no other way can it be explained. Consider these words from a writer who has a high appreciation of Jonah as literature but a low estimate of its historicity: "It would be humanly impossible for one speaking a foreign language to enter the capital of a great nation and by a single proclamation to convert king and city to obedience to the true God."†[1] What an exposé of the shallowness of unbelief! "It would be humanly impossible." Of course it would! Every conversion is humanly impossible. Christian ministers should know that it is not possible for them as individuals to convert a single soul. <u>Conversion is always the result of the mighty power of God working through His divinely commissioned servants.</u> Have the doubters never read the words of Christ in the nineteenth chapter of Matthew, where, after His arresting statement, "It is easier for a camel to go through the eye of a needle, than for a rich man to enter into the kingdom of God," we are told that the disciples asked in amazement, "Who then can be saved?" To which question Jesus replied, "With man this is impossible; but with God all things are possible" (Mt 19:23-26). <u>God delights to do the impossible, and never more so than in turning men to Himself.</u> Instead, then, of denying on the grounds of its "human" impossibility the repentance that swept over Nineveh, let us see it as an evidence of divine power. For this, not the episode of the sea monster, is the greatest miracle in the book.

In discussing the repentance of Nineveh some scholars suggest that a severe plague which visited the city in 765 B.C., followed by a total eclipse of the sun in 763 and another plague in 759, might have predisposed the king and people to look for a total catastrophe.[2] Other expositors of Jonah refer to Layard's state-

---

†"The greatest of the improbabilities [in the book of Jonah] is a moral one. Can we conceive of a large heathen city being converted by an obscure foreign prophet?" *Encyclopaedia Britannica*, 1938 ed., s.v. "Jonah." "The sudden conversion on such a large scale as is evidently implied of a large heathen population, is contrary to analogy. It is remarkable also that the conversion of Nineveh, if it took place upon the scale described, should have produced so little permanent effect, for the Assyrians are uniformly represented in the Old Testament as idolators" (S. R. Driver, cited in John Kennedy, *On the Book of Jonah*, p. 43).

ment: "I have known a Christian priest to frighten a whole
Mussulman town to tents and repentance by publicly proclaiming
that he had received a divine mission to announce a coming
earthquake or plague."[3] History contains minor resemblances to
what happened at Nineveh. For instance, there was a time
when the whole city of Florence was under the sway of
Savanarola's eloquence. Nor will those who heard Orson Welles'
radio broadcast in 1938, based on H. G. Wells' science fiction
novel *War of the Worlds*, forget the widespread panic that
resulted. Such things, however, do not explain what happened
at Nineveh any more than data about sharks and whales prove
the miracle of Jonah and the fish.

No comment on the miracle of Nineveh's repentance is complete without some reference to our Lord's words as reported in
Luke 11:30. Matthew speaks of "the sign of the prophet Jonah"
(12:39), but Luke uses the significant phrase "as Jonah was a
sign unto the Ninevites." These words, "a sign unto the Ninevites," point to some awareness on the part of the inhabitants of
Nineveh of Jonah's marvelous experience. For them he was a
living lesson in the sure judgment and great mercy of God.
" 'The sign of Jonas' . . . includes not only his 'death' and 'resurrection,' but also his preaching, by virtue of that 'resurrection,' to
Gentile Nineveh. Ponder the great importance of this sign for
Christ's generation . . . and for our own."[4] We may suggest that
this "sign" of the prophet himself may have been a real factor in
the conversion of the city.

Observe further that, once Jonah delivered his message to
Nineveh, his name is not mentioned again in this chapter. Nor
does the record say, "The people of Nineveh believed Jonah." A
tendency of the human heart is to place faith in the messenger
rather than the message. To make the contemporary application,
there are churches where members are more devoted to the
minister than to God. Happy is the preacher who has the Jonah-
like quality of imparting to his hearers God's message so fully
that he himself is forgotten.

The remainder of the verse tells us that the people themselves
proclaimed the fast and put on the sackcloth of humility. Distinctions of rank were forgotten, as indicated by the phrase "from

the greatest of them even to the least of them." Their conviction of peril was urgent, and they apparently acted by consensus.

The king's repentance and proclamation (3:6-9)

> For word came unto the king of Nineveh, and he arose from his throne, and he laid his robe from him, and covered him with sackcloth, and sat in ashes. And he caused it to be proclaimed and published through Nineveh by the decree of the king and his nobles, saying, Let neither man nor beast, herd nor flock taste any thing: let them not feed, nor drink water: But let man and beast be covered with sackcloth, and cry mightily unto God: yea, let them turn every one from his evil way, and from the violence that is in their hands. Who can tell if God will turn and repent, and turn away from his fierce anger, that we perish not? (Jon 3:6-9).

In a city the size of Nineveh it must have ordinarily taken considerable time for news to reach the king, surrounded as he was by a complex and luxurious Oriental court. However, this clamor was too great to escape his ears. With comparatively little delay the word reached him.

But who was this king of Nineveh? Realizing that we are only in the realm of probability and bearing in mind that Jonah lived before or during the reign of Jeroboam II (c. 793-753), we may venture the opinion that the monarch at this time may have been Adad-nirari III (810-782 B.C.) or possibly, Shalmaneser IV (781-772), or Ashur-dan III (772-775).‡ The king's response to Jonah's preaching was no less direct and decisive than that of the populace. Promptly he got up from his magnificent throne, laid aside his gorgeous robes of office, and, covering himself with the harsh cloth of mourning, sat in the ashes of humiliation. In a sense his action was a spiritual abdication of his power before Almighty God. Whatever else this monarch may have been, he now showed greatness.

The word for "robe" is the same one used in Joshua 7:21 for

---

‡Dates are based on the *New Bible Dictionary* and *Unger's Bible Dictionary*.

the garment that led to Achan's fatal covetousness. Layard describes a bas-relief showing an Assyrian king "in vestments consisting of a long flowing garment, edged with fringes and tassels, descending to his ankles, and confined at the waist by a girdle. Over this robe a second, similarly ornamented and open in front, appears to have been thrown. From his shoulders fell a cape or hood, also adorned with tassels, and to it were attached two long ribbons or lappets. He wore the conical mitre, or tiara, which distinguished the monarch in Assyrian bas-reliefs, and appears to have been reserved for him alone."[5]

There is something affecting in the picture of this Oriental monarch so swiftly casting aside such gorgeous robes and taking the place of the penitent. He had the virtue of not holding back in his approach to God.

"And he caused it to be proclaimed and published through Nineveh by the decree of the king and his nobles, saying, Let neither man nor beast, herd nor flock, taste any thing: let them not feed, nor drink water" (Jon 3:7). Having himself turned to God, the king acted for the whole nation in publishing a proclamation. This proclamation contains an interesting provision, linking the domestic animals of the city with the human inhabitants. Scholars tell us that this is the only instance in ancient times wherein beasts are portrayed as wearing sackcloth, although the custom of having horses participate in mourning goes back to the Persians, who, after their commander Massistius died, clipped their horses and mules. And the participation of black-draped horses in funeral processions continues into modern times.[6] (A riderless horse added a poignant touch to President Kennedy's funeral procession.) No Bible student, however, should be too much perplexed by the terms of this proclamation. It is an instance of the deep humanitarian note in the Bible that recognizes the relationship between man and beast and that is found in Psalm 36:6 and again at the close of this book of Jonah. Moreover, it is an unconscious testimony on the part of this Gentile monarch to the profound truth of Romans 8:18-25, where Paul, looking back to the fall of man that involved not only Adam and Eve but also the brute creation and the fruit of the ground, says, "The whole creation groaneth and travaileth in pain together until now" (Ro 8:22).

"But let man and beast be covered with sackcloth, and cry mightily unto God: yea, let them turn every one from his evil way, and from the violence that is in their hands" (Jon 3:8). The remainder of the proclamation narrows down the sin of Nineveh to the individual and isolates the cardinal transgression of this people. That it does so is one of the surest proofs of the reality of the repentance that swept the city. When men confess their sins to God, not in general but in specific terms, then we may be sure that the Spirit is dealing with them. Note the phrase "Let them turn every one from his evil way." Archeology is unanimous in substantiating the cruelty of the Ninevites. Violence was their national sin, and for it they were especially to cry unto God.

It is easy to read about the violence and barbarity of the Assyrians and shudder, forgetting the violence of our own times and our own society. If Nineveh stood under the judgment of God for its cruelty, what of so many of us who live all too comfortably with the persistent violence and inhumanity of man toward man today? We have little difficulty in acknowledging that Moscow and Peking need to repent. But what about Washington and New York, Los Angeles, and Chicago?

We have now reached the place in our study where an analysis of the steps by which Nineveh came to repentance is in order. One deals with this subject under a deep sense of humility. The experience of most of us concerning revival is meager. To be sure, we may have participated in meetings where there was much blessing or have witnessed§ many conversions. But none of us has ever beheld revival to the extent to which it came upon Nineveh, and very few today have seen real revival of modern times.|| To declare that revival of religion is one of the most pressing needs of our day is easy. What is more important

§While what happened at Nineveh was not strictly speaking "revival," which means a return to religion, yet it was in a broader meaning of the term—a spiritual awakening.

||The Uganda revival, for instance.

is to learn something of its conditions. Now in what happened at
Nineveh these four distinct steps may be traced:

1. *Revival in that ancient capital began with hearing the Word
of God.* Jonah boldly proclaimed it, and Nineveh stopped to
hear it. This suggests that the reason modern nations, cities,
communities, and churches lack revival is their unwillingness to
hear the Word. Any country, the vast majority of whose inhabitants are outside church on the Lord's day and who read the
Word of God very infrequently, if ever, is doing much to cut
itself off from revival as long as this indifference continues. Paul's
principle, "So then faith cometh by hearing, and hearing by the
word of God" (Ro 10:17), is true. The nation or individual that
will not even listen to God's messengers is in desperate straits.
Nineveh heard.

2. *But the city did more than hear.* No sooner did the divine
message reach the ears of the people than belief followed. As
has been pointed out above, the result of Jonah's preaching was
that the Ninevites believed God. The message having been
heard, faith resulted. There is an intimate connection between
revival and the Bible. For any true revival of Christianity and
any widespread repentance, there must be more than the
preaching of man's word, eloquent though it may be. There must
be preaching rooted in and saturated with the Word of the
living God. So far as Jonah was concerned, his was a God-given
message ("The preaching that I bid thee," 3:2). This is not to
say that preaching today must consist only of Scripture, but it
surely means that the preaching that brings men to their knees
before the holy God and leads them to the cross must be
Bible-centered.

3. *When the Ninevites heard the message and believed in
God, they took action upon their faith.* Even before the royal
edict, they proclaimed their own fast and as one man donned
the garments of humility. The test of any conversion lies in what
happens after it.

4. *Another aspect of the repentance of this great city had to*

do with the revelation of its specific sin. When God deals with men to bring them to Himself, He points His holy finger at the evil in their lives and lays bare their besetting sins. Then the individual must put away his sin. So the king of Nineveh issued a proclamation that commanded every man to turn from his evil way and the whole nation to repent of its violence.

Truly this subject of revival is a humbling one, not to be discussed merely impersonally and theoretically. You and I never have seen a Nineveh turned to God, but, if we are Christians, we have all seen conversion in at least one instance. That instance is ourselves. We who belong to Christ must know the meaning of repentance in our own hearts. We must know what God has done to awaken us to our sin through His word and to bring us to Christ.

God's "repentance" (3:10)

Some commentators assert that the repentance of Nineveh was neither city-wide nor genuine. But the text implies that the city as a whole turned to God, and this is reinforced by the royal proclamation. It is quite true that Nineveh later apostatized and was finally destroyed in judgment, according to Nahum's prophecy. But there is a period of many years between Jonah's time and that of Nahum shortly before the fall of Nineveh in 612 B.C. Conversion is always individual and never inherited. That Jonah's generation in Nineveh turned to the true God does not mean that their successors could not have fallen back into idolatry.

> And God saw their works, that they turned from their evil way; and God repented of the evil, that he had said that he would do unto them; and he did it not (Jon 3:10).

Having considered the repentance of Nineveh, we now face the larger and more difficult question of God's repentance toward the city. That this verse and others like it# speak of God as repenting or changing His mind is plain. But it is equally plain that other passages** state that God never changes. Representative of these are the words of Balaam: "God is not a man, that he should lie; neither the son of man, that he should repent: hath he said, and shall he not do it? or hath he spoken, and shall he not make it good?" (Num 23:19). And in the New Testament James speaks of "the Father of lights, with whom is no variableness, neither shadow of turning" (Ja 1:17). The question is, What is to be done with this apparent discrepancy in describing God's dealings with men?

To claim a complete solution of the problem would be unwarranted. In regard to every question concerning the divine character and sovereign purpose, man must be properly humble. There is wisdom in the words of Luther on this subject: "I stick to this rule, to avoid such questions as entangle us with the throne of the Divine Majesty, as much as I can. It is much better and safer for one to sit down by the cradle of our Lord Jesus Christ, Who has become man, than to puzzle one's soul with the Deity."[7] Yet it will not do completely to ignore this difficulty. Like other seeming discrepancies there are some helpful things that may be said about it without "entangling" oneself "with the throne of Divine Majesty." For example, there is the fact that, when the Bible speaks of repentance in respect to God, it does so, as the note in the New Scofield Reference Bible on Zechariah 8:14 says, "phenomenally," i.e., the word "repentance" applied to Deity "is used *phenomenally* according to Old Testament custom. God *seems* to change His mind. The phenomena are such as, in the case of a man, would indicate a change of mind." This is another way of saying that verses like Jonah 3:10 are anthropomorphic; God is thought of in manlike terms. But God is infinitely greater than human language; the difficulty we are facing relates to His inscrutable nature and essential unknowableness for the human mind.

Granting these things, we inquire further into the question before us. Did God really repent or change His mind in not destroying Nineveh? There are those who say He did not. His repentance, they claim, was more apparent than real. Defending their point of view, they reason thus: God is always on the side

---

#See Genesis 6:6; 2 Samuel 24:16; Joel 2:13.
**Numbers 23:19; 1 Samuel 15:29; Malachi 3:6; Romans 11:29.

of the right. It is impossible for Him to change His attitude toward righteousness and unrighteousness. The change referred to in Jonah 3:10 was really a change in Nineveh. After the city had truly repented of evil, if God had not seemed to change His purpose in destroying it but had carried out the original sentence of destruction, the problem would indeed have been serious; for in destroying a repentant city God might have acted in violation of His justice. But He did not do so. In perfect consistency with His justice and righteousness He spared Nineveh, because by heeding the warning the city had qualified for mercy. As Mitchell comments, "The man who should act and feel toward his son, when obedient, just the same as when disobedient would receive from sensible parents, not the praise of consistency, but condemnation for his indifference to morality. A dog or a horse may view sinful and holy actions with no difference of emotion; but not so a good man. Like a faithful mirror, which remains itself unchanged, uncolored, and undimmed while it reflects white light, blue light, red light, as it may fall on it, so a good man's mind reflects according to the character of the object presented, itself remaining good. And so God's holiness requires Him to present different aspects to different conduct. . . . His principles of action remain ever the same; their outworkings and applications are endlessly varied."[8]

Helpful also is the analogy of the thermometer.[9] Is it changeable or unchangeable? The superficial observer says it is changeable, for the mercury certainly moves in the tube. But just as certainly it is unchangeable, for it acts according to fixed law and invariably responds precisely to the temperature.

Finally, we note that the Bible contains certain principles of God's dealings with nations. A basic passage on this subject is Jeremiah 18. After watching the potter take clay and fashion it on the wheel, as it seemed good to the potter, Jeremiah received this message from the Lord: "At what instant I shall speak concerning a nation, and concerning a kingdom, to pluck up, and to pull down, and to destroy it; if that nation, against whom I have pronounced, turn from their evil, I will repent of the evil that I thought to do unto them. And at what instant I shall speak concerning a nation, and concerning a kingdom, to build and to plant it, if it do evil in my sight, that it obey not my voice, then I will repent of the good, wherewith I said I would benefit them" (Jer 18:7-10). These principles assuredly apply to Nineveh. Although the conditional element is not directly stated in Jonah, nevertheless it is unquestionably implied. God threatened to overthrow the wicked city. But the city repented and turned back to Him. Therefore, acting in conformity with His declared principles of dealing with nations, God did not carry out the sentence of doom.

6

THE WIDENESS OF GOD'S MERCY

In some respects the fourth chapter is the richest portion of the book of Jonah. The narrative began with God and Jonah. It has gone on to portray Jonah's flight, his relationship to the mariners, his strange experience in the great fish, and the marvelous repentance of a world capital. Now it ends, as it began, with God and Jonah. As suggested in the introduction, this closing chapter may be characterized by the title "The Wideness of God's Mercy." It is full of spiritual lessons. And one of its most significant features is that it contains no less than three more miracles. For God was not through with Jonah. In chapter 3 He was dealing with a city of hundreds of thousands of people. Now He has to do with one man. Jonah was a true servant of the Lord, though sadly mistaken. But God did not let him go. He who used His mighty power for the repentance of Nineveh employed the same power to teach just one of His children, and an obdurate one at that. So the conclusion of the book shows us that when we are the Lord's He Himself is our teacher.

> But it displeased Jonah exceedingly, and he was very angry. And he prayed unto the LORD, and said, I pray thee, O LORD, was not this my saying, when I was yet in my country? Therefore I fled before unto Tarshish: for I knew that thou art a gracious God, and merciful, slow to anger, and of great kindness, and repentest thee of the evil. Therefore now, O LORD, take, I beseech thee, my life from me; for it is better for me to die than to live (Jon 4:1-3).

Here is a picture of Jonah's mood after he had delivered his message. Vivid, indeed, is the Hebrew expression translated "very angry." It means "hot." Nineveh was spared, and Jonah did not like it. In modern parlance, he was "burned up." We may say that he had "learned nothing from his experiences."[1] But that is not quite fair. Remember that Jonah had been obedient to God's command. Submerging his own feelings, he had gone to Nineveh and faithfully delivered the divine message. Certainly the prophet would have done better to have rejoiced in Nineveh's pardon; yet we may acknowledge that he is not entirely the same man as the fugitive who took passage for Tarshish. For one thing, Jonah "prayed unto the LORD." Unlike many, even in this age of grace, he did not complain *of* God. Instead he took his complaints directly *to* God. The very freedom with which he brought his troubles "unto the LORD" tells much about his spiritual state. He knew God to be consistently gracious and merciful. And he also knew that, whenever men repent, God is *for* them even to the extent of turning aside the threatened judgment.

Knowing all this, Jonah did not like it; he still feared Nineveh. He had not yet learned to look beyond the horizon of his own people to the wideness of God's mercy. Therefore, he pled for death. Think of it! The prophet who had been instrumental in the repentance of the great city of Nineveh was so disappointed that he would rather die than live. Why? How could Jonah fail to be happy? A Christian who knows his own heart will not find it hard to answer that question. As with many of us today, Jonah lacked peace, because, although he had obeyed God, he was not wholly reconciled to the will of God. God had had His way with Nineveh and Jonah. But Jonah had not truly accepted God's way. And for this he was indeed blameworthy. True peace comes only from full acquiescence in everything to the will of God. Nothing saps spiritual activity more effectively than hidden rebellion against the divine will.

Another consideration is the nervous reaction from which Jonah may well have been suffering. The episode of the sea monster followed by the strain of entering boldly into Nineveh with his awful proclamation, must have taken a great physical and mental toll. Consider a parallel from the life of Elijah (1 Ki 19:1-7). After his tremendous victory over the priests of Baal on Carmel, that great prophet ran away from Jezebel, and, under the juniper tree, "requested for himself that he might die; and said, It is enough; now, O LORD, take away my life; for I am not better than my fathers." Then the Lord graciously cared for His over-wrought servant through the ministry of an angel who pointed him to the food and drink he desperately needed. So it may have been with Jonah. For the time being he was dejected and distressed, even to the extent of desiring death. But as we shall see, God was not through with him. By a series of gracious acts, He kept on working with him until he learned the full lesson Deity would teach him.

JONAH TAUGHT HIS FINAL LESSONS (4:4-11)

> Then said the LORD, Doest thou well to be angry? So Jonah went out of the city, and sat on the east side of the city, and there made him a booth, and sat under it in the shadow, till he might see what would become of the city (Jon 4:4-5).

As the chapter continues, the lengths to which the divine love goes become increasingly apparent. It is all a living illustration of the hymn "O Love, That Wilt Not Let Me Go." God has had His way both with Nineveh and with Jonah. But there is much yet to be done in Jonah's heart. As Paul reminded the Philippians, "He which hath begun a good work in you will perform it until the day of Jesus Christ" (Phil 1:6). That, of course, was written after Christ had come; yet God is ever the same, and His patience in Jonah's time was just as long as it was in Paul's day or as it is when He deals with us.

"Doest thou well to be angry?" That question was God's answer to the prophet's bitter request for death. And the same Lord who questioned Jonah speaks to us whenever our wrath rises. There is a natural tendency toward easy self-justification of anger. How readily we excuse ourselves by saying, "Oh, well, righteous anger is permissible." But there is always the question as to *how* righteous our anger really is. Though there are some things that justly provoke wrath, on what trivialities most human anger is expended! Whenever our feelings grow heated, we do well to remember God's question, "Doest thou well to be angry?"

Returning to the prophet, we observe that, though he answered not a word, he replied very plainly by what he did. So we see him going outside Nineveh, perhaps to some rise of ground. There on the eastern edge of the city he built a little hut to shelter him from the burning Oriental sun. Alone he sat, determined to see things through. God had said that Nineveh would be destroyed in forty days. True, Nineveh had repented. But Jonah wanted to be certain of the outcome.* He was still hoping for the city's destruction. Like the elder brother in the parable of the prodigal son, he was not big enough to rejoice in the forgiveness of the penitent. Moreover, he had what we might call an irreverent solicitude for God's care of His people, Israel. There was something akin to Jonah's attitude in Peter at Joppa, when he saw the vision of the great sheet and the voice from heaven ordered him to "rise, kill, and eat." When Peter replied, "Not so, Lord; for I have never eaten anything that is common or unclean" (Ac 10:14), he was acting as though he were too good for the Lord's command. But God does not need correction from any man; His way is perfect, and He does not require human solicitude for the justice of His acts.

THE GOURD, WORM, AND WIND

> And the LORD God prepared a gourd, and made it to come up over Jonah, that it might be a shadow over his head, to deliver him from his grief. So Jonah was exceeding glad of the gourd. But God prepared a worm when the morning rose the next day, and it smote the gourd that it withered. And it came to pass, when the sun did arise, that God prepared a vehement

---

*Jonah 3:10 tells us that God did not do the evil He had promised would come upon Nineveh. However, that statement may be anticipative and need not necessarily imply that chapter 4 takes place after the forty days had passed. The clause in verse 5 of this fourth chapter, "till he might see what would become of the city," probably means that the forty days were not yet completed.

east wind; and the sun beat upon the head of Jonah, that he fainted, and wished in himself to die, and said, It is better for me to die than to live (Jon 4:6-8).

By building the hut, Jonah had answered God's question about his anger. Now God speaks again, this time by preparing a gourd to shade Jonah's booth. "The LORD God prepared a gourd." The same verb† has already appeared at the end of the first chapter, where the text says, "Now the LORD had prepared a great fish" (1:17). What a contrast! The appointment of a sea monster and the appointment of a plant!

Regarding identification of the gourd, it was probably the *Ricinus communis*,[2] better known as the castor-oil plant. Because of the shape of the leaves, it is sometimes called the "Palma christi," or, in the English form of the word, the "palmcrist." It grows rapidly and is found in the Near East. Such may have been the plant God used in dealing with Jonah. Its natural rate of growth was supernaturally accelerated,‡ so that, as the prophet was sitting in his little hut with the blazing sun beating down on it, God caused one of these plants to spring up suddenly and give him needed shade.

Behind this act of divine mercy is a spiritual lesson. "And the LORD God prepared a gourd . . . that it might be a shadow over his head to deliver him from his grief." One looks at these words and thinks of the comfort of the shadows God allows to come into our lives. The old medical principle of homoeopathy declared that "like cures like." Likewise there is a divine homeopathy. Sometimes God lets the shadow of a great grief come upon His children. And sometimes such a shadow is used to strengthen them or to deliver them from even greater grief. Many a Christian knows the refining influence and ultimate blessing of the sorrows God has allowed to come into his life.

---

†Hebrew, *manah*, which has the meaning of "appoint." Cf. p. 130.

‡"God approaches nature when He does anything beyond nature: this is not indeed always the case; but generally we find that God so works as that He exceeds the measure of nature, and yet from nature does not wholly depart" (John Calvin, cited in E. Huxtable, The Bible Commentary, *Jonah*, p. 605).

> But God prepared a worm when the morning rose the next
> day, and it smote the gourd that it withered (Jon 4:7).

Step by step the instruction of Jonah continued. Having prepared the gourd, the Lord prepared the worm. What an effective
answer that simple fact is to those who are timid about bringing
small things to the heavenly Father! The difference between the
sea monster that swallowed Jonah and the little caterpillar that
killed the gourd now sheltering his head was vast, but there was
no difference in the Lord's oversight of the prophet. And who
will say that it was less of a miracle for God to appoint a worm
to take the life of the palmcrist than it was for Him to prepare a
great fish to save the life of the prophet. The supernatural
cannot be measured quantitatively. When God hears our prayers
and acts in our behalf He shows Himself to be just as great as
when He delivered Jonah out of the raging sea. The observer
passing by Jonah's hut overshadowed by the withering plant
would never have given it a second thought, yet behind that
seeming triviality was the power of the Creator exercised in
behalf of His angry and recalcitrant servant.

> And it came to pass, when the sun did arise, that God pre-
> pared a vehement east wind; and the sun beat upon the head
> of Jonah, that he fainted, and wished in himself to die, and
> said, It is better for me to die than to live (Jon 4:8).

The gourd destroyed, God took another step in bringing Jonah
to his senses. For the fourth time we read that God "prepared"
something. In this instance it is "a vehement east wind." No experienced traveler in the Near East can fail to appreciate this
aspect of Jonah's testing. The hot, burning wind of that region is
called the sirocco. The Septuagint describes it by a picturesque
word meaning "scorcher."[3] Once more God used an existing
natural phenomenon for His purpose. Jonah's misery was now
complete. There he sat under his miserable little hut, dogged in
his obstinacy of spirit and parched in body, as the burning wind
blew on him and the sun beat down on his head. No wonder he
wished for death!

GOD'S FINAL WORDS TO JONAH

> And God said to Jonah, Doest thou well to be angry for the
> gourd? And he said, I do well to be angry, even unto death.
> Then said the LORD, Thou hast had pity on the gourd, for the
> which thou hast not laboured, neither madest it grow; which
> came up in a night, and perished in a night. And should not I
> spare Nineveh, that great city, wherein are more than sixscore
> thousand persons that cannot discern between their right hand
> and their left hand; and also much cattle? (Jon 4:9-11).

Then God spoke again. "And God said to Jonah, Doest thou
well to be angry for the gourd?" This question is identified with
that in verse 4 but with an important exception; here Jonah's
anger is specifically related to the gourd. Before the prophet had
left the city, built the booth, and had the experience of the
gourd, the worm, and the wind, his anger was divided between
the city and God for sparing it. But God had been working with
Jonah. And the effect of the divine use of gourd, worm, and
wind was to change the direction of the prophet's anger. Now, it
centers on one thing—the loss of the gourd. So we read that
Jonah replied, "I do well to be angry, even unto death." Under
God's discipline, he has been brought to the place where the loss
of even a plant can affect him so deeply as to make him long to
die.

One of the masterly touches in this wonderful narrative is the
consummate handling of the close. There is no anticlimax; the
ultimate lesson of the book is succinctly stated, and the story ends
without a single unnecessary word. God is now ready to speak
directly to Jonah and Jonah is at last prepared to hear. The book
does not tell us the effect of these final words upon the prophet,
but who that has read the narrative closely and has endeavored
sympathetically to understand the prophet's experience can
doubt that the lessons were learned? That Jonah was able so
plainly and unsparingly to write of his own obstinacy is in itself
evidence that he was a changed man.

So the divine word goes straight to Jonah's heart. He was a
man, the Lord was showing him, who was crushed by the death
of a plant he had not in any way cultivated; because of the

withering of an inanimate growth whose life was measured by a single day, he wanted to die. Why, then, should God not spare a great city like Nineveh, containing over 120,000 innocent children below the age of discernment and also a great number of harmless cattle?

With this great question ringing in our ears the book closes. It is as if God through these words opened to all the world a door of mercy. This is what Jonah needed to learn—that God cares for *all* men, regardless of nation, race, or outward circumstances. It is true that "There's a wideness in God's mercy, like the wideness of the sea." Yet, beautiful though it is, the figure is inadequate. Not even the spacious sea can fully represent the dimensions of God's mercy. The greatest symbol of the heart of God toward man is not the sea but the cross; it is the outstretched arms of the crucified Saviour that most truly portray the measureless expanse of divine mercy toward sinful men. Between the lines of this history of the Lord's dealing with Jonah, and particularly in these concluding words, we see the same God who "was in Christ reconciling the world unto himself." Let us never, like Jonah, try to exclude anyone§ from the mercy of God. Christ died not only for us and our people but also for the whole world. "Salvation *is* of the LORD" (Jon 2:9).

---

§One is tempted to write "anything" in a sentence like this, remembering the tender humanitarian note sounded in the very last phrase of the book, "and also much cattle." Who will deny that God's mercy is wide enough to comprehend even the animals? As Coleridge beautifully put it at the close of *The Rime of the Ancient Mariner*, "The dear God who loveth us, He made and loveth all."

7

JONAH AS PROPHET: THE OUTREACH OF GOD'S LOVE

Having come to the end of our exposition, it is time to step aside, as it were, and take a larger view of the territory that has been traversed. This we may do by looking first at Jonah as a prophet and then by looking at his message for today.

JONAH AS PROPHET

The designation is not so obvious as it seems. To call a man a prophet in the authentic Old Testament sense of the term is to place him in a unique category. Israel alone among the nations had, as Abraham Heschel says, a succession of prophets that, "stretching out over many centuries . . . is a phenomenon for which there is no analogy."[1] And while the book bearing Jonah's name has in the Hebrew canon its unchallengeable place among the latter prophets, what of the man himself? In contrast with the hundreds and thousands of words spoken and written by the other prophets, we have in Jonah just one utterance in direct quotation: "Yet forty days, and Nineveh shall be overthrown" (3:4). Nevertheless, Jonah surely stands among the prophets. His few God-given words, the preaching he was inspired to base on them, and the results of that preaching have reverberated down through the corridors of history to the Ninevehs of our day.

Jonah was a great prophet apart from his proclamation to Nineveh. In paucity of recorded words he is like Abel, from whom no utterance has come down yet who is classed by our

Lord Himself as one of the prophets.* But if this is true of Abel,
how was he a prophet? He was a prophet, because, as the author
of Hebrews asserts, "By faith Abel offered unto God a more
excellent sacrifice than Cain . . . and by it he being dead yet
speaketh" (Heb 11:4). He accomplished his great prophetic work
not by what he said but by what he did. Similarly with Jonah;
he also being dead yet speaks. Powerful as his words to Nineveh
were, his life stands as a still more eloquent prophecy not only
because of what he did but also because of what God did to him
and through him. Among the Old Testament prophets, he is an
outstanding example of what might be called biographical typology.

The modern mind does not find typology congenial. And it is
only fair to admit that, from the time of Origen down
to our own day, there have been those who have run
into strange excesses through misuse of allegory and symbol-
ism in the interpretation of Scripture. Nevertheless, typology
remains a vehicle for divine truth, provided that it has biblical
warrant. This principle is impressively illustrated in the case of
Jonah. The statement has just been made that his life has a
prophetic, typical meaning. This statement, however, has value
only as authorized by Scripture other than Jonah. Is there such
Scripture? Immediately there come to mind our Lord's references to Jonah as a "sign"† (Greek, *semeion*) pointing to "a
greater than Jonah."

Now it is significant that of all the Old Testament prophets
Jonah is the only one with whom Jesus directly compared Himself. Primarily and on His own authority, His death, burial, and
resurrection were foreshadowed by this prophet. Yet there are
other parallels[2] and contrasts between Jonah and the One who
directed our attention to him. Some of these, mentioned for
reverent but not dogmatic consideration, are the following:

(1) Jonah had a special commission from God; Christ was

---

*"That the blood of all the prophets, which was shed from the foundation
of the world, may be required of this generation; from the blood of Abel
unto the blood of Zacharias which perished between the altar and the
temple" (Lk 11:50-51).
†Mt 12:39; 16:4; Lk 11:29.

divinely sent into the world for His unique work. But Jonah's commission was one of judgment; Christ's was primarily a commission of salvation (Jn 3:17). (2) Jonah disobeyed God, repudiated his commission and fled; Christ perfectly obeyed God, fully embraced His commission, and faithfully drained His cup of suffering. (3) Jonah was in a storm at sea; Christ was in a storm on Galilee. But Christ did what Jonah could not do; He rebuked the winds and the waves, and they obeyed Him. (4) Jonah sacrificed himself, and blessing and salvation resulted for others. But he sacrificed himself because of his own sin in displeasing God. Christ sacrificed Himself, not because of any sin of His own, for He was sinless, but for the sin of the whole world. (5) Jonah in being swallowed by the great fish endured an experience figurative of death. But Christ actually died according to the Scriptures and was really buried. (6) Jonah cried out from the belly of the fish. So from the depths of His sufferings on the cross Christ cried out, "My God, my God, why hast thou forsaken me?" The final meaning of Jonah's prayer is Messianic, made up as it is of quotations from Messianic psalms. (7) The third day of Jonah's figurative death and burial ended in his deliverance from the fish. Christ, the "greater than Jonah," rose from the grave the third day.‡ (8) Jonah came out of the fish to preach the Word of God to the Ninevites. And our Lord after His actual resurrection preached to those who beheld Him. In his preaching

---

‡Redford is probably correct when he says: "It has been suggested that the other instances in which the '*third day*' is mentioned, as Luke 24:21; I Corinthians 15:4, etc., may be allusions to this veiled anticipation in the Book of Jonah. Genesis 22:4 and Psalm 16:10 both fail to satisfy the precision of the language. 'We may in all reverence infer,' says Professor Huxtable in *Speaker's Commentary*, Vol. VI, p. 577, 'that this most strange and otherwise utterly unaccountable circumstance was ordered by Divine Providence for the very purpose of furnishing a typical prediction in which both the Lord Jesus Himself (Luke 18:31, 33), and His church as taught by Him, should recognize the distinctive foreshadowing of his pre-ordained death and resurrection . . . The all but consummated sacrifice of Isaac by his father is a piece of history which stands in this respect by the side of Jonah's three days' burial in the fish. Either narrative, if regarded by itself, shocks all sense of probability; either, when regarded as typical, is seen to be in strict accordance with the main purpose of divine revelation which is the exhibition to the world of Christ' " (R. A. Redford, *Studies in the Book of Jonah*, pp. 283-84).

Jonah was so marvellously successful that the whole city was converted. But who can measure the results of our Lord's unceasing ministry through His Spirit's use of His witnesses. Truly, He who has "brought many sons into glory" continues His great work of reconciliation.

Meditation on Jonah as a type of Christ teaches the beautiful lesson of yieldedness in the hand of God. "It was," says Pusey, "where Jonah was passive, where nothing of his own was mingled"[3] that he was most fully a type of our Lord. For when he committed himself to the raging sea and underwent the experience of typical death and resurrection, then he most faithfully portrayed the Saviour. So may Christians learn that the essential qualification for serving their Lord is wholehearted submission to Him.

But although Jonah is by Christ's own designation a type of Himself, in a secondary sense the prophet may be said to portray his own people.§ The Hebrew Christian scholar C. L. Feinberg calls Jonah "a picture of Israel," and sees in him an historical "prefiguring of the dealings of God with His chosen people."[4] This is recognized by the Jews themselves. In their synagogue ritual Jonah is read on the Day of Atonement. As an orthodox Jew said on being asked by A. C. Gaebelein[5] why this book should be read on that great day of prayer and fasting, "We are the Jonah."

It is true that just as Jonah turned away from the Lord, so Israel has turned away from Him. And just as Jonah was recommissioned and restored to the Lord, so in the future, as Feinberg says, "Israel will be used of God to accomplish that which has never been wrought before, the conversion of the world." Paul refers to this in Romans 11:12,15, where he speaks of the fall of Israel as the source of present blessing to the Gentiles and declares that their "fulness" will mean even greater blessing in the future: "Now if the fall of them be the riches of the world,

---

§It is significant that critical scholars like Cheyne and George Adam Smith, who refer to Jonah as "the type of Israel," adopt this allegorical interpretation and link it to their nonhistorical view of the book. (Cf. George A. Smith, *The Twelve Prophets*, pp. 492-93; T. K. Cheyne, *Encyclopaedia Britannica*, 1938 ed., s.v. "Jonah.")

and the diminishing of them the riches of the Gentiles; how much more their fulness? For if the casting away of them be the reconciling of the world, what shall the receiving of them be, but life from the dead?"

JONAH'S MESSAGE FOR TODAY

Yes, Jonah *is* among the prophets. Like all in the great succession of which he was a part, he was a witness to the living God. Therefore, we must take his message seriously as it applies to us today. For when the prophets of the Lord speak by word or life, what they declare is not optional advice but truth to be obeyed here and now. "They speak," as R. B. Y. Scott says, "not *of* our age but *to* it, because the Word of God is in their mouth."[6]

The book of Jonah is like a window through which we are permitted to see something of the heart of God. Though written in a time when foreign missions were unknown, it reveals the God "who will have all men to be saved, and to come unto the knowledge of the truth" (1Ti 2:4). It is the earliest and, with the exception of Acts, the greatest of missionary books. And the man whose name it bears, unwilling though he was, did a unique work in calling a wicked and alien people to repentance.

In a day when prejudice and hate inflame men's emotions and pervert their judgment, Jonah speaks with compelling force about limiting our love and sympathies only to some of our fellow human beings and excluding others from our pity and compassion. One of the anomalies in church history was the slowness of the whole church, following the early centuries during which Christianity swept the Roman empire, to proclaim the gospel to the uttermost parts of the earth. And one of the sad paradoxes of the church in modern times is its sending of missionaries to minister to the spiritual and physical needs of people on "the foreign field," while at the same time remaining indifferent to or oblivious of the spiritual and physical needs of the Ninevehs at home. We know little of the poignant relevancy of Jonah if we do not recognize in it God's rebuke of exclusivism that shuts the doors of our hearts on the deprivation and suffering all around us, on racial and other hatreds wherever and however manifested, and on contempt for alien peoples, including the despised among us as well as the foreigners beyond our shores. No matter how far some men may be from what we think is right nor how low they may have fallen, no human beings, the book of Jonah reminds us, are beyond the pity of the God who so loved lost men and women that He gave His only Son to save them. How then can any of us who, solely by God's grace, are members of Christ's body refuse to have compassion on any man? In the broadest and yet the most specific sense, according to our need for warning and rebuke, Jonah is a tract for us in a day when affluence coexists with misery.

Another contemporary aspect of Jonah is its dramatic emphasis upon judgment and upon the repentance which alone can avert its consummation. God knew all about the sins of Nineveh—its idolatries, its pagan vices, above all its cruelty and violence. "Their wickedness," He said, "is come up before me" (1:2). Yet in the wideness of His mercy and the riches of His longsuffering, He sent the prophet to this great city that it might repent. And today to a violent people in a violent age, when God's moral law is not only flouted but ridiculed, the ancient warning of Jonah—that unless men and nations repent judgment is sure—sounds with insistent logic backed by the long record of history. But whereas Nineveh had only the brief preaching of Jonah, our modern society has the full message of the redeeming love of Christ presented to it through many witnesses. God's everlasting mercy holds the door of repentance and faith open, but Scripture gives us no warrant to believe that He will hold it open indefinitely.

We may study Jonah as a problem in historicity, we may debate the various ways of interpreting it, we may defend its miracles, we may scrutinize its text word by word; yet unless we take to heart its deep and wonderful meaning, we shall not only fail to be helped by it but we may even be harmed by our study. "O brethren," exclaimed G. Campbell Morgan when lecturing on this book years ago at Northfield, Massachusetts. "O brethren, how much of the attitude of Jonah is in us, without his honesty!"[7] It is not only the unbelievers in the Ninevehs of today who need to repent; it is also we who are modern Jonahs.

For no one begins to understand this profound and searching little book unless he discovers the Jonah in himself and then repentantly lays hold upon the boundless grace of God.

APPENDIX

THE MIRACLE OF THE GREAT FISH

The purpose of this discussion is not to prove the miracle reported in Jonah 1:17 and 2:10. The biblical supernatural rests upon the unique authority of the inspired Word of God. While historical, scientific, or archeological information may shed light on it, essentially "the miraculous in Scripture is not subject to rational proof—it is to be received by faith."[1] Yet in a time when popular rejection of the Jonah miracle is still largely based upon outworn misconceptions and upon uncritical acceptance of the pronouncements of scholars who minimize the biblical supernatural, a review of some of the material bearing on it is not irrelevant. This material is of four kinds: (1) zoological; (2) archeological; (3) teleological (relating to the purpose behind the miracle); (4) mythological.

1. Many relegate this miracle to the realm of fiction out of ignorance of certain elementary facts. It has often been said that a whale has a throat so small that it would have difficulty swallowing an orange. The Greenland whale does indeed have a very small throat. But there are other whales which can swallow a man;* in fact, some can engulf objects larger than a horse. Robinson refers to a thirty thousand pound sperm whale captured off Florida in 1912 and later exhibited at the Smithsonian Institution in Washington that was found to have in its stomach a black fish of about fifteen hundred pounds.[2]

The German critic König, who rejected the historical inter-

---

*Speaking of the sperm whale, *The New International Encyclopedia* says: "The mouth is large and wide; the throat, unlike that of the Greenland whale is very wide, sufficiently so as to admit the body of a man" (s.v. "Whale").

pretation of Jonah, cites[3] (and apparently accepted as authentic) an account in the *Neue Luth. Kircheuzeitung,* 1895, p. 303f., of the experience of James Bartley, a seaman on the whaler *Star of the East.* In February, 1891, this sailor disappeared when one of the ship's boats was demolished by a huge whale in its death throes. When the creature was cut to pieces, Bartley was found alive but unconscious in its stomach. However, two articles in the *Expository Times*[4] which were based on investigation of this famous incident repudiate its authenticity.

Pusey tells of the case, reputed to have happened in 1758, of a sailor who, on falling overboard, was seen to be swallowed by a shark. The captain shot a gun at the fish which cast out the sailor and he was taken aboard alive. The fish was harpooned and dried. The sailor had the good fortune to be presented with the fish by the captain. He toured Europe, exhibiting the shark, which was twenty feet long and weighed 3,924 pounds.[5] Whatever one thinks of this story, it has one very significant feature— the monster that swallowed the man was a shark, not a whale.

Actually, the familiar words "Jonah and the whale" are misleading. In the Hebrew the word used in Jonah 1:17 and 2:10 is *dag,* which means "fish" and is so translated. But a whale, of course, is not a fish but a mammal. It was through the rendering of Matthew 12:40 in the King James Version, where the word *whale* is used, that "Jonah and the whale" came into common parlance. However, the Greek word in this text is *kētos,* which simply means "sea monster." While it might include a whale, it certainly includes great fish. Modern translations, such as Weymouth, Berkeley, Phillips, The New English Bible, and The Jerusalem Bible, all have "sea monster" instead of "whale."

While there are whales capable of swallowing a man, it seems more likely that Jonah was swallowed by a great shark. According to the *Encyclopaedia Britannica,*[6] the *Rhineodon,* also known as the "whale shark" or at the Seychelles as the "chagrin," is the largest of all sharks and is said to reach seventy feet. These monsters do not have the terrible teeth that other sharks do but are "harmless giants that subsist on plankton strained through modified gill rakers."[7] Fully capable of engulfing a man, the *Rhineodon* is of worldwide distribution. In the 1930s a comparatively small specimen of only a ton or so in weight but with a throat quite wide enough to admit a man was captured off Islip, Long Island.† And in his widely-read *Kon-Tiki,* Thor Heyerdahl describes a huge whale shark that followed his raft in mid-Pacific: "It was the head of a veritable sea monster . . . broad and flat like a frog's, with two small eyes right at the sides, and a toadlike jaw which was four or five feet wide and had long fringes drooping from the corners of the mouth. Behind the head was an enormous body ending in a long tail fin which stood straight up. . . . The monster was a whale shark, the largest shark and the largest fish known in the world today. . . . The whale shark has an average length of fifty feet, and according to zoologists it weighs fifteen tons."[8]

These things do not, of course, prove the reality of the supernatural event. Yet because skepticism has made so much of the "impossibility" of Jonah's being swallowed by a whale, or a fish, and also because these things relate to the natural means God used in doing this miracle, they have their place in a discussion of it. For this was one of the instances, not uncommon in the Bible, of a miracle in the realm of nature. For example, certain of the plagues God sent upon Egypt during Moses' contest with Pharaoh were a miraculous heightening of natural processes. Likewise in His final dealing with Jonah, God made supernatural use of the gourd, the worm, and the east wind. In the New Testament we have such miracles as the wonderful draught of fishes, the feeding of the multitudes, and the stilling of the storm on Galilee.

Now while God could have created on the spot a sea monster to swallow Jonah, the Hebrew text (Jon 1:17) tells us that He "prepared" a great fish to do this. The Hebrew word *manah* which is translated "prepared" has no implication of an act of special creation but definitely means "appoint" or "assign." It is, as Orelli remarks, "a favorite word of this narrator for the ruling of Divine Providence."[9] The miracle, therefore, consisted in

---

†This whale shark is on display in the Vanderbilt Museum, Northport, Long Island, New York.

God's divine appointment and control of the sea monster (whatever it might have been) in making it play its creaturely part in His dealing with His disobedient prophet. And this was the unexplained and unexplainable supernatural act of the sovereign God.

2. There are a number of ancient links, overlooked by many students of Jonah, between Nineveh and the prophet. Robinson calls attention to one of these. "The archeologist, Knight," he writes, "in his remarkable volume . . . entitled *Nile and the Jordan,* 1921, page 344, calls attention to a seal belonging to the reign of Amasis II, 570–526 B.C., of Egyptian history, which shows a minute drawing, executed with remarkable clearness, of a man emerging from a sea monster, which Petrie identifies as Jonah; hence the date of Jonah, Knight declares, must be anterior to the date of Nebuchadnezzar."[10] In 1892, H. Clay Trumbull, then editor of *The Sunday School Times,* published a paper [11] entitled *Jonah in Nineveh.* The booklet is only fifteen pages long, but contains much valuable material. Trumbull first points out the similarity between the ten plagues of Egypt and the story of Jonah, stressing that the plagues of Egypt "were successful strokes at the gods of Egypt, beginning with a stroke at the popular river-god and passing on and up to the royal sun-god in the heavens and terminating with a stroke at the first-born, or priestly representative of the gods, in every household in Egypt."[12] He then demonstrates that one of the permanent divinities of ancient Assyria was Dagon—a strange creature, part man and part fish. Sometimes he was portrayed upright with the head of a fish above the head of a man, the open mouth of the fish being a sort of miter or sacred headdress, while the feet of a man extended below the tail of a fish. At other times the body of a man was joined at right angles to the body of a fish. Trumbull shows that images of this fish-god have been found at palace and temple entrances in the ruins of Nineveh, that they appear on ancient Babylonian seals, and that the name "Dagon" is found on early cuneiform inscriptions. It is clear that this fish-god was worshiped from early times in Babylon and Assyria. "What better hearlding, as a divinely sent messenger to Nineveh, could Jonah have had," asks Trumbull, "than to be thrown up out of the

mouth of a great fish in the presence of witnesses, say, on the coast of Phoenicia, where the fish-god was a favorite object of worship?"[13] He goes on to suggest that such an appearance of God's prophet might well have had a bearing on the amazing response of the whole city.

Trumbull also calls attention to the fact that Berossus, a Babylonian historian, gives the name of the Assyrian fish-god as "Oannes," a form of the name that might have been employed by Berossus as a Greek equivalent of "Jonah."‡ It is well known that the very location of ancient Nineveh was lost to the civilized world until the epoch-making discoveries of Layard[14] over a hundred years ago. Not until he excavated the mound that had for centuries been known as "Neby Yunas" were there found the ruined palaces of old Nineveh.

3. The teleological aspect of the miracle—that is, the purpose behind it—is significant. The great difference between the biblical supernatural and the miracles of mythology of uninspired writings, such as the Apocrypha (especially the New Testament Apocrypha), lies right here. The God of the Bible is not a deity of caprice; He does nothing without adequate purpose. Is there, then, sufficient occasion for this wonderful thing that happened to Jonah? In answer we may list three reasons for it. The first is the obvious fact that in this miracle God was disciplining His rebellious prophet. The second is that He used it to prepare Jonah for preaching with such power that a great city turned to Him. The third is that behind God's performing this miracle there was also His purpose to set forth a great pre-Christian foreshadowing of the burial and resurrection of His Son.

The book of Jonah is historical. It is also allegorical. Like other portions of the Old Testament, such as the story of Abraham and Isaac or that of Joseph and his brethren, it has a definite typical meaning. This is not conjecture; it is the plain declaration of our Lord Himself (Mt 12:38-42; Lk 11:29-44).

In 1 Corinthians 15:1-4, Paul affirms the elements of the gospel—that "Christ died for our sins according to the scriptures;

---

‡König argues against Trumbull's conclusions, but not all will agree with his criticisms (*Hastings Bible Dictionary*, s.v. "Whale").

and that he was buried, and that he rose again the third day according to the scriptures." Now the Old Testament contains many prophecies of the death of Christ for the sins of men. (Such passages as Ps 22 and Is 53 come readily to mind.) But to recall Old Testament passages relating to His burial and resurrection is more difficult. The clearest of these is the miraculous experience of Jonah in the great fish. Indeed Paul's statement might even be thought of like this: "that he was buried, and that he rose again the third day according to the scriptures [in Jonah]."

While the meaning of our Lord's use of "three days and three nights" (Mt 12:40) in applying Jonah 1:17 to His own burial has already been discussed (cf. p. 88), two quotations illuminate the idiomatic use of these words.

The first is from the Hebrew Christian scholar, David Baron: "According to the Jewish law part of the day stands for the whole. . . . If a child is born in the last hour or even in the last few minutes of a day it is counted as a whole day of the period of time within which he must be circumcised. Thus *legally*, according to Jewish reckoning, the crucifixion and burial of our Lord having taken place before the 16th Nisan actually commenced, He may be said to have been in the grave 'three days and three nights,' viz., *Friday*, to which legally belonged the night of what we should call Thursday; *Saturday*, consisting of the night of Friday and the day of Saturday; and *Sunday*, to which belonged the night of Saturday and the very early morn of Sunday."[15]

The other quotation is from the writings of Sir Robert Anderson, a distinguished lawyer and Bible student who was chief of the criminal investigation department of Scotland Yard: "A prison chaplain would find no difficulty in explaining this ['three days and three nights'] to his congregation. Our civil day begins at midnight, and the law reckons any part of a day as a day. Therefore while a sentence of three days means three days of twenty-four hours, equal to seventy-two hours, a prisoner under such a committal is seldom more than forty hours in gaol: and I have known cases where the period was in fact only thirty-three hours. And this mode of reckoning and of speaking was as familiar to the Jews as to the habitués of our criminal courts. 'A day and a night make an *Onah,* and a part of an *Onah* is as the whole.' Dr. Lightfoot quotes this Jewish saying in his *Horae Hebraicae* (Matt. 12:40); and he adds: 'Therefore Christ may be truly said to have been in his grave three *Onoth,* . . . the consent of the schools and the dialect of the nation agreeing thereunto.' "[16]

4. To end this discussion of the miracle of Jonah and the great fish, we turn to theories of its alleged pagan or mythological derivation. Some critics have attempted to discredit the record of the miracle by linking it with such fables as the story of Hercules and Hesione or the similar myth of Andromeda and Perseus. In each case, a beautiful maiden was exposed as food for the sea monster, sent up on a floodtide by Poseidon. In each case also the maiden was liberated by the hero who slew the monster. This tale appears in various forms in pagan mythology and is related by authors like Diodorus Siculus and Ovid. Jerome uses it as an illustration of the folly of the pagans who believed their own foolish myths yet rejected Scripture. Pliny says that a certain "M. Saurus, when Aedile, exhibited at Rome, among other marvels, the bones of the monster to which Andromeda was said to have been exposed, which bones were brought from Joppa, a city of Judaea, being forty feet long, in height greater than the ribs of the Indian elephant, and the vertebrae a foot and a half thick." He even speaks of "a projecting rock, in which they show the traces of the chains of Andromeda."[17]

Burn[18] cites the story of Arion, the ancient musician, who had become very rich and had committed himself and his wealth to a crew bound for Corinth. The sailors determined to murder him and steal his riches; Arion asked leave to dress in his best robes and sing them a parting song. The song finished, he jumped overboard, harp in hand, and landed on the back of a dolphin which had been lured alongside by the music. This creature brought Arion to Corinth ahead of the vessel. When the crew landed, they were denounced by the musician, convicted of their crime, and punished by crucifixion.

To summarize such stories answers the claims that the narrative of Jonah is derived from them. They are far removed from the character of the Scripture record. Moreover, they postdate the prophecy. If there is any connection, which seems unlikely, it may be, as Burn suggests, that they are vague reflections and corruptions of the marvelous thing that happened to the prophet. Possibly such a phenomenal event passed into folk lore. However, such explanations, and there have been many of them,§ are no more than conjecture.

---

§For example, some have tried to establish a link between Jonah's experience and the initiatory rites of the Elusinian Mysteries. (Cf. W. Simpson, *The Jonah Legend,* cited in Robinson, *The Twelve Minor Prophets,* p. 83.) Others have resorted to such suppositions as that the prophet happened to find the carcass of a dead whale floating on the sea and took refuge in its jaws, or that he was picked up by a ship with a great fish as its figurehead, or that he simply dreamed the whole story.

NOTES

INTRODUCTION

1. *Encyclopaedia Britannica*, 14th ed., s.v. "Jonah."
2. C. A. Dinsmore, *The English Bible as Literature*, pp. 254-56.
3. J. G. Hill, *The Prophets in the Light of Today*, pp. 123-24; see also Mary Ellen Chase, *The Bible for the Common Reader*, pp. 195-99.
4. *The Jerusalem Bible*, p. 1141.
5. H. E. Fosdick, *The Modern Use of the Bible*, p. 163.
6. James D. Smart, *The Interpreter's Bible*, 6:871 f.
7. C. H. Cornill, *The Prophets of Israel*, p. 170.
8. Herbert Spencer, cited in D. E. Hart-Davies, *Jonah: Prophet and Patriot*, p. xvi.
9. E. B. Pusey, *The Minor Prophets*, 1:373 ff.
10. Cf. *The New Bible Dictionary*, s.v. "Chronology of the Old Testament," "Jeroboam."
11. G. L. Robinson, *The Twelve Minor Prophets*, p. 84.
12. Ibid.
13. Ibid.
14. Ibid.
15. E. J. Young, *Introduction to the Old Testament*, p. 255.
16. G. L. Archer, *A Survey of Old Testament Introduction*, p. 298.
17. Young, p. 255.
18. H. K. von Orelli, *The Twelve Minor Prophets*, p. 167.
19. Charles Reade, cited by Dinsmore, p. 256.

CHAPTER 1

1. T. T. Perowne, The Cambridge Bible for Schools and Colleges, *Obadiah and Jonah*, p. 59.
2. E. Huxtable, The Bible Commentary, *Jonah*, 6:584.
3. E. B. Pusey, *The Minor Prophets*, 1:397.
   Cf. Charles A. Blanchard, *An Old Testament Gospel*, pp. 78-79.
5. Cf. Huxtable, p. 586.

CHAPTER 2

1. E. B. Pusey, *The Minor Prophets*, 1:403.
2. Alexander Raleigh, *The Story of Jonah*, p. 134.
3. Pusey, p. 404.

4. R. F. Horton, ed., The New Century Bible, *The Minor Prophets*, 1:206.
5. Pusey, p. 405.
6. See Samuel Clift Burn, *The Prophet Jonah*, pp. 107-8.
7. Thomas John Carlisle, *You! Jonah!* p. 21. Used by permission.
8. G. K. Chesterton, *The Amazing Adventures of Father Brown*, p. 8.
9. E.g., G. Herbert Livingstone, *The Wycliffe Bible Commentary*, p. 845; D. W. B. Robinson, *The New Bible Commentary*, pp. 716-17.
10. H. K. von Orelli, *The Twelve Minor Prophets*, p. 177.

CHAPTER 3

1. E. B. Pusey, *The Minor Prophets*, 1:407; T. T. Perowne, The Cambridge Bible for Schools and Colleges, *Obadiah and Jonah*, p. 68.
2. Alexander Raleigh, *The Story of Jonah the Prophet*, p. 152.
3. D. E. Hart-Davies, *Jonah: Prophet and Patriot*, pp. 77-78.
4. John Calvin, cited in Perowne, p. 68.
5. Charles A. Blanchard, *An Old Testament Gospel*, pp. 73-75.
6. Cf. William L. Banks, *Jonah the Reluctant Prophet*, p. 63.
7. E. Huxtable, *The Bible Commentary*, 6:590.

CHAPTER 4

1. Flavius Josephus, *Antiquities*, B, ix, c.x., 2.
2. Hugh Martin, *The Prophet Jonah*, pp. 290 ff.
3. T. T. Perowne, The Cambridge Bible for Schools and Colleges, *Obadiah and Jonah*, p. 74.
4. D. W. B. Robinson, *The New Bible Commentary*, p. 74.
5. D. W. Deere, *The Twelve Speak*, 1:70.
6. Stuart Mitchell, *Exposition of the Book of Jonah*, pp. 166-67.
7. *New Bible Dictionary*, s.v. "Nineveh."
8. E. B. Pusey, *The Minor Prophets*, 1:381.
9. R. A. Redford, *Studies in the Book of Jonah*, p. 114.

CHAPTER 5

1. C. A. Dinsmore, *The English Bible as Literature*, p. 354.
2. Cf. J. E. Steinmueller, cited in Gleason L. Archer, *A Survey of Old Testament Introduction*, pp. 299-300.
3. Sir Austen H. Layard, *Nineveh and Babylon*, p. 367.
4. D. W. B. Robinson, *New Bible Commentary*, p. 718.
5. Sir Austen H. Layard, cited in T. T. Perowne, The Cambridge Bible for Schools and Colleges, *Obadiah and Jonah*, p. 78.
6. Stuart Mitchell, *Exposition of the Book of Jonah*, p. 179; C. L. Feinberg, The Major Messages of the Minor Prophets, *Jonah, Micah, and Nahum*, p. 36.
7. Mitchell, p. 191.
8. Ibid., pp. 189-90.
9. Samuel Clift Burn, *The Prophet Jonah*, p. 178.

Chapter 6

1. William Scarlett in *The Interpreter's Bible*, 6:889.
2. See E. Huxtable, *The Bible Commentary*, 6:605; E. B. Pusey, *The Minor Prophets*, 1:388.
3. Stuart Mitchell, *Exposition of the Book of Jonah*, p. 224.

Chapter 7

1. Abraham Heschel, *The Prophets*, pp. 474-75.
2. Augustine, cited in R. A. Redford, *Studies in the Book of Jonah*, p. 293.
3. E. B. Pusey, *The Minor Prophets*, 1:393.
4. C. L. Feinberg, The Major Messages of the Minor Prophets, *Jonah, Micah, and Nahum*, pp. 38-39.
5. See A. C. Gaebelein in *The Annotated Bible*, 5:163. This work contains a significant discussion of the typical meaning of Jonah.
6. R. B. Y. Scott, *The Relevance of the Prophets*, p. 216.
7. G. Campbell Morgan, *The Minor Prophets*, p. 68

Appendix

1. H. E. Freeman, *An Introduction to the Old Testament Prophets*, p. 168.
2. George L. Robinson, *The Twelve Minor Prophets*, p. 78.
3. *Hastings Bible Dictionary*, s.v., "Jonah."
4. L. Williams, *Expository Times* (Aug. 1906, Feb. 1907), cited in D. E. Hart-Davies, *Jonah: Prophet and Patriot*, p. 106.
5. E. B. Pusey, *The Minor Prophets*, 1:385.
6. *Encyclopaedia Britannica*, 14th ed., s.v. "Shark."
7. *Encyclopaedia Britannica*, 1967 ed., s.v., "Shark."
8. Thor Heyerdahl, *Kon-Tiki*, pp. 120-21.
9. H. K. von Orelli, *The Twelve Minor Prophets*, p. 176.
10. Robinson, p. 183.
11. H. Clay Trumbull, "Jonah in Nineveh" (paper read before Society of Biblical Literature and Exegesis), pp. 4-5.
12. Ibid.
13. Ibid., pp. 10-11.
14. See Sir Austen H. Layard, *Nineveh and Its Remains*; idem., *Nineveh and Babylon*.
15. David Baron, cited in D. E. Hart-Davies, *Jonah: Prophet and Patriot*, pp. 123-24.
16. Sir Robert Anderson, cited in ibid., p. 124.
17. Pliny, cited in Pusey, pp. 389-90; see also Orelli, p. 171.
18. Samuel Clift Burn, *The Prophet Jonah*, pp. 147-48.

THE PROPHECY OF

HABAKKUK

INTRODUCTION

THE IMPORTANCE OF THE BOOK

Among the twelve books known as the minor prophets, none is of more significance than Habakkuk. Its author struggles with the deepest questions of God's ways with men and nations; the truth he proclaims is in the mainstream of redemptive religion; and he mounts to some of the loftiest ground reached by any Old Testament writer. In three brief chapters, the prophet compresses a wealth of spiritual insight expressed in beauty of style unsurpassed by the other minor prophets. The most philosophical of the prophets, Habakkuk is strikingly original both in the content and expression of his book.

When the prophet wrote, "The just shall live by his faith" (2.4), he penned one of the most dynamic ideas in world history. Every Bible student knows Paul's quotation of these words in stating the theme of his epistle to the Romans: "I am not ashamed of the gospel of Christ: for it is the power of God unto salvation to everyone that believeth; to the Jew first, and also to the Greek. For therein is the righteousness of God revealed from faith to faith: as it is written, The just shall live by faith" (1:16-17.) Nor is this the only time the sentence is quoted by the apostle to the Gentiles. In Galatians he uses it again in speaking of the impossibility of being made righteous by the law. "But that no man is justified by the law in the sight of God, it is evident: for, The just shall live by faith" (3:11.) And the words appear a third time in the New Testament, as the author of the espistle to the Hebrews uses them to introduce his great chapter on faith: "Now the just shall live by faith: but if any man draw back, my soul shall have no pleasure in him. But we are not of them who draw back unto perdition; but of them that believe to the saving of the soul" (10:38-39).

It is plain, therefore, that Habakkuk is in the central current of biblical truth. Any fair estimate of his remarkable little book demands recognition of its outstanding importance. If he must be classed among the minor prophets, he should at least be called a *major* minor prophet.

THE AUTHOR

Aside from the book he wrote, little is known with certainty of the life of Habakkuk. While his words speak eloquently of his genius and his spiritual experience, his personal life is obscure. The prophet's name, however, is significant, being related to the Hebrew root *habhak,* "to embrace." Davidson suggests that "the name is really an abstract noun used in the concrete sense of an object that is embraced and so means 'darling.'"* Luther's comment is well known. "Habakkuk," he says, "has a right name for his office. For Habakkuk means a heartener, or one who takes another to his heart and his arms, as one soothes a poor weeping child, telling it to be quiet."[1]

Several clues to the prophet's life are found in the book. The first occurs in the opening verses: "The burden which Habakkuk the prophet did see." According to F.C. Cook, "the prophet" is a designation "generally admitted to denote a recognition of official position." He suggests that the statement in 2:2, "And the LORD answered me, and said, Write the vision, and make it plain upon tables" may indicate that Habakkuk was in a position of prophetic leadership qualifying him to give authoritative expression to the prophecies.[2]

Another clue is the musical ascription with which the book closes, "To the chief singer on my stringed instruments." Those who accept the entire book as the work of Habakkuk see in this an indication that the prophet was a Levite. On the other hand, those who hold the book to be of composite authorship usually

---

*Cf. G. W. Wade, Westminster Commentaries, *Zephaniah, Nahum and Habakkuk,* pp. 141-42. Wade points out that the Septuagint calls the prophet *'Ambakoum* both in the book itself and also in Bel and the Dragon. This leads to the conjecture that the name is derived from the Assyrian, *hambakuku*—a kind of plant. The alternate derivation, however, is not generally accepted.

deny that the third chapter is by the prophet and therefore discard this clue.

When we come to legend, there are a number of references to Habakkuk. Some of the old rabbis imagined a connection between the name of the prophet and Elisha's words to the Shunammite woman, "Thou shalt embrace a son" (2 Ki 4:16). Thus they conjectured that the prophet was the son of the Shunammite. Another tradition links Isaiah 21:6 ("For thus hath the Lord said unto me, Go, set a watchman, let him declare what he seeth") with Habakkuk 2:1 ("I will stand upon my watch, and set me upon the tower, and will watch to see what he will say unto me, and what I shall answer when I am reproved"), and thus identifies Habakkuk with the watchman appointed to watch for the fall of Babylon. And according to *The Lives of the Prophets*, a compilation of extrabiblical Jewish traditions dated from first century A.D., Habakkuk was of the tribe of Simeon.[3] This traditional work also refers to the fantastic story in the apocryphal book Bel and the Dragon in which the prophet, carrying food to workers in the field, was lifted up by the hair of his head and transported through the air to Babylon, where he fed Daniel in the lions' den a bowl of pottage and some bread!

In contrast is what the book says to us about Habakkuk's inner life. Students of Scripture through the ages have been fascinated by the unique quality of the prophet's mind and thought. He begins with a complaint to God about the wickedness of the people. The reply is that the Chaldeans will be raised up to punish the people, a vivid description being given of their ruthless power. But the prophet is not satisfied. He expostulates with God on the ground that the enemy raised up to punish the people is worse than the people being punished. The second chapter finds Habakkuk waiting before God on his watchtower. There the vision is given him and he receives the great word, "The just shall live by his faith," coupled with a declaration of the essential perversity of the wicked. The remainder of the chapter details a series of woes upon the enemy. As to the third chapter, it is in the form of a psalm. One of the most exalted visions in all Scripture, it culminates in a sublime attitude of personal resignation; whatever calamities may come, Habakkuk says, "Yet I will rejoice in the LORD, I will joy in the God of my salvation" (3:18).

It is plain from even such a brief summary as this that Habakkuk wrestles with profound questions. Here is a believer who knows what to do with his problems. An honest doubter, he take his troubles boldly to God. Then, waiting upon God, he receives the answer and progresses from his doubt to a faith that is willing to trust God no matter what happens. George Adam Smith calls him "the prophet as skeptic," and speaks of his book as "the beginning of speculation in Israel."[4] George A. Robinson refers to him as "Habakkuk the philosopher,"[5] while W. J. Farley says he is "the prophet of honest doubt."[6] According to C. A. Dinsmore, he is "a voice from the crowd."[7] L. Fuerbringer calls his book on Habakkuk *The Eternal Why,* and H. K. von Orelli characterizes the prophet as "the suppliant among the prophets."[8]

There is much to be said for this emphasis upon the speculative and questioning element in Habakkuk. But it is by no means the whole story. While the prophet certainly questioned God, he was a great deal more than a doubter; as A. C. Gaebelein put it, "much of his message is in the form of communion with the Lord."[9] And F. C. Cook and others see Habakkuk as essentially the prophet of faith.[10] After all, trial and perplexity are not incompatible with real trust. A profound paradox of the spiritual life is that a man may be confused and even in the dark as to God's purposes and ways and at the same time be a fully committed believer. The very fact that this prophet struggled with skepticism and by the grace of God came through to such triumphant faith that he was singled out as the vehicle for one of the greatest spiritual insights of all time justifies us in thinking of him as the prophet of faith as well as of skepticism. For he was a kind of Job of the prophets; like the afflicted patriarch, he wrestled with the hard problem of permitted evil, and also like Job he found peace through an overwhelming vision of the greatness of the Lord.

DATE

The date of the book of Habakkuk is closely linked to the

events of the first chapter. Taken at their face value, these events are relatively simple. The prophet, indignant at oppression and corruption in Judah, cries out to God against this evil (vv. 2-4). In answer God points to the impending punishment by the Chaldeans, whose might and cruelty are vividly described (vv. 5-11). But Habakkuk is still troubled. Addressing himself to the holiness of God, he expostulates that the wickedness of the Chaldeans exceeds even that of those whom they are sent to chastise (vv. 12-17).

Such are the contents of the chapter. The problem of dating the book is to locate the historical background which best fits these events. With this in mind let us consider the possibilities. First of all, there is the reign of Manasseh (686-642 B.C.). Following the great revival (2 Ch 29:3–31:21) under his godly father, King Hezekiah, Manasseh took Judah into the depths of apostasy (2 Ki 21:1-16). Therefore, some scholars, like Pusey, date Habakkuk in the reign of Manasseh on the ground that the injustices described in verses 2 to 4 reflect the conditions of his time. But surely this is too early a date, if for no other reason than that the Chaldeans, or Babylonians, were not yet the towering menace implied in verses 5 to 17.

Another attempt must accordingly be made to match the conditions described at the beginning of the first chapter. Manasseh was succeeded by Amon (2 Ki 21:19-26) whose wicked reign of only two years was terminated by assassination. Then Josiah came to the throne. In his reign (c. 639-609 B.C.) there was another great revival (2 Ki 22:3–23:25), but it seems to have been more external than internal (cf. the conditions reflected in Jeremiah 2–6, which refer to this time). And it is not clear that the moral climate in the latter years of Josiah actually swung from national revival to the extremes of evil reflected in verses 2 to 4. Furthermore, it was not until the fall of Nineveh in 612 B.C. and the battle of Carchemish in 605 B.C. that the full structure of Babylon as a world-conquering nation was revealed.

And so the search for the period that most exactly accords with the first chapter continues. Josiah was slain at Megiddo, fighting against Pharaoh-necoh of Egypt (2 Ch 35:20-27) and was succeeded by Jehoahaz (2 Ki 23:31-33). After only three months, Pharaoh-necoh deported him and placed Eliakim, another son of Josiah, on the throne, changing his name to Jehoiakim. During the reign (609-598 B.C.) of this perversely evil king (2 Ki 24:1-5; 2 Ch 36:4-8), world power was passing to the Chaldeans, and finally Nebuchadnezzar came up against Jerusalem, making Jehoiakim his tributary for three years, after which Jehoiakim rebelled but was punished by Nebuchadnezzar's sending against the city a mixed expedition of Chaldeans, Syrians, Moabites, and Ammonites. Jehoiakim himself was bound in fetters (2 Ch 36:6, 8) to be carried to Babylon but died on the way to captivity. This was the king who had the audacity to whittle up Jeremiah's prophetic scroll with his penknife and throw the pieces into the fire (Jer 36:21-23). Of him the record in 2 Kings says that he repeated the sins of Manasseh and was punished "for the innocent blood he shed: for he filled Jerusalem with innocent blood" (24:4).

All in all, a date during the closing part of Jehoiakim's reign seems best to fit the picture painted in Habakkuk 1:2-4. As usually happens at the fall of a nation, the last days of Judah were marked by gross wickedness and callous injustice. Not only that, but the Chaldeans loomed on the horizon much as the Russians have threatened the security of other nations since World War II.

Aside from these considerations, the very position of Habakkuk among the prophets confirms a date at the end of Jehoiakim's reign. As Cook puts it, "Nahum had predicted the fall of Nineveh and the total overthrow of the Assyrian Empire. . . . That 'yoke' was then broken . . . and the princes and people of Jerusalem, indulging dreams of security, relapsed into old habits of violence and injustice. Habakkuk was then commissioned to announce the near approach of heavier woes than any which had hitherto been inflicted."[11]

For the above reasons the most likely date for the book seems to be about 600 B.C. Of course, the exact year is not to be dogmatically insisted upon. The general time, however, seems plain, and we may think of Habakkuk as a contemporary of Jeremiah, prophesying in the days of national apostasy that preceded the Babylonian captivity.

But there is another view of this first chapter and the events it describes. It begins by questioning the application of verses 2 to 4 to conditions in Judah, assuming instead that Habakkuk is crying out against a foreign oppressor like Assyria or Egypt. So some European higher critics,† such as Hitzig, Ewald, König, and Wellhausen, denied the reference of this passage to Judah. Similarly George Adam Smith, along with other British and American critics, saw the oppressor as an outsider, possibly Assyria or Egypt.‡

Once this theory§ is accepted, a process of transposition begins. Verses 5 to 11 no longer fit their original position and are therefore moved to a place after the fourth verse of chapter 2. Thus the critic becomes an editor, adjusting the text to fit his assumptions.

Although the Hebrew text of the first chapter actually names the Chaldeans (v. 6), there are some scholars who deny that the reference really means the Chaldeans. For example, Sellin, following Duhm, insists that the oppressor is not Nebuchadnezzar at all but Alexander the Great.[12] Therefore he moves the date of the book, commonly regarded as having been written sometime in the latter days of Judah, several hundred years forward to the time of Grecian world rule. Despite the plain fact of the original reference to the *Chasdim* (*Kasdim*)—that is, the Chaldeans, the supporters of the Grecian theory get rid of the term. This they do by arbitrarily changing *Chasdim* to *Kittim,* a name originally derived from the Cyprian town of *Kition* and applied in 1 Maccabees to the Greeks. Also the words in Habakkuk 2:5, "Wine is a treacherous" ("He transgresseth by wine," KJV) are made to read "the treacherous Greek."

---

†It is a mistake, sometimes made by conservative Christians, to condemn *all* higher criticism. The term is in itself a technical one, referring to that branch of scholarship which inquires into such things as the authorship, date, and style of the biblical documents. It stands in contrast to lower criticism which has to do with the transmission of the text and allied questions. Obviously there are conservative as well as liberal higher critics.

‡Cf. for an excellent account of the various critical views *The Book of the Twelve Prophets* by George Adam Smith, 2:117 f.

§There are, of course, a good many variants of the theory. Wellhausen, for example, thought that 1:5-11 predates the remainder of the book and so threw this passage out completely.

Habakkuk's prophecy covers only three brief chapters. Many critics question its unity. In fact, one critic, Marti, credits him with having written no more than 1:5-10, and 14-17—ten verses in all.

The genuineness of the third chapter has frequently been challenged. Some have claimed that Habakkuk did not write it because they think that its musical notations point to a postexilic origin. They also think that the marked difference of mood in chapter 3 indicates different authorship. But certain of the earlier psalms have similar notations, and the difference of mood is essential for the resolution of Habakkuk's theodicy. Other critics point to the fact that the Habakkuk commentary in the Qumran (Dead Sea) Scrolls deals only with Habakkuk 1:4—2:20. But this commentary relates the prophecy to the Qumran sect, and Habakkuk's psalm was hardly relevant to this purpose.[13] The logical place of the psalm in Habakkuk's thought and personal development is the most convincing evidence of its genuineness. Among contemporary scholars who accept Habakkuk's authorship of chapter 3 is W. F. Albright.[14]

LITERARY QUALITY

It is refreshing to turn from this maze of conjecture to a consideration of Habakkuk's style. For scholars join in acclaiming the literary excellence of his book. "If Habakkuk is to be compared . . . with the best prophets, he.excells in his lyrical piece, ch. iii, everything which Hebrew poetry has to show of this kind; he commands the greatest strength and richness, the loftiest enthusiasm, along with a due measure of beauty and clearness."[15] So writes DeWette. According to F. Delitzsch, "his language is classical throughout, full of rare and select turns and words, which are to some extent exclusively his own, whilst his view and mood of presentation bear the seal of independent force and finished beauty. Notwithstanding the vivid rush and lofty soaring of the thoughts, his prophecy forms a finely organized and artistically rounded whole. Like Isaiah, he is, comparatively speaking, much more independent of his predecessors, both in contents and form, than any of the other prophets."[16] And S. R. Driver pays tribute to the literary genius of Habakkuk in these words: "The literary power of Habakkuk is considerable. Though his book is a brief one, it is full of force; his descriptions are graphic and powerful; thought and expression are alike poetic; he is still a master of the old classical style, terse, parallelistic, pregnant. . . . And if ch. 3 be his, he is moreover a lyric poet of high order; the grand imagery and the rhythmic flow of this ode will bear comparison with the finest productions of the Hebrew muse."[17]

F. C. Eiselen may well be right when he says: "Only the Hebrew student can get an adequate idea of the literary excellence of the book of Habakkuk,"[18] an opinion shared by William Hayes Ward: "It is impossible in translation to reproduce the abounding alliterations of the original or the prevailing poetical measure consisting of three principal words in a line."[19]

To the Christian who takes the Bible seriously, no portion of it is without significance. Yet he cannot but feel it a special privilege to study a book of such excellence as Habakkuk. Probably no other of the minor prophets offers the reader greater rewards than this short prophecy of only three chapters. Nor is there any book in the Old Testament of comparable size that is more important than it is.

The book may be outlined as follows:
   I. The topic sentence (1:1)

  II. Habakkuk's first complaint (1:2-4)
      A. The prophet's questions (1:2-3*a*)
      B. The moral and civil condition of Judah (1:3*b*)
      C. The prophet's conclusions (1:4)

 III. The Lord's reply (1:5-11)
      A. The marvellous work announced (1:5)
      B. The Chaldeans and their might (1:6-11)

  IV. Habakkuk's confidence in the Lord (1:12)

   V. Habakkuk's second complaint (1:13-17)

  VI. The waiting prophet (2:1)

VII. The Lord's answer (2:2-4)
    A. The vision to be written plainly (2:2)
    B. The vision surely to come (2:3)
    C. The vision (2:4)

VIII. The five woes (2:5-19)
    A. Introduction (2:5-6a)
    B. The five woes upon the Chaldeans (2:6b-19)
        1. The first woe (2:6b-8)
        2. The second woe (2:9-11)
        3. The third woe (2:12-13)
        4. The earth to be covered with the knowledge of the Lord's glory (2:14)
        5. The fourth woe (2:15-18)
        6. The fifth woe (2:19)

IX. The summons to silence before Jehovah (2:20)

X. Habakkuk's psalm (3:1-19)
    A. The title (3:1)
    B. The plea (3:2)
    C. The Lord's answer by theophany (3:3-15)
    D. Habakkuk's response (3:16-19a)
    E. The musical ascription (3:19b)

1

THE DIALOGUE WITH GOD

The burden which Habakkuk the prophet did see (Hab 1:1).

This sentence might well stand as the superscription or title of the whole prophecy. Brief as it is, it sets the tone of the book and contains several words that are worthy of comment. There is first of all Habakkuk's use of the term *burden*. The Hebrew word has both the meaning of a heavy load such as might be borne upon the back of a man or animal and the meaning of an utterance, particularly a prophetic vision or oracle. It is in the latter sense that Habakkuk uses it. When so used, it generally has a dark connotation of foreboding, as in Isaiah 13:1; Nahum 1:1; and 2 Kings 9:25. The prophet who had a burden was a man of God bearing on his mind and heart a heavy load of divinely imposed concern.

Next there is the reference to Habakkuk as "the prophet." Except in Haggai, this is the only instance of such a designation being used of the writer in the first sentence of a prophetic book. The significance may be, as has already been pointed out, that Habakkuk probably held an official public position that gave him status in the eyes of the people as an accredited prophet of the Lord.

Finally there is the verb *did see*. For the English reader, there is something paradoxical in the thought of *seeing* a burden, when ordinarily we speak of *bearing* a burden. But, as this first chapter shows, the terrible things Habakkuk saw cannot be divorced from the oracle God laid upon his heart. It is also significant that the word translated "did see" is used particularly of the prophetic vision.

HABAKKUK'S FIRST COMPLAINT (1:2-4)

O LORD, how long shall I cry, and thou wilt not hear! even cry out unto theé of violence, and thou wilt not save! Why dost thou shew me iniquity, and cause me to behold grievance? (Hab 1:2-3*a*).

With dramatic suddenness the prophet begins. Like a man who has witnessed awful things against which his whole being protests, Habakkuk cries out. The words in verse 2, "how long" (literally "until when"), imply that the wickedness Habakkuk is seeing has gone on for a considerable period of time. The Hebrew word for "cry" means to "cry for help."

"And thou wilt not hear!" Here the moral problem of the prophet comes before us for the first time. He has cried out to God many times and nothing has happened. Therefore it seems to him as though God has deliberately shut His ears to his appeal. The next statement is extremely vivid. The word rendered in the King James Version "cry out" actually means "scream." Thus Habakkuk wrote something like this: "Scream unto Thee, 'Violence!' " It is as if a man today, coming upon a crime being committed, would scream out a single word like "Robbery!" or "Murder!" "Violence" is a term occurring rather frequently in the Old Testament, and has special reference to unjust aggression and assault. Back in Genesis 6:11, 13, we find it used to point out the particular sin which brought on the deluge.

In His Olivet Discourse, the Lord Jesus made a classic comparison between the time of Noah and our own day. "But as the days of Noe were," He said, "so shall also the coming of the Son of man be" (Mt 24:37). If the antediluvian age was characterized by violence, what of our day when lawlessness and violence threaten the very existence of civilization? Surely we are living in an age when God's people have laid upon their hearts, by the very sight of what is going on, a great burden.

"And thou wilt not save." Again the prophet, impatient in his indignation, voices his concern that God is not doing anything about the conditions that so stir his soul.

> Why dost thou shew me iniquity and cause me to behold
> grievance? (Hab 1:3*a*).

The complaint continues. Not only does Habakkuk accuse
God of not doing anything about the violence in Judah but
he also questions why he should be made to see the
sins that so outrage righteousness. The words *show me* may be
rendered "cause me to see." As to the words *iniquity* and
grievance, the former means "trouble" and refers to the sorrow
occasioned by human oppression; the latter has the sense of
"perverseness" or "mischief."

> For spoiling and violence are before me: and there are that
> raise up strife and contention (Hab 1:3*b*).

Here is a terse description of the state of society in Judah. To
be sure, there are scholars who think that the reference is not so
much to the Judah of Habakkuk's time as to some oppressing
nation outside Judah. But for the reasons given in the Introduction it seems clear that the prophet is speaking of the internal
affairs of his own nation. The term *spoiling* holds the meaning of
robbery. It was a case then, back in the seventh century B.C., of
the rich and powerful oppressing the poor, just as it has been
down through the ages. In the prophet's day, sin of this kind was
aggravated rather than lessened by the terrible danger from
Babylonian might in which the nation stood. And recent history
has shown that, when a country stands at the brink of catastrophe, it does not necessarily mean that righteousness will increase. Sometimes the response is a reckless plunge into sin and
violence, as in the days of Habakkuk.

The "strife and contention" referred to were probably the
result of quarrels between the nobility of Judah and the common
people whom they were oppressing. Everyone who is familiar
with the Hebrew prophets knows that they spoke out with great
boldness against such injustice. Likewise the ministry today,
which corresponds to the Old Testament order, is obligated to
speak out in denunciation of social evil. The church needs to
remember that a sensitiveness to corruption in society goes with

love for the Lord and the gospel. The divorce between preaching the gospel of grace and a concern for what is happening to our neighbor is not scriptural. The present-day evangelical ministry needs to declare itself more boldly against injustice; it should be free to exercise this God-given obligation without being criticized for preaching merely a social gospel. Proclaiming the gospel is not incompatible with responsible exercise of the prophetic ministry.

> Therefore the law is slacked, and judgment doth never go forth: for the wicked doth compass about the righteous; therefore wrong judgment proceedeth (Hab 1:4).

With this statement, Habakkuk sums up his complaint. Deeply concerned about evil, he falls into the error of jumping to a conclusion. In his double use of the word *therefore* there is a judgmental tone. "The law," he goes on, "is slacked" (literally "paralyzed"). So he concludes that, because in his time he has not seen the wicked judged, justice is *never* done.

This is an audacious way for any man to talk to God. But before we condemn Habakkuk for speaking like this, let us remind ourselves of how easy it is for us today to jump to similar conclusions. Have we not all heard questions like these: Why doesn't God stop war? Why does God let these terrible things go on? Where is God, that such wickedness can continue? The fact is that the words of this great prophet of long ago have in them a note of universality that speaks to our problems today.

Yes, Habakkuk dares to question God. It is true that he begins as a complainer and something of a skeptic. But though he complains, he never does so, as Robinson points out, "*against* God, but to God."[1] And there is all the difference in the world between the two kinds of complaining. Every thoughtful person with any experience of life meets insoluble problems. Every such person faces the seeming triumph of evil and the seeming defeat of good. To do as Habakkuk did and take these problems to God, even with a boldness like his, is right, provided that we do this with belief in God like that of the prophet. Instead, therefore, of censuring Habakkuk for the boldness of his speech under such great emotional and spiritual stress, we should follow him in taking our doubts, perplexities, and problems first of all to the living God, while continuing our efforts to deal with injustice and violence as best we know how.

THE REPLY (1:5-11)

> Behold ye among the [nations], and regard, and wonder marvellously, for I will work a work in your days, which ye will not believe, though it be told you (Hab 1:5).

Having complained that evil is rampant in Judah and that nothing is done about it, Habakkuk is now answered. The Lord speaks—not just to him but to the nation as a whole (note the plural pronoun *ye*). Habakkuk and his people are to be on the watch among the nations. They are to do more than look; they will also "wonder marvellously" at what they see. Here Habakkuk uses the same Hebrew verb in two different forms. The effect is one of great emphasis, indicative of extreme amazement, to the extent even of terror. It might be rendered, "be amazed, amazed."[2] The wonder will result in part from the immediacy of what will happen. The work the Lord is going to do will come to pass "in your days," by which is meant either at once or within the existing generation. More than that, however, it will be amazing because of its nature; it will be a work so startling as to seem unbelievable. Thus the prophet learns that, contrary to his complaint, God is *not* inactive. And not only is God not inactive: He will also intervene so speedily that His work, coming as it will "in your days," will be contemporary.

Paul's use of this verse (Ac 13:41) along with his citation of 2:4 in Romans 1:17 and also in Galatians 3:11 shows his familiarity with the prophet. It is significant that he quoted the Septuagint (Greek translation of the Old Testament) of Habakkuk 1:5 in his great address in the synagogue at Antioch at Pisidia (Ac 13:14-41) on his first missionary journey, using it to warn the Jews against rejecting Christ. The work to be done in their days that they would not believe he interpreted as God's calling of the Gentiles into the church.

> For, lo, I raise up the Chaldeans, that bitter and hasty nation, which shall march through the breadth of the land, to possess the dwelling places that are not theirs (Hab 1:6).

Now the nature of the marvelous work is revealed. A scourge is to be raised up against Judah for judgment. Punishment will come through the Chaldeans, described as a "bitter and hasty nation," or, in more modern parlance, a cruel and rash people.* They are to invade Judah and rush through it from one end of the land to the other.

Who were these Chaldeans? History tells us that they were a Semitic people (Hebrew, *Kasdim*). Of ancient lineage, they sprang from Kesed (Chesed), the son of Nahor and brother of Abraham (Gen 22:20-22). About the time of Habakkuk they came into sudden prominence with the rise of Babylonia. As recently as 626 B.C., Nabopolassar had founded the Neo-Babylonian Empire. And with the accession of his son Nebuchadnezzar to the throne in 605 B.C., the Chaldeans became a world power. Just as the smaller European nations such as Holland or Poland witnessed the swift inflation of might in Nazi Germany, or just as Czechoslovakia has faced Communist power, so little Judah saw the mounting strength of the Chaldeans.

> They are terrible and dreadful: their judgment and their dignity shall proceed of themselves. Their horses also are swifter than the leopards, and are more fierce than the evening wolves: and their horsemen shall spread themselves, and their horsemen shall come from far; they shall fly as the eagle that hasteth to eat (Hab 1:7-8).

So the vivid description of the Chaldeans continues. The gist of verse 7 is that they are a law unto themselves. Like the totalitarian powers against which free nations have struggled in the twentieth century, they are not only terrible in cruelty but also arbitrary and self-sufficient in action. At this point we are reminded of one of the lessons of history—namely, that evil

---

*C. L. Feinberg calls verse 6 "the classic passage for the characteristics of the Chaldeans, as Isaiah 5:26-30 is for the Assyrians" (The Major Messages of the Minor Prophets, *Habakkuk, Zepaniah, Haggai, and Malachi*, p. 15).

remains essentially unchanged. If wickedness today has assumed such gigantic proportions, one reason is that the facilities for its accomplishment have been vastly enlarged through the discoveries of science which, not dedicated to the blessing of humanity, are perverted to its destruction.

There is a modern ring about verse 8, with its mention of the speed of the Chaldeans in conquest. In fact, it might be aptly summed up by one word—*blitzkrieg*. The mounted troops of the Chaldeans are to descend upon Judea with fearful haste. They are characterized as "more fierce than the evening wolves," the reference being to wolves that, emboldened by hunger, descend upon a village at nightfall. Or, as the figure changes, the horsemen, coming from afar, are to fan out in all directions ("spread themselves") and swoop down upon their victims as birds of prey upon a carcass.

> They shall come all for violence; their faces shall sup up as the east wind, and they shall gather the captivity as the sand. And they shall scoff at the kings, and the princes shall be a scorn unto them: they shall deride every strong hold; for they shall heap dust, and take it (Hab 1:9-10).

The purpose of the Chaldeans is plainly to do violence. Yet there is an ironic nuance here, pointing back to Habakkuk's initial cry against the iniquity of Judah, "O LORD, how long shall I cry, and thou wilt not hear! Even cry out unto thee of violence, and thou wilt not save!" (Hab 1:2).

The description goes on with words that have puzzled commentators: "Their faces shall sup up as the east wind." The reference in the original to the east as a point of the compass is doubtful; what is probably meant is that the Chaldeans in their attack always faced forward, the picture being one of irresistible advance.† And when they are said to "gather the captivity as the

---

†The New Scofield Reference Bible replaces these words with "the set of their faces is forward," and the Revised Standard Version has "terror of them goes before them." The Jerusalem Bible, however, has "their faces scorching like an east wind," which reflects the Qumran comment on Habakkuk (found in 1947) and the Vulgate. (Cf. note in loc. in The Jerusalem Bible.) The Hebrew text is uncertain.

sand," the image is of the utter ease with which the Chaldeans are to conquer Judah, a nation no more resistant than the shifting sands.

Scoffing at kings and princes was thoroughly characteristic of cruel Babylonia. According to Chaldean custom captive rulers were put in cages and exhibited as public spectacles. Their eyes were put out, as in the case of Nebuchadnezzar's treatment of Zedekiah (2 Ki 25:7). As to the deriding of strongholds and the heaping of dust spoken of in verse 10, this pictures a common mode of ancient warfare in which immense amounts of earth were heaped up against the wall of a city to make a platform for the battering rams and the attacking armies.

> Then shall his mind change, and he shall pass over, and offend, imputing this his power unto his god (Hab 1:11).

The description of the Chaldeans closes with a plain hint of their downfall. The implication is that guilt is incurred by the Chaldeans as they sweep over Judah. Here in their self-deification is the reason for the conqueror's ruin. The terse words "imputing this his power unto his god" (Berkeley, "but they are guilty men, for their might is their God") express the seed of Babylonia's fall. Indeed, they may look forward to Nebuchadnezzar's own downfall, after he surveyed Babylon and said, "Is not this great Babylon, that I have built?" (Dan 4:28-33).

Perhaps the most searching temptation that can come to a nation is for it to gain great power. The stronger a people the more liable they are to rely upon themselves. History has demonstrated over and over again that power leads to ruin. When munitions and armies are multiplied, it is all too easy for nations to forget God and to rely upon their might even to the extent of practically deifying it. Moreover, what applies to nations applies also to individuals. Personal power and independence from other men all too readily lead to independence from God. When any man, however great, forgets that he is only a creature of the Almighty, he too may go the way of the Chaldeans and offend by making his power his god.

HABAKKUK'S CONFIDENCE IN THE LORD (1:12)

Art thou not from everlasting, O LORD my God, mine Holy One? We shall not die. O LORD, thou hast ordained them for judgment; and, O mighty God, thou hast established them for correction (Hab 1:12).

The Lord has spoken. Now the dialogue gives us Habakkuk's reply. This twelfth verse is one of the noblest in the Old Testament. It begins with a question that is in reality a great affirmation of faith. There is nothing of skepticism in this question; it comes out of faith and an affirmative answer is implied. Having seen what God is going to do about the sin of Judah, the prophet acknowledges the eternal, unchangeable, and holy character of God: "Art thou not from everlasting, O LORD, my God, mine Holy One?" Observe the twice-repeated possessive pronoun *my*. Habakkuk has the first qualification for an intercessor—a personal hold upon the Lord. For him religion was more than ritual; it was a matter of his own individual grip upon the holy One of Israel.

The point may seem a simple one, but it is nevertheless of highest importance. Nothing can take the place of a personal grasp on the Lord. Habakkuk had the same kind of faith David had, when David wrote: "I will love thee, O LORD *my* strength. The LORD is *my* rock, and *my* fortress, and *my* deliverer; *my* God, *my* strength, in whom I will trust; *my* buckler, and the horn of *my* salvation, and *my* high tower" (Ps 18:1-2). In its New Testament aspect, this is the kind of faith Paul had, when he said to the church at Philippi: "But *my* God shall supply all your need according to his riches in glory by Christ Jesus" (Phil 4:19). Behind these words of the apostle is an intercessory purpose. It is not the supply of his own needs of which Paul is speaking, but the supply of the needs of the Philippian church. He is able to assure them of the full adequacy of God, because for him God in Christ Jesus was "*my* God." So with us Christians; we can only assure others that the Lord will help them and meet their need if we have first of all experienced for ourselves what He does for the person who fully trusts Him.

Returning to Habakkuk, consider also his emphasis upon the holiness of God. For him the Lord was not only "from everlasting"; He was also holy. This was the ground of the prophet's forthcoming expostulation. No wonder he was able to see the divine purpose in the predicted judgment. In humble faith, he acknowledged that God ordained the Chaldeans for judgment; he saw that the mighty God had established them for the correction of Judah. With the essential rightness of the impending chastisement, he had no quarrel, although he was really crying out in behalf of the very Judah against whose sins he had been speaking.

HABAKKUK'S SECOND COMPLAINT (1:13-17)

In the midst of his perplexity, Habakkuk has paused to consider the nature of God. Having voiced his complaint about the wickedness of Judea and having received the divine assurance of imminent judgment through the Chaldeans, he has lifted his heart to God. Out of a personal grip on the holy One who is from everlasting, he realizes the Lord's sovereign purpose in using the Chaldeans as a scourge upon His unfaithful people. It is lofty ground on which Habakkuk is standing in verse 12. But he is not yet ready to stay there. Too many questions remain unanswered, too many doubts are active. Thus not in unbelief but in a spirit of faith that knows God well enough to trust Him with even the most persistent doubts, Habakkuk voices another complaint.

> Thou art of purer eyes than to behold evil, and canst not look on iniquity: wherefore lookest thou upon them that deal treacherously, and holdest thy tongue when the wicked devoureth the man that is more righteous than he? (Hab 1:13).

The prophet, though recognizing the judgment aspect of the Chaldean invasion, is still troubled. This second complaint is inconsistent but very human. The man who has cried out so bitterly against the sins of Judah, charging God with slackness in not avenging the oppression of the innocent, now complains against the appointed instruments of vengeance. For Habakkuk's objection is simply this: the avengers are even more wicked than those they are punishing. And this, he is saying, is wrong, for God is "of purer eyes than to behold evil" and of Him it must be said, "Thou . . . canst not look upon iniquity."

The writer remembers talking with a young student. In endeavoring to substantiate the view that evil is nonexistent, the student quoted this verse, arguing that if God, who is omniscient, is of too pure eyes to behold evil, then evil does not exist! The answer to such twisting of Scripture is simple. The connotation of the words "Thou art of purer eyes than to behold evil, and canst not look on iniquity" is that God cannot look at wickedness with favor. What Habakkuk meant in this remonstrance was that God, because of His transcendent holiness, cannot view with complacence anything evil. Yet He seems to the prophet to be countenancing the awful wickedness of the Chaldeans who in their depravity are far worse than the sinful Jews upon whom He is executing divine judgment. The complaint, then, is made on the ground that "the wicked devoureth the man that is more righteous than he."

> And maketh men as the fishes of the sea, as the creeping things that have no ruler over them? (Hab 1:14).

There follow several vivid figures of speech, based upon the sea with its teeming life. The first of these figures (Hab 1:14) refers to "the Lord who is said to do what he permits others to do. As a result of God's seeming indifference to destruction, men become like fish caught from the sea by a fisherman who uses every conceivable means—fishoook, net, drag (v. 15)—to increase his catch."[3]

> They take up all of them with the angle, they catch them in their net, and gather them in their drag: therefore they rejoice and are glad (Hab 1:15).

Here the Chaldeans are compared with the fisherman with his drag net. The prophet portrays the helplessness of the fish and the gloating force of the angler as he sweeps more and more of the vainly struggling creatures into his net.

Therefore they sacrifice unto their net, and burn incense unto their drag; because of them their portion is fat, and their meat plenteous (Hab 1:16).

At this point the figure takes on a profound shade of meaning that points to the great truth so briefly expressed in the first half of the fourth verse of the second chapter. "Therefore," says the prophet, "they sacrifice to their net and burn incense to their drag." In other words, the Chaldeans worship their might. In the figure Habakkuk is using, the net and the drag stand for the military power with which the Chaldeans overwhelm and en- slave their helpless enemies. And now, without comment, it is stated that the aggressor is making his power the object of his worship.

Ancient Babylon, as the prophet suggests, bowed down to its might. In this lay the seeds of its inescapable ruin. How often we hear it said, "We must be strong. We must build up our national power." No sensible man would deny the necessity, tragic as it is, for reinforcement of national defense. But woe to the nation that trusts in its armed forces and nuclear power, and forgets God! Woe to the country that, with Henley in his stirring but thoroughly unchristian *Invictus,* declares:

I am the master of my fate;
I am the captain of my soul.

Shall they therefore empty their net, and not spare continual- ly to slay the nations? (Hab 1:17).

This rhetorical question is of a summary nature. The picture is of the aggressor filling and emptying his net with a monotonous succession of victims. How long, Habakkuk is asking the Lord, is this to go on? How long are the unspeakably wicked Chaldeans to be permitted to devour, unrebuked and unchecked, the other nations?

2

THE LORD'S ANSWER

THE WAITING PROPHET (2:1)

I will stand upon my watch, and set me on my tower, and will watch to see what he will say unto me, and what I shall answer when I am reproved (Hab 2:1).

Although the text does not directly indicate it, we shall do well in this place to think of a pause in the prophet's inner struggle. The mood changes: Habakkuk turns from remonstrating to waiting. Moreover, this attitude seems to be the result of definite decision. "I will," he says, "stand upon my watch and set me on my tower." What is this place of watching? Are we to believe that Habakkuk actually went to some special tower and there waited for God to answer him? It may be that this was the case. Certainly there is nothing impossible in the prophet's withdrawal for a retreat, and he may indeed have had a place for meditation. But whatever the physical setting, the important thing is that he took time to be alone with God in an attitude of waiting before Him.

In the seventy-third psalm, Asaph says, after describing the prosperity of the ungodly, which is always so perplexing to the righteous: "When I thought to know this, it was too painful for me, until I went into the sanctuary of God; then understood I their end" (73:16-17). And while the verse before us does not suggest that Habakkuk actually made the temple his watchtower, in his heart he was in the sanctuary of the Lord.

The watchtower—what is it for Christians today? It may be some quiet place where we are undisturbed. Or for those in the midst of crowded family life, it may be the early morning or late evening hours when the activity of the home is stilled. Even if no place of quietness is available—and some may be so situated as to have practically no privacy*—Christians may still go to their watchtower. For the real place of withdrawal into the presence of God, the true sanctuary of communion with Him, is in the heart.

A devotional writer tells of a young woman in domestic service whose work kept her so busy that she seldom had time for prayer and meditation. But in her imagination she cherished the picture of a quiet little room with an open Bible on the table, a chair to kneel by, and a window opening on a view of forest and hill. There in her thoughts she would wait upon the Lord, when the round of duties made it impossible for her to be physically alone. So it is not literally going apart from daily life that is most important, although to have a place of actual quiet and solitude is helpful. The one essential is to learn how to be alone with God inwardly. For most of us there are opportunities to go to some place of undisturbed quiet for meditation. ⌈But the difficulty is that many of us do not take these opportunities, because we lack the spiritual discipline to give time daily to God.⌋

We now turn to the latter part of verse 1. The prophet is in the place of withdrawal, waiting upon the Lord. He is waiting for a specific purpose—to determine, as he puts it, "What I shall answer when I am reproved," or, as the American Standard Version translates it, "what I shall answer concerning my complaint." The reference is obviously to Habakkuk's words in 1:2-4, 13-17. Although the Hebrew and the Septuagint read, "what I shall answer," the better reading may be, "what he shall answer," as suggested by Stephens-Hodge, who says, "the person has been changed by some scribe out of a sense of reverence."[1] What the prophet is waiting for, then, is the Lord's reply to his perplexed expostulations. However, if the more common reading, "what I shall answer," is followed, then the meaning is that Habakkuk is thinking about the reply he must make regarding his complaint, which has seemed to impute injustice or inconsistency to God.

---

*The soldier in the barracks or the patient in the hospital ward, for example.

THE LORD'S ANSWER (2:2-4)

> And the Lord answered me, and said, Write the vision, and make it plain upon tables, that he may run that readeth it (Hab 2:2).

The reply now comes to Habakkuk in the form of a definite vision or revelation. The prophet's waiting is rewarded and his questions answered. As Raymond Calkins reminds us, "The Bible . . . never ends in an interrogation point. Always it ends in a period. Bible writers ask questions, but always also they get answers. . . . Modern writers ask many questions, raise many doubts, project all kinds of difficulties. But they present no answers, offer no solutions."[2] In the verse before us Habakkuk is told exactly what to do with the vision he is to receive. He is to write it. The word translated "write" has the meaning of "engrave." It signifies a clear and unmistakable type of inscription. The "tables" are tablets, probably of clay, to be set up in some prominent place. Apparently the prophets had the right of placing such tablets somewhere in the temple. On them they wrote or engraved key prophetic passages. Later such tablets might be taken down and assembled.[3]

Habakkuk's writing was to be so plain that it would be thoroughly legible. It is interesting that the common misquotation, "that he that runs may read," has become almost proverbial. But the prophet did not write it that way; his words are "that he may run that readeth." The difference is by no means trivial, for what Habakkuk actually wrote shows us something important about the purpose of prophecy. Despite widespread opinion, biblical prophecy is not necessarily an obscure subject. Although it has difficulties, its main currents are plainly discernible for the careful reader. And the purpose of prophecy in its plain meaning is not for the student to become entangled in details and finespun interpretations. On the contrary, prophecy has a dynamic urgency—"that he may run that readeth it." It should issue in faithful proclamation of its message and obedient action upon what God has revealed.

> For the vision is yet for an appointed time, but at the end it shall speak, and not lie: though it tarry, wait for it; because it will surely come, it will not tarry (Hab 2:3).

Having been told what to do with the vision, Habakkuk is next given a vivid description of it and its manner of coming. First of all, he is told that the vision will come exactly at the time of divine appointment. The import of this is that the evil of which the prophet has been complaining is to be judged by God at a predetermined time.

This whole verse is paradoxical in its expression and striking in the perspective it gives of time under God. As Calkins says, "God's train is never late. It will arrive on schedule time. A time limit is set in the counsels of God to the triumph of evil over good."[4] Or, as it also may be put, God *always* keeps His appointments.

"At the end it shall speak and not lie." The language is vivid. The vision seems almost personified. The thought is that it hastens or strives to the end. The words imply panting or gasping for breath. "The prophecy is, as it were, filled with the impetus and impulse to be fulfilled."[5] Though to Habakkuk, looking at it from the human point of view, it seemed that the fulfillment would be delayed, he is assured that it will surely come and will not be a moment late. Peter says of the divine chronology: "But, beloved, be not ignorant of this one thing, that one day is with the Lord as a thousand years, and a thousand years as one day" (2 Pe 3:8).

> Behold, his soul which is lifted up is not upright in him: but the just shall live by his faith (Hab 2:4).

Only twenty words in length in the King James Version, this verse covers a vast amount of territory. In its first half there is compressed a whole philosophy of history. Its second half contains the germinal truth out of which there blossoms in the New Testament the profound doctrine of how a sinner may become righteous in the sight of a holy God.

"Behold, his soul which is lifted up is not upright in him." This is God's ultimate statement regarding the Chaldean and all who through history have followed his tyrannical example. George

Adam Smith translates it: "Lo! swollen, not level is his soul within him."[6] The thought is that the aggressor, puffed up with pride, is in his nature essentially crooked. The great truth behind these words is that, as Smith also puts it, "Tyranny is suicide."[7] When a nation is committed to self-aggrandizement through oppression of others, it has written its own obituary. There is a self-destroying power in evil that time always reveals. Ultimately the wicked power falls of its own weight. In respect to the Chaldean, therefore, the vision is simply the statement of his true character. Inflated with pride and thoroughly crooked, he is doomed.†

Brief as it is, the first half of the verse may well be of comfort to Christians today. At a time when world powers are lifted up with pride and dedicated to the policy that a lie, repeated often enough and insisted upon strongly enough, will be believed in place of the truth, it is reassuring to realize that the final collapse of such a system is inevitable. Whether in ancient Babylon, Soviet Russia, Communist China, or any other nation, it is still true that tyranny is suicide.

Even more concise is the second half. It too is simply packed with meaning. (In the Introduction the use of this declaration in Ro 1:16; Gal 3:11-12; and Heb 10:38 has already been mentioned.) Every student of Romans knows that upon Habakkuk 2:4b Paul built his great exposition of justification by faith. Here, then, is one of the seminal ideas in Christian theology. Because of it Habakkuk 2:4 must rank among the very greatest single statements in the entire Old Testament.

The meaning of the statement that "the just shall live by his faith" is this. The word *just* refers, of course, to the man who is righteous in the sight of God. Such a man lives in God's sight by faith. Or, as the idea is developed in the New Testament, a man is made right (justified) before God not by what he himself does but by his faith in the finished work of Christ. There can be no question that Habakkuk's words are used in the New Testament in support of this central evangelical doctrine.

---

†Cf. G. Campbell Morgan, *Living Messages of the Books of the Bible,* 1:273 ff., for an impressive elaboration of this point.

Some scholars, however, imply that the words translated "the just shall live by his faith" mean practically the opposite of justification by faith alone. They base their opinion upon the Hebrew word *'ĕmûnâh* in Habakkuk 2:4. Instead of being translated "faith," this word, they say, should be translated "faithfulness" in the sense of steadfastness and trustworthiness in the performance of duty. According to them, Habakkuk is saying that the just man lives by his faithful acts and his steadfast life.

Now without denying that *'ĕmûnâh* does indeed have the meaning of steadfastness, we cannot agree that the deeper idea of living by faith is ruled out. In the first place, there is the context of 2:4*b*. The attitude of the just man in a firm attachment to God is clearly contrasted with the pride and crookedness of the Chaldean. In the preceding verse, Habakkuk is exhorted to "wait for" the vision. This surely is an attitude of faith, waiting upon God to take action. Again, there is Genesis 15:6, "Abraham believed God and it was counted to him for righteousness." Here the verb translated "believe" is from the same root as *'ĕmûnâh*. Smith says of *'ĕmûnâh,* "Of course, it has faith in God as its secret—the verb from which it is derived is the regular Hebrew term to believe—but it is rather the temper which faith produces of endurance, steadfastness, integrity."[8] The meaning of "faithfulness" for *'ĕmûnâh* is not incompatible with the evangelical concept of faith. For it is a reminder that the faith of the heart must find expression in faithful, steadfast living, a principle repeatedly stressed in the New Testament.

Finally and most important of all, there is the plain use Paul makes of Habakkuk's great statement. There is no doubt about the meaning he attached to it. He was a rabbinical scholar of the first order. Not only so but he was an inspired writer.

All things considered, this is a place where the student must choose the best interpreter. So the question is simply this: Who *is* the ultimate interpreter of this Scripture? Is it not the Holy Spirit, who inspired both Habakkuk and the apostle to the Gentiles, who made such dynamic use of this passage in developing one of the central doctrines of Christian theology?

3

THE TAUNT SONG

INTRODUCTION

> Yea also, because he transgresseth by wine, he is a proud man, neither keepeth at home, who enlargeth his desire as hell, and is as death, and cannot be satisfied, but gathereth unto him all nations, and heapeth unto him all people: Shall not all these take up a parable against him, and a taunting proverb against him (Hab 2:5-6a).

The remainder of this second chapter consists of a taunt song made up of a series of "woes" upon the Chaldeans. The form is quite regular, consisting of five strophes with three verses in each strophe. Taken together, they provide a striking exemplification of the principle, so concisely stated in the first part of verse 4, that the despot has within him the seeds of his own destruction. If tyranny *is* suicide, these vivid maledictions show us exactly why. The five strophes make up a taunt song ("a taunting proverb"). And inasmuch as Babylon was at the apex of its power when the passage was written, the strophes are also a prophetic pronouncement of doom upon that proud and cruel power, a preview, as it were, of leading features of its sure ruin.

Verses 5 and 6a introduce the taunt song. The reference to wine ("he transgresseth by wine") poses a problem because of the obscurity of the text. There are scholars who insist that "wine" is a corruption and that an emendation is demanded. Some, as Sellin, for example, arbitrarily change the word *hayyayin* by changing the text to make it mean "Greek."[1]

So the translation becomes, "How much more the treacherous Greek." This fits in with the attempt to turn the word for

"Chaldean" in the first chapter (1:6) into *Kittim,* a term sometimes applied to the Greeks. But, as has already been pointed out, this is twisting the text to fit preconceived notions of what it should mean. Moreover, agreement about "wine" is by no means general. Ward says, "The word *wine,* which must be retained, gives the key to emendation. . . ."[2] The Qumran commentary sustains the Hebrew text.[3] And it is a fact that the Chaldeans were proverbial for their drunkenness. One of the most elaborate debauches in history was Belshazzar's feast. Herodotus and Xenephon confirm this aspect of the Chaldean character. It is, therefore, not difficult to see the connection between the mention of wine and the remainder of verse 5, with its description of Chaldean pride, coupled with insatiable thirst for conquest.

Have we today anything to learn from Habakkuk's reference to one of Babylon's besetting sins? When a people spends for alcoholic beverages over $72 a year for every man, woman, and child, or an annual total of $14,451,000,000 (over twice as much as all contributions for religious and charitable purposes), and when the number of alcoholics in the population is estimated at 6.5 million, serious questions arise. (These are recent figures for the United States and they should be of concern to every American Christian.) Neighbor-love is a Christian responsibility, as is an informed conscience about social issues. In the light of the many millions being spent annually on advertising to promote the sale of alcoholic beverages, Christians (especially those responsible for the nurture and education of youth) need to know three key facts: (1) that the risk every drinker runs of becoming an alcoholic is one in eighteen;[4] (2) that there is no way of knowing who among those who begin to drink will become alcoholics; (3) that "the only absolute insurance against alcoholism is lifelong abstinence."[5]

The Chaldean, Habakkuk goes on to say, "enlarges his desire as hell, and is as death, and cannot be satisfied." He is speaking here of the Hebrew *sheol.* This is not hell in the sense of a place of punishment, but is the equivalent of the Greek *hades,* the place of the departed spirits. The thought is that as death and the grave increasingly devour human life, so Babylon continues ravenous for victims of its ambition.

Having described the Babylonian lust for conquest, the prophet represents the conquered people as lifting up their voices in "a proverb against him" (the Chaldean). There will come a time, he is saying, when the oppressed will see retribution descending upon their oppressors, and in that day they will taunt them in proverbs. Thus the underdog will be in the position of heaping scorn and derision upon his erstwhile conqueror. In form this taunt song is a riddle, which is what the word translated "proverb" means.*

THE FIVE WOES UPON THE CHALDEANS (2:6B-19)

The first woe

> Woe to him that increaseth that which is not his! how long? and to him that ladeth himself with thick clay! Shall they not rise up suddenly that shall bite thee, and awake that shall vex thee, and thou shalt be for booties unto them? Because thou hast spoiled many nations, all the remnant of the people shall spoil thee; because of men's blood, and for the violence of the land, of the city, and of all that dwell therein (Hab 2:6b-8).

This first woe refers to the inordinate greed of the Chaldean shown by his spoiling of subject peoples. The idea of unlawful possession, even to the extent of robbery, underlies the declaration, "Woe to him that increases [multiplies] that which is not his!" Less clear is the next statement, "And to him that ladeth himself with thick clay!" The King James Version "thick clay" results from breaking up the word *pledge* or *debt* into "thick cloud" or "clay."⁶ The prophet is saying something like this: "Woe to the Chaldean who is burdening himself with a great load of pledges or debts!" These debts consist of the belongings of oppressed nations, stolen from them as a usurer would extort unlawful gain.

In verse 7 the King James Version is again obscure. Here the original seems purposely enigmatic, for the Hebrew does indeed speak of "biters." This word, however, also means "creditors,"

---

*Cf. Ludwig E. Fuerbringer, *The Eternal Why*, pp. 45-65, for a good exegesis not only of this passage but of all five woes.

and this is the present meaning. The tables are turned. Having spoiled weaker peoples, the Chaldeans are going to experience poetic justice, when those from whom they have extracted unlawful gain will turn on them and exact by force their just due. All this is ethically on Old Testament ground and belongs with the Mosaic law of retribution. It reminds us that God's vengeance is never outdated. History shows that ultimately He deals with nations that flout His sovereignty.

As to the last clause of verse 7, the modern reader would understand it better were "spoils" to be substituted for "booties." Some years ago the writer was teaching Habakkuk to an adult Bible class. Following a lesson in which this chapter was discussed, a woman physician attending the class asked why the prophet mentioned little shoes ("booties"). It took only a minute to point out that Habakkuk was not speaking of infant footwear, but that the seventeenth century translators were simply using the plural of booty, a plural that has an intensive force. The incident reminds us of the necessity for verifying the meaning of Bible words. However much we value the Bible as the inspired Word of God, we must use common sense in interpreting it.

The next verse is a restatement of the retribution that is surely to come upon Babylon. The word *blood,* being in the plural, vividly brings to mind the almost incalculable number of casualties resulting from the Chaldean's conquests. Regarding the execution of the predicted judgment · upon the Babylonian empire, the major prophets have much to say. Daniel in particular describes the final overthrow of Babylon (chap. 5), a doom also recounted in the secular history of Herodotus,[7] and Isaiah gives a remarkable picture of the continuing desolation of the ruined city (13:19-22). Today the remains of Babylon bear grim witness to the law of retribution. Exactly as prophecy foretells, the very site of the ancient capital is bleak and uninhabited. Although extensive remains of Babylon were uncovered by German archeologists up to the time of the First World War, the place itself is desolate. "There are various superstitions current among the Arabs that prevent them from pitching their tents there, while the character of the soil prevents the growth of vegetation suitable for the pasturage of flocks. The whole site is a desolate waste, with the caves and holes in the ruins occupied only by wild animals of the desert. Lions, jackals, and various other animals sport among the ruins, and their cries re-echo through the caverns of the ancient palace walls, but human beings are seldom seen in the vicinity. The prophecy might well be written now as a description of the site of Babylon, yet we know that it was written over twenty-five hundred years ago!"[8]

The second woe

> Woe to him that coveteth an evil covetousness to his house, that he may set his nest on high, that he may be delivered from the power of evil! Thou hast consulted shame to thy house by cutting off many people, and hast sinned against thy soul. For the stone shall cry out of the wall, and the beam out of the timber shall answer it (Hab 2:9-11).

Condemnation is now directed against the rapacity of the Chaldean, a leading feature of whose conquests was plunder. Motivated by a covetous spirit, he amassed huge stores of ill-gotten riches, which were used to build up material security. In verse 9 the prophet reverts to the eighth verse of the first chapter, wherein the Chaldeans are likened to the eagle. The figure reminds us also of Obadiah 4: "Though thou exalt thyself as the eagle and though thou set thy nest among the stars, thence will I bring thee down, saith the LORD." The word *house* in verse 9 refers to the Chaldean empire or dynasty, not to an individual dwelling. Likewise the expression *nest* is to be taken as a symbol of the Chaldean's purpose to make himself so secure as to be out of reach of his enemies.[9]

To the English reader, verse 10 is rather puzzling. But when the expression *consulted shame* is read as "plotted" or "devised shame," it becomes clear. Actually, the statement is ironical. The Chaldean has schemed to build up his own power and glory through the destruction of many peoples. But this cruel ambition will boomerang. All these plans for glory will bring shame and ruin upon the wicked oppressor.

Verse 11, making the transition to the next woe, stigmatizes the propensity of godless civilizations to build imposing structures. Such outward evidences of swollen pride stand as a silent condemnation of oppression. The very stones and the beams have a voice; unitedly they cry to high heaven against the slave labor with which they were built into man-glorifying monuments.

But a house speaks of more than the character of its builder. It also reflects the personality of those who dwell in it. In his short story "They," Rudyard Kipling says, "Men and women may sometimes, after great effort, achieve a creditable lie; but the house, which is their temple, cannot say anything save the truth of those who have lived in it." The idea is one worth thinking about by Christians. What do our homes say of us? Suppose that, during our absence, some discerning strangers went through our homes. What would they learn of our character, our culture—most of all, of our devotion to the Lord? Kipling is right. A house cannot lie; silently it will, through its order, the pictures on the walls, the books on the shelves, the music on the piano, the presence or absence of the Bible and other religious literature, tell what we are and how we live.

The third woe

> Woe to him that buildeth a town with blood, and stablisheth a city by iniquity! Behold, it is not [margin] of the LORD of hosts that the people shall labor in the very fire, and the people shall weary themselves for very vanity (Hab 2:12-13).

This verse intensifies the thought of building upon a foundation of injustice and cruelty. Indirectly it reminds us of the familiar word of the psalmist, "Except the Lord build the house, they labor in vain that build it" (Ps 127:1). To put it in another way, it is the antithesis of Paul's affirmation, "For other foundation can no man lay than that is laid, which is Jesus Christ" (1 Co 3:11). Verse 13 cries out against the fire of affliction in which conquered peoples have been forced to toil throughout the ages. How little godless men have progressed! Today, so long after Babylon fell, slave labor is still a tragic fact, and the United Nations cannot stop it.

The earth to be covered with the knowledge of the Lord's glory

> For the earth shall be filled with the knowledge of the glory of the LORD, as the waters cover the sea (Hab 2:14).

It is with a sense of relief that we come to verse 14. Here, in this dark passage, is a glorious parenthesis that opens a window through which we may see God's judgments in the perspective of His future, sovereign plan. An Old Testament critic says of this verse: "The quotation from Isa. 11:9 (the reference is to verse 14) is not metrical, nor has it any particular bearing on the subject, but is merely a pious reflection thrown in at hazard."[10] Is this true? Is this facile dismissal of Habakkuk 2:14 all that there is to be said about it? Certainly not. In quoting Isaiah 11:9 the prophet modifies it significantly: "For the earth shall be full of the knowledge of the Lord" (Is); "For the earth shall be filled with the knowledge *of the glory* of the LORD" (Hab; italics added). Habakkuk is referring to "God's power and majesty."[11] In doing so, he looks forward to the magnificent display of God's might in chapter 3. And at the same time the context of Isaiah 11:9 with its emphasis on men knowing God is a classic description of the future kingdom age when the wolf will dwell with the lamb, the leopard with the kid, the calf and young lion will be at peace together, and a little child will lead them. Instead of calling Habakkuk's use of Isaiah's words "merely a pious reflection thrown in at hazard," we should rejoice in the glorious prospect it presents. Civilizations come and go. Arnold Toynbee identifies about twenty cycles of them. But God is ever working toward His final purpose in the coming millennial kingdom. For the day is inevitably approaching when the earth *will* overflow with the knowledge of the glory of the Lord. So the quotation points to the reign of Him who is King of kings and Lord of lords. It reminds us who share with Habakkuk the experience of living in a time of corruption and injustice, turmoil and judgment, that there is a brighter day ahead. Evil will be dealt with and, judgment having been meted out, God will clothe the earth with His glory.

The fourth woe

> Woe unto him that giveth his neighbour drink, that puttest thy bottle to him, and makest him drunken also, that thou mayest look on their nakedness! Thou art filled with shame and not glory: drink thou also and be as one uncircumcised [American Standard Version]†: the cup of the Lord's right hand shall be turned unto thee, and shameful spewing shall be on thy glory. For the violence of Lebanon shall cover thee, and the spoil of beasts, which made them afraid, because of men's blood, and for the violence of the land, of the city, and of all that dwell therein. What profiteth the graven image that the maker thereof hath graven it; the molten image, and a teacher of lies, that the maker of his work trusteth therein, to make dumb idols? (Hab 2:15-18).

Drunkenness was a besetting sin of the Chaldeans (cf. comment on 2:5). Not only did they drink to excess but they were also possessed with the desire to make others drunk. At this point Habakkuk's language is terribly severe, as it lays bare the disgraceful motive of the Chaldean in plying others with drink. In verse 16 we have a Hebrew word for vomiting that occurs only here and that connotes the ultimate in scorn.[12]

There is, however, more behind Habakkuk's words than this picture of bestial drunkenness. While the disgraceful scene was drawn from life, the true force of the figure is retributive. The likening of fury and wrath to the intoxicating cup is a familiar prophetic figure. Jeremiah has a powerful passage on the "wine cup of fury" in which he portrays nation after nation imbibing the cup of wrath which drives them to the madness of war (25:15-38). Obadiah also uses the same figure at the close of his brief but severe prophecy (v. 16). So, with that double application so unique in the prophetic word, the intemperance of the Chaldean turns into retribution, as "the cup of the LORD's right hand," which is the cup of His terrible wrath, is poured out against them.

---

†This is the meaning of the King James .Version, "let thy foreskin be uncovered"—i.e., to show in the Chaldean's shameless intoxication his non-Jewishness.

In verse 17 the prophet shifts to another iniquitous act of the Chaldean. "The violence of Lebanon" undoubtedly refers to the devastation of the forests of that region, while "the spoil of beasts" points to the resulting destruction of wild life, as the forests were denuded. This judgment, then, is against the Chaldean's wanton waste of natural resources, such waste being the inevitable concommitant of the passion for building which characterized Babylon. It is one of the earliest references in ancient literature to the conservation of the natural resources with which God has blessed humanity.

Only in comparatively recent years have we begun to realize how important conservation is, as man-made pollution despoils not only the land but also the air we breathe and the water we drink. God created man to use, not to destroy, his environment, and he must accept responsibility for his stewardship of natural resources. The biblical basis of conservation is a neglected subject among many Christians.

Once more the focus of judgment shifts; verse 18 brings to the fore another sin of Chaldea. As the woes come to their end, a climax is reached with the mention of the crowning sin of idolatry and sorcery, denunciation of which is carried over to the fifth woe. "What profiteth the graven image that the maker thereof hath graven it; the molten image, and a teacher of lies, that the maker of his work trusteth therein, to make dumb idiols?" (Hab 2:18). Scripture has a great deal to say about the idolatry and sorcery of Babylon. The very term *Chaldean* was synonymous with a practitioner of hidden arts; "Chaldeans" are prominent in Daniel, one of the sources for knowledge of ancient Babylon.‡ And it is significant that in Revelation the great dirge over the "overthrow of Babylon the great" sums up her iniquity in these words: "for by thy sorceries were all nations deceived" (18:23).

The fifth woe

Woe unto him that saith to the wood, Awake; to the dumb

---

‡Cf. Daniel 2:2, 4-5; 3:8; 4:7; etc.

stone, Arise, it shall teach! Behold, it is laid over with gold and silver, and there is no breath at all in the midst of it (Hab 2:19).

Habakkuk now pronounces judgment against the Chaldean for presuming to give speech to idols of wood and "dumb stone." Whether by a kind of ventriloquism or some other deceit, or possibly by Satanic power, the ancient sorcerer claimed to give speech to wood and stone. And his modern counterpart, the spiritualist, follows the same old path.

Or, to ask another question, what should be the Christian attitude toward this matter of modern spiritualism? The only safe principle is to keep completely away from it. Any dabbling in these things is expressly forbidden by the Word of God. One of the New Testament signs of the last days is that "some will depart from the faith, giving heed to seducing spirits and doctrines of demons" (1 Ti 4:1). Such practices are often fraudulent; they are also perilous because of the danger of emotional imbalance and the possibility of demonic influences. It is paradoxical that in this age of science and education, credulous followers of spiritualism, theosophy, astrology, and other kinds of occultism number in the millions. And among them are some widely known leaders.§ Neither out of curiosity nor from any other motive should a Christian have anything to do with mediums and their "communication" with the dead.

Some years ago a well-known religious periodical printed the following paragraph, which stands as a strange modern comment on Habakkuk 2:19: "Spiritism might sometimes be described as the art of waking wood. Regarding table-tipping, etc., Sir Oliver Lodge is quoted: 'A light table seems no longer inert; it behaves as if animated. It can exhibit certainty, it can seek for information, it can convey it.' In the *Outlook* (30 January, 1920) Mr. J. Vine Milne wrote: 'I had been spending an evening with a

---

§Cf., the book by the late James A. Pike with Diane Kennedy, *The Other Side: An Account of My Experiences with Psychic Phenomena,* in which the author told of alleged communication with his dead son. Cf. also Rev. Arthur A. Ford, *Unknown But Known: My Advent into the Meditational Dimension.*

friend, an M.A. and D.Sc. of London. It was not long before we heard knocks, which we spelt out aloud. It was a reference to Habakkuk. We eagerly turned up the passage, which read: 'Woe to him that saith to the *wood*, Awake; to the *dumb stone*, Arise, it shall teach!' A great silence fell on us. I took it as a personal warning, and this was forty years ago: I have not touched the unclean thing since."[13]

The Summons to Silence Before Jehovah (2:20)

> But the Lord is in his holy temple: let all the earth keep silence before him (Hab 2:20).

Habakkuk's complaint has been heard. The Lord has answered him not only by announcing the coming of the Chaldeans but by the profound revelation of 2:4. The taunt song with its five woes is ended.

Suddenly the mood changes. It is as though the prophet puts his finger to his lips and says with a note of awe, "Hush! Remember the presence of the Lord and be quiet." As with the interjection in Psalm 46:10 of "Be still, and know that I am God," here also man is summoned to silence before the Almighty. The verse provides an impressive transition to the sublime imagery of the third chapter.

The reference to the Lord "in his holy temple" need not be limited to His presence in the temple at Jerusalem. It may well refer to the Lord's abode in heaven, as Kerr suggests on the basis of Psalms 11:4; 18:6, 9; 2 Samuel 22:7, 10.[14] This view is reinforced by the theophany of 3:3-15.

4

THE PSALM

THE TITLE

The last chapter of Habakkuk is one of the most majestic portions of the Old Testament. Not only its form but also its content give it a distinctive place among the prophetic Scriptures.

> A prayer of Habakkuk the prophet upon Shigionoth (Hab 3:1).

This opening verse is like the titles found about one hundred times in the Psalms and points in particular to the superscription of Psalm 7, where we find *Shiggaion*, the singular form of the word. Here we have its plural, *Shigionoth*. The exact meaning of the Hebrew word is uncertain. Some think that it refers to a musical instrument. More probable, however, is the meaning of a song or hymn characterized by rapid movement, strong emotion, and swift transition of thought—in short, the kind of expression usually called rhapsodic.

Significant also is the use of the word *prayer*. Strictly speaking, the prayer, as Pusey shows,[1] is confined to verse 2. Considered in this light, most of what follows in the chapter (vv. 3-15) constitutes the Lord's answer, while the closing verses (16-19) give the prophet's response. However, in a broader sense verses 3-15 may also be considered prayer in that they imply a plea for future deliverance and a celebration of God's greatness.

The chapter as a whole is a sublime psalm.* As an example of powerful utterance, it is very great literature. It seems likely from the use of the word *Selah* in verse 3 and from the closing

---

*For a discussion of the authorship of chapter 3 see the Introduction.

reference (v. 19), "To the chief singer upon my stringed instruments," that the psalm was meant to be sung or accompanied by instrumental music. One of the great works in organ literature is the *Sonata on the Ninety-fourth Psalm* by Reubke. But it would challenge a master of sublimity like Beethoven to set Habakkuk's psalm to music.

THE PLEA

> O LORD, I have heard thy speech, and was afraid: O LORD; revive thy work in the midst of the years, in the midst of the years make known; in wrath remember mercy (Hab 3:2).

Here is the prophet's petition after his dialogue with the Lord and after the vision has been given him upon the watchtower. Observe his reaction. When he speaks of being "afraid," we are not to think just of fright or intimidation. Rather is his attitude the deep awe the Old Testament calls "the fear of the Lord." God has condescended to take the prophet into His counsels and show him what He will do not only about punishing Judah but also about the wickedness of Babylon.

The word translated "revive" means "to call into life." It is important to see the primary historical meaning of Habakkuk's prayer. It is not a plea for religious revival, important as such revival always is. Instead Habakkuk is plainly beseeching God to bring into being the judgment work He promised against the Chaldeans. Involved also in this judgment work, and prior to it, is the punishment of Judah that, as Habakkuk has learned, will be carried out by Babylon. Now that the prophet knows what will happen, he is praying for it to take place swiftly. It is as if a Christian were to pray, "O Lord, Thy will be done—and soon." Then the prophet adds to his petition the eloquent phrase, "in wrath remember mercy." He knows that judgment is inevitable.

If Habakkuk, in a day when the wickedness and corruption that had so perplexed him were comparatively localized, knew that judgment was sure, how much more should we, looking upon a world scene of turmoil and evil, realize the inescapability of the divine reckoning with sin. Though the believer longs for the consummation of the age in Christ and though he knows that

it inevitably entails judgment, yet the love for all men that
should characterize Christians compels him to join Habakkuk in
the plea, "in wrath remember mercy."

THE LORD'S ANSWER BY THEOPHANY

> God came from Teman, and the Holy One from mount Paran.
> Selah. His glory covered the heavens, and the earth was full of
> his praise (Hab 3:3).

The next passage describes a stupendous storm and astound-
ing disturbances in heaven and earth. The imagery is overpow-
eringly vivid, as phrase piles upon phrase in picturing various
cataclysms of nature. But there is more behind the words than
natural catastrophes. The passage portrays a theophany with
reminiscences of God's mighty deliverance of His people at the
time of the Exodus. In spirit it is akin to other Old Testament
poems like Exodus 15, the song of Deborah (Judg 5), and Psalm
68. Unquestionably Habakkuk is describing a visible manifestation of God in the splendor of His might and the awful power of
His judgment. And he portrays it with such awe-inspiring majesty as to justify fully George Adam Smith's designation of the
passage as "the Great Theophany."[2]

In the verse before us God is visualized as appearing from the
high mountain regions south of Sinai. The name Teman is linked
with Edom in the Old Testament. Paran is also in the region of
Seir. It may be that the theophany of Sinai is in the prophet's
mind, although he does not definitely mention this locale.

The word *Selah,* which appears here and also in verses 9 and
13, is well known to every reader of the Psalms. Its precise
meaning is not certain, but it may well designate a pause or
interlude in those psalms that were set to music. During this
pause the instruments would play and the worshiper would have
an opportunity to meditate. Significantly enough, the only instances of the use of this word outside Psalms are in this third
chapter of Habakkuk. Its occurrence here is evidently one of the
indications that this portion of the prophecy is in structure
actually a psalm.

> And his brightness was as the light; he had horns coming out
> of his hand: and there was the hiding of his power (Hab 3:4).

Habakkuk now pictures the effulgence of the Lord's glory. The
first clause, speaking of "brightness," calls to mind many portions
of Scripture in which light is associated with the Lord. There is,
for example, the transfiguration scene where momentarily the
essential glory of the Lord Jesus Christ shone through His physical body with blinding brilliance (Mt 17:2; Mk 9:3; Lk 9:29).
There is also the great picture of the risen Christ in the first
chapter of Revelation (1:14-15) where His resplendent glory is
emphasized. And in the grand opening sentence of the espistle
to the Hebrews, we are reminded that the Son is "the brightness
of [God's] glory."

The Rev. Alex Dodds of the Sudan Interior Mission described
an incident that occurred in a school for blind men in Africa.
During a question period, one of the men asked, "What is brightness?" In telling the story Mr. Dodds said, "How would one
answer a blind man?" In this case, one of the other blind men
suggested that brightness might be like lightning. But he was a
man who had not been born blind. When the missionary asked
the inquirer if this had been helpful, he received a negative
shake of the head. The suggestion was then made that brightness was like the warm light of the sun that made the light of
the moon seem cold by comparison. The blind man could sense
that the moon does give off some kind of feeling, but that it was
far weaker than the heat of the sun, especially in the tropics.
This helped a little bit. Finally, the missionary said, the Lord
brought to mind this answer, "Brightness is the light which
shines in the heart when we put our trust in Jesus as our
Saviour." With that the question was answered, and the blind
man was enabled to grasp the concept of brightness. And the
proof of his understanding was his shining face.

Puzzling to the English reader is the reference to "horns" in
verse 4. The word is a fairly common Oriental term, signifying
power and strength; here it could be better translated "rays."
In commenting on this verse Pusey alludes to the hands of the
Redeemer, pierced for the sin of the world, relating this thought

to the clause, "there was the hiding of his power." "And what has been the weapon of His warfare," he asks, "whereby He has subdued the might of Satan and the hearts of men, but the horns of His cross, whereto His Sacred Hands were once fastened by the sharp nails, where was the hiding of His Power, when His Almightiness lay hid in His Passion, and He was a worm and no man; a reproach of men and the despised of the people?"[3]

Another interpretation points out that behind the glory of God is always His omnipotence. For light is the garment God wears when He appears to men. And a study of the theophanies in Scripture shows this to be generally true. As Fuerbringer puts it, "The radiance is . . . the visibility of the invisible God."[4]

> Before him went the pestilence, and burning coals went forth at his feet. He stood, and measured the earth: he beheld, and drove asunder the nations; and the everlasting mountains were scattered, the perpetual hills did bow: his ways are everlasting (Hab 3:5-6).

There is tremendous vigor in these two verses. In the first, Habakkuk portrays the Lord's devastation of evil. The second, which is wonderfully dramatic, should perhaps be translated in the present tense as might the whole theophany. The following rendering is vivid: "He stands, and rocks the earth: He looks and makes nations tremble; and the everlasting mountains burst into pieces, the eternal hills sink down: He walks the ways of olden time."[5]

The image suggests a giant striding across the world and, by his insuperable might, shaking the very earth and tossing the mountains to and fro. Dull of apprehension is the person who, when in the great mountains, can fail to be awed by their magnitude. But God is greater than the mountains and anything else on earth or in the whole universe. The transcendent Creator is infinitely above His creation, and can do as He wills with all He has made.

> I saw the tents of Cushan in affliction: and the curtains of the land of Midian did tremble. Was the LORD displeased against the rivers? was thine anger against the rivers? was thy wrath against the sea, that thou didst ride upon thine horses and thy chariots of salvation? (Hab 3:7-8).

The theophany goes on to single out Cushan (probably Ethiopia) and Midian as quailing under judgment. The mention of these two lands indicates the widespread effects of the Lord's might; Ethiopia represents the peoples to the west of the Red Sea; Midian refers to the inhabitants of the peninsula of Sinai to the east of the Red Sea.[6]

With verse 8 the scene shifts to rivers and to the sea. In the former case, the allusion may be to the miracle of the dividing of the Jordan, while the reference to the sea may point to the passage of Israel through the Red Sea. In any case, the Lord is now seen as a great warrior going forth with horses and chariots to execute vengeance upon his enemies.

> Thy bow was made quite naked, according to the oaths of the tribes, even thy word. Selah (Hab 3:9a).

The sentence preceding the next "Selah" is one of the most difficult in the minor prophets. The meaning of the first clause, "Thy bow was made quite naked," apparently refers to the baring of the warrior's bow preparatory to shooting. But the second clause is a puzzle, because the Hebrew is obscure. According to Davidson, the words of this clause "form a riddle which all the ingenuity of scholars has not been able to solve. Delitzsch calculates that a hundred translations of them have been offered."[7] Smith translates it as follows: "Thou gluttest thy shafts."[8] The King James Version—"according to the oaths of the tribes"—is based on Jerome, who holds that the meaning is "the oaths which thou spakest to the tribes."[9] But newer translations give quite a different meaning. The Revised Standard Version has "and put the arrows to the string" and The Jerusalem Bible renders it "you ply its string with arrows." The passage is one about which it is not possible to be certain.

> Thou didst cleave the earth with rivers. The mountains saw thee, and they trembled: the overflowing of the water passed by: the deep uttered his voice, and lifted up his hands on high. The sun and moon stood still in their habitation: at the light of thine arrows they went, and at the shining of thy glittering spear (Hab 3:9b-12).
>
> Thou didst march through the land in indignation; thou didst thresh the [nations] in anger.

Perhaps the prophet had in mind the great rift of the Jordan valley when he wrote, "Thou didst cleave the earth with rivers." Surely those who have seen the Grand Canyon can realize the forcefulness of the figure. And let no one be so literal-minded as to object that it takes hundreds of thousands of years for a river to cut a deep valley or canyon! Though the word *cleave* denotes swift action, God is beyond time. What are aeons with men are in His sight eternally present.

The next sentences picture convulsions of nature. The mountains are personified as writhing,† cloudbursts pour down, and the abysmal depths are seen as suppliants wringing their hands, a startling image based perhaps upon the breaking up of "the fountains of the great deep" at the time of the deluge (Gen 7:11). Even the sun and the moon must render obeisance to the arrows of the Lord and the shining of His glittering spear. All nature trembles. For the Lord Himself stalks through the land in His wrath and threshes the nations in His fierce anger.

> Thou wentest forth for the salvation of thy people, even for salvation with thine anointed; thou woundest the head of the house of the wicked, by discovering the foundation unto the neck. Selah (Hab 3:13).

Here in the first clause of the verse we see the purpose behind the great theophany. All of this mighty power is for the salvation of God's people. It is as if the Lord were reminding men that the illimitable resources of omnipotence are forever arrayed on the side of His own. Moreover, the Messianic implication of the words *Thine anointed* is plain. Not so plain, however, is the second half of verse 13. At this point the wicked power, summed up for Habakkuk in Chaldea but representative of all godless world rule down to the Antichrist, is portrayed under the figure of a house, the upper part of which is smashed and the foundation then laid bare.[10] It reminds us that God always has the last word with human power. No empire, however great, is able to withstand His judgment.

---

†A more accurate translation for the King James Version "tremble."

> Thou didst strike through with his staves the head of his villages: they came out as a whirlwind to scatter me: their rejoicing was as to devour the poor secretly. Thou didst walk through the sea with thine horses, through the heap of great waters (Hab 3:14-15).

The word translated "villages" is perhaps better rendered "princes." The scene is that of a tremendous conflict. Though the attack has the force of a whirlwind, it is as nothing against a Lord who is described in words of awe-inspiring sublimity, reminiscent again of the overthrow of Pharaoh and his hosts in the Red Sea: "Thou didst walk through the sea with thine horses, through the heap of great waters."

HABAKKUK'S RESPONSE (3:16-19A)

> When I heard, my belly trembled; my lips quivered at the voice: rottenness entered into my bones and I trembled in myself, that I might rest in the day of trouble: when he cometh up unto the people, he will invade them with his troops. Although the fig tree shall not blossom, neither shall fruit be in the vines; the labour of the olive shall fail, and the fields shall yield no meat; the flock shall be cut off from the fold, and there shall be no herd in the stalls: yet I will rejoice in the LORD, I will joy in the God of my salvation. The LORD God is my strength, and he will make my feet like hinds' feet, and he will make me to walk upon mine high places. To the chief singer on my stringed instruments"‡ (Hab 3:16-19).

Suddenly the scene changes. The theophany is over. Now we see Habakkuk's response to the theophany. He is in a state of collapse, the very picture of shuddering awe. "My belly trembled . . . my lips quivered . . . rottenness entered into my bones . . . I trembled." But he does not remain that way; he pulls himself together and voices his chastened feelings.

The prophet who began as a skeptic has learned the greatest of all lessons—that God is fully adequate. The man who had complained against the justice of God has come to the place

---

‡The "chief singer" was probably the conductor of the choir and orchestra (stringed instruments).

where he can say (v. 17) that, although everything fails and the land is completely desolate, he will yet rejoice in the Lord. For he now realizes who it is that is his strength. Mark the significant pronouns in the final verse: "The LORD God is *my* strength, and he will make *my* feet like hinds' feet, and he will make *me* to walk upon *mine* high places."

The reference to "hinds' feet" expresses poetically power and strength. Just as the feet of the deer, as it bounds along, are energy personified, so will the prophet go joyfully on. There come to mind the reassuring words of Isaiah: "He giveth power to the faint; and to them that have no might he increaseth strength. Even the youths shall faint and be weary, and the young men shall utterly fall: but they that wait upon the LORD shall renew their strength; they shall mount up with wings as eagles; they shall run, and not be weary; and they shall walk, and not faint" (Is 40:29-32).

What happened to change Habakkuk's outlook so radically? Simply this. God had shown the prophet what He is able to do. God had revealed His power. He had not explained everything to Habakkuk, nor had He answered all his "whys." He had done more: He had made the prophet see something of His greatness. And that was enough. As a writer on Job points out, "God does not explain, but He does give to the anguished spirit such a sense of the Divine that questioning ceases in the peace of submission. He does not answer the interrogations of the mind but does satisfy the profound yearnings of the spirit."[11] So Habakkuk came from questioning—not to faith; he had that all along down underneath his doubts—but to faith plus joy in the God of his salvation. There he found strength and reassurance in a day of impending ruin for his nation. He knew the secret that Ezra told the returned captives of a latter day: "The joy of the LORD is your strength" (Neh 8:10).

And what of us? The lessons learned by Habakkuk are timeless. Translated into the language of today, they tell us who are living in a time when world revolution and world-judgment are on the threshold that the Lord Jesus Christ is not only necessary; He is enough. If we have Him, we have all, potentially and actually. Without Him we are infinitely poor; with Him, no matter

what happens, we are infinitely rich. As T. R. Glover said, it is
with us, as with the Christians in the first century, "Jesus or
nobody."[12]

5

THE MAN OF FAITH AND THE
NEEDS OF TODAY

Of the twelve minor prophets none wrestled more earnestly with the problem of evil in a disordered society than Habakkuk. To follow step by step the progress of thought in his profound little book is to be impressed with the similarity of his situation to that in which we live. His time, which was marked by corruption and violence, stands as a prototype of these troubled decades at the close of the twentieth century. Habakkuk spoke to God about the awful things he saw, and he received from God the answer to his questions. Nearly twenty-six centuries separate him from us; yet the gulf is bridged by the common ground which the responsible Christian of today shares with him.

This prophet had what we in our situation must have if we are to witness and minister with godly relevance to our alienated and ailing society. His was a burning solicitude regarding injustice and strife among his people and a deep concern as to what God would do about these things. He cared enough about the wrongs that demanded rectifying to agonize with God. He lived in no ivory tower of unconcern. A man with an intensely personal relationship to the Lord whom he addressed as "O LORD my God, mine holy One" (1:12), he could not keep silent regarding the evil he saw. In this respect he was unlike some in our day who, while talking much about what the Lord of all love and compassion means to them, are strangely unmoved by the plight of others though quick to react to any threat to their own privileges.

But Habakkuk not only had his eyes wide open to the problems of his time; he knew who was making him look at the iniquity that wrung his heart. "Why," he asked the Lord, "dost thou shew me iniquity, and cause me to behold grievance?" (1:3). So God gave him the burden, or oracle, which we have in the pages of his book.

Habakkuk belonged to the noble company of those who care deeply about the ethical problems of their times. The other prophets—and notably, Isaiah, Jeremiah, Ezekiel, Amos, Micah— had this concern. Our Lord was its supreme exemplar. We find it in the epistles and especially in that of James, the brother of the Lord. History is studded with the record of men motivated by solicitude for humanity. Francis of Assisi reached out in compassion to all, even the Muslims. Luther, converted through the truth of justification as expressed by Paul, who drew upon Habakkuk (Ro 1:17; Hab 2:4*b*), saw the corruption of the church in his time, and out of his concern God brought the Reformation. Tyndale saw Scripture locked away from the people by the hierarchy, acted upon the vision of opening God's Word to the common man, and paid for his concern with his life. Because Wesley's heart was "strangely warmed" when, as he wrote in his diary, "I felt I did trust in Christ, Christ alone, for my salvation," he looked at the moral and spiritual need around him and took up the burden of evangelizing England. When Wilberforce's Christian conscience was stirred by the iniquity of slavery, he led his nation to abolish it. Likewise, Shaftesbury's moral indignation at the cruelties of child labor resulted in its eradication. So too with the great succession of missionary leaders from Zinzendorf to Zwemer, from Carey to Strachan, whose burden for the lost was used by God for the worldwide outreach of the gospel.

But what of the man of faith and the needs of today? An understanding of Habakkuk and his times, a realization of the way in which the Lord dealt with him, raises probing questions. Have some Christians fallen into the unbiblical notion that verbal proclamation of the gospel is all that is required of them? Is concern for human deprivation suspect among them as savoring of "the social gospel"? Do they interpret Paul's challenge to those who are constrained by the love of Christ to be ambassadors for Him as relating only to words, forgetting that John's question addressed to the first-century church still speaks to us in this time of affluence: "But as for the well-to-do man who sees his brother in want but shuts his eyes—and his heart—how could anyone believe that the love of God lives in him?" (1 Jn 3:17, Phillips). Or, to put it more personally, how much do we Christian people really care about the problems of our time like racism, poverty, war, disregard for human welfare resulting from putting profit above people, squandering the natural resources entrusted to men as a stewardship, and polluting the environment in which God has placed us. We deplore—and with good reason—the flouting of law and order, the wave of crime and drug addiction, the breakdown of sexual morality. But to be indifferent to other acute human problems reveals a heartlessness ill-becoming a disciple of the Lord Jesus Christ. He did not stand aloof from this lost world but involved Himself in it even to the death of the cross.

There is profound significance in the fact that God gave one of the very greatest of all spiritual insights—"the just shall live by his faith" (Hab 4:2*b*)—to a man who cried out to Him against injustice and violence. For Habakkuk there was no incompatability between impassioned concern for social righteousness and the faith by which a man is justified. In this prophet's perplexity, God revealed to him the moral pattern of history that tyranny and oppression are self-destroying but that faith in the Lord is life-giving. God showed this concerned man how He would use the Babylonians as a scourge to punish the wickedness of His people and then how He would require the Babylonians for their cruelty. His ultimate response to Habakkuk's perplexity about the problem of evil came through the great theophany described in the third chapter of the book. In it God showed the prophet something we too need to know—that the divine logic in answering our profoundest problems transcends our human reason. For when He shows us in His Word, as He showed Habakkuk in the theophanic vision, something of His sovereign greatness and when He makes Christ real to our hearts, then we begin to see our perplexities in respect to the divine perspective.

The study of Habakkuk, like that of any other portion of the Bible, should be more than an exercise in historical and literary analysis. While it is essential to understand as fully as we can the meaning of what this prophet wrote, interpretation must issue in response. Unless we allow Habakkuk's words to take the measure of our attitude to the problems of our time, we shall have frustrated the function of this Scripture to teach us, to reprove and correct us, to train us in right living so that we may be equipped for every good work.

Thoughtful Christians who face problems candidly and realistically—and what Christian is excused from doing this—can hardly fail to see that among those who are most concerned about such things as poverty, hunger, and injustice there are, through God's common grace, many who make no claim to evangelical faith, while among those who pass by on the other side of so much of human misery there are many who profess a saving relationship to Christ. Man's deepest need *is* that of salvation through faith in Christ crucified. The needs of the soul do transcend those of the body. Yet we do not have the privilege of forgetting that the Bible tells us to minister to the whole man. A great thinker once pointed out that in the Lord's parable of the lost sheep, the shepherd who left the ninety-nine sheep to find the one that had strayed into the wilderness saved the whole sheep. And so long as men are physically hungry as well as spiritually lost, it remains as inadequate to offer them bread for their souls while letting their bodies starve as to feed their bodies while letting their souls go hungry.

If Habakkuk speaks with unfading relevance to us today, as indeed he does, it is because he was a man of faith who cared with all his heart about what was happening to human beings in his time and who brought his concern to God. So he shows us who hold what James in his practical epistle called "the faith of our Lord Jesus Christ, the Lord of glory," our responsibility for Christ-like involvement with the human problems of our day.

NOTES

INTRODUCTION

1. A. B. Davidson, cited by George L. Robinson, *The Twelve Minor Prophets*, p. 118.
2. F. C. Cook, *The Bible Commentary*, 6:651.
3. C. C. Torrey, *The Lives of the Prophets: Greek Text and Translation*, pp. 28, 43.
4. George Adam Smith, *The Book of the Twelve Prophets*, 2:131, 133.
5. George A. Robinson, *The Twelve Minor Prophets*, p. 118.
6. W. J. Farley, *The Progress of Prophecy*, p. 133.
7. C. A. Dinsmore, *The English Bible as Literature*, p. 227.
8. H. K. von Orelli, *The Twelve Minor Prophets*, p. 242.
9. A. C. Gaebelein, *The Annotated Bible*, 5:212.
10. F. C. Cook, *The Bible Commentary*, 6:657; Cf. C. L. Feinberg, The Major Messages of the Minor Prophets, *Habakkuk, Zephaniah, Haggai, and Malachi*, p. 12; G. C. Morgan, *The Minor Prophets*, pp. 94, 98.
11. Cook, 651.
12. Cf. G. W. Wade, Westminster Commentaries, *The Book of the Prophet Habakkuk*, ed. N. B. Stonehouse and G. W. Wade, pp. 158-59.
13. Cf. *The Wycliffe Bible Commentary*, pp. 871-72; *The New Bible Dictionary*, p. 496.
14. W. F. Albright, "The Psalm of Habakkuk," *Studies in Old Testament Prophecy*, ed. H. H. Rowley.
15. W. M. L. De Wette, cited in Orelli, pp. 242-43.
16. F. Delitzsch, cited in A. C. Gaebelein, *The Annotated Bible*, 5:212.
17. S. R. Driver, cited in *The International Standard Bible Encyclopaedia*, 2:1312.
18. F. C. Eiselen, cited in ibid.
19. William Hayes Ward, *The International Critical Commentary*, Habakkuk, p. 7.

CHAPTER 1

1. G. L. Robinson, *The Twelve Minor Prophets*, p. 121.
2. Ludwig E. Fuerbringer, *The Eternal Why*, p. 14.
3. D. W. Kerr in *The Wycliffe Bible Commentary*, p. 875.

CHAPTER 2

1. L. E. H. Stephens-Hodge, "Habakkuk," *The New Bible Commentary*, p. 734.
2. Raymond Calkins, *The Modern Message of the Minor Prophets*, p. 94.
3. Ludwig E. Fuerbringer, *The Eternal Why*, p. 35.
4. Calkins, p. 96.
5. Fuerbringer, p. 37.
6. George Adam Smith, *The Book of the Twelve Prophets*, 2:136.
7. Ibid., pp. 144 ff.
8. Ibid., p. 142.

CHAPTER 3

1. Sellin, as cited in Westminster Commentaries, *Zephaniah, Nahum, and Habakkuk*, ed. N. B. Stonehouse and G. W. Wade, p. 185.
2. William Hayes Ward, The International Critical Commentary, *Habakkuk*, p. 14.
3. Cf. *The Wycliffe Bible Commentary*, ed. Charles F. Pfeiffer and Everett F. Harrison, p. 877.
4. Public Health Information Branch, National Institute of Mental Health, *Alcohol and Alcoholism* (Public Health Service Publication No. 1640), cf. p. 11.
5. Ibid.
6. George Adam Smith, *The Book of the Twelve Prophets*, 2:146.
7. *Clio* (191), Rawlinson translation.
8. Floyd E. Hamilton, *The Basis of Christian Faith*, p. 310.
9. Ludwig E. Fuerbringer, *The Eternal Why*, p. 50.
10. William Hayes Ward, The International Critical Commentary, *Habakkuk*, p. 17.
11. Cf. *Wycliffe Commentary*, p. 878.
12. Ludwig E. Fuerbringer, *The Eternal Why*, p. 59.
13. *The Sunday School Times*, June 16, 1934.
14. Cf. David W. Kerr. In *The Wycliffe Bible Commentary*, p. 879.

CHAPTER 4

1. E. B. Pusey, *The Minor Prophets*, 2:204.
2. George Adam Smith, *The Book of the Twelve Prophets*, 2:151.
3. Pusey, p. 216.
4. Ludwig E. Fuerbringer, *The Eternal Why*, p. 78.
5. Ibid., p. 79.
6. H. K. von Orelli, *The Twelve Minor Prophets*, p. 253.
7. George Adam Smith, *The Book of the Twelve Prophets*, 2:155.
8. Ibid.
9. *The Bible Commentary*, 6:673.
10. Cf. Smith, p. 156, and Fuerbringer, pp. 91-92.
11. C. A. Dinsmore, *The English Bible as Literature*, pp. 195-96.
12. T. R. Glover, as cited in Robert E. Speer, *The Finality of Jesus Christ*, p. 57.

THE PROPHECY OF

HAGGAI

INTRODUCTION

THE MAN AND HIS TIMES

In most estimates of the relative prominence of the minor prophets, Haggai finds a place among the more obscure. Nevertheless, he is a prophet whose message should not be underrated. Though his book is surpassed in brevity in the Old Testament only by that of Obadiah, yet hidden between the lines of its two small chapters are moral and spiritual principles relevant to every age. Not only that, but in certain of its features his prophecy is unique. His importance is therefore not to be measured by the shortness of his book nor by the seemingly prosaic character of his ministry. The truth is that few prophets have succeeded in packing into such brief compass so much spiritual common sense as Haggai did.

The known facts of the prophet's personal life are extremely few. There is, of course, his name. As with the names of so many of the other prophets, Haggai signifies something, the meaning in his case being "festal," or "festive." From this it has been inferred that he was born on one of the Jewish feast days. Be that as it may, nothing is known either of his parentage or early life. To be sure, it is generally supposed that he prophesied when an old man, and there is much to be said for this inference. Solomon's temple was destroyed by the Babylonians in 587 B.C., and work on the second temple was begun in 520 B.C. Now if Haggai was, as seems likely, one of the venerable group of captives who could remember Solomon's temple in all its glory, then he must have been an aged man, perhaps even an octogenarian, when he delivered the discourses comprising his book. Pusey calls him the "silver-haired prophet . . . rebuking the people."[1] Certainly there is no scriptural objection to this supposition; on the contrary, Haggai's advanced age may help explain the short duration of his ministry, which covered a period of only about four months.

Evidence of the veneration in which the ancient Jews held

199

Haggai and his colleague Zechariah is found in the fact that the Septuagint attributes Psalm 138 and Psalms 146, 147, and 148 to these two prophets. It is interesting also that the Vulgate heads Psalms 111 and 145 with the names of Haggai and Zechariah.[2]

But if our information regarding the personal life of the prophet is scanty, we know a good deal regarding the times in which he lived and the work to which God called him. The first six chapters of Ezra describe the situation out of which Haggai spoke for Jehovah. Twice in these chapters (5:1; 6:14) he is mentioned by name. It will be remembered that the northern kingdom of Israel, made up of the ten tribes which had revolted under Jeroboam I, was overthrown by Assyria and Samaria, its capital, fell in 722 B.C. This left only the southern kingdom of Judah, comprising the tribes of Judah and Benjamin. These, however, continued with Jerusalem as their capital until the final overthrow of the city in 587 B.C.

Now the events recorded in the first six chapters of Ezra have to do with the return to Jerusalem and Judea of a large company of Jews from Persia, the empire which had succeeded Babylon. It was by royal permission of King Cyrus that these colonists set forth. According to Ezra 2:64-70, they consisted of 42,360 individuals plus 7,337 slaves and 200 singing men and women.* Also with them were a large number of horses, mules, camels, and asses, to say nothing of considerable treasure in gold and silver. Some have suggested that the remnant was actually much larger than indicated in the text of Ezra, the thought being that the 42,360 were free men only and that women and children were not counted. By such a reckoning, the returning remnant would number some 200,000.[3]

In charge of this remnant was Zerubbabel, the son of Shealtiel, as civil leader, and Joshua, the son of Josedech, as ecclesiastical head.† On their return to Jerusalem by express permission of King Cyrus of Persia, one of their first acts was to set up the altar and reestablish the ancient worship of Israel in 536 B.C.

---

*The lists that precede the total of 42,360 do not add up to this number and so with the parallel passage in Neh 7. Scribal errors may account for the discrepancies.

(Ezra 3:1-7). Shortly thereafter, they laid the foundations of the new temple amid a time of great rejoicing and thanksgiving. The record in Ezra puts it vividly in these words: "And when the builders laid the foundation of the temple of the LORD, they set the priests in their apparel with trumpets, and the Levites, the sons of Asaph, with cymbals, to praise the LORD, after the ordinance of David king of Israel. And they sang together by course in praising and giving thanks unto the LORD, because he is good; for his mercy endureth for ever toward Israel. And all the people shouted with a great shout, when they praised the LORD, because the foundation of the house of the LORD was laid" (Ezra 3:10-11).

However, the original enthusiasm of the colonists waned. As their zeal for the temple cooled, they devoted themselves to their own affairs. Money-making became important, and some of the more wealthy built themselves elaborate dwellings with expensive wood paneling. But there was no real prosperity; instead there came drought and failure of crops. Then God called Haggai to challenge the indifference and neglect of the remnant. He had as his companion in prophecy Zechariah, the son of Iddo, a much younger man, whose book follows that of Haggai. "Then the prophets, Haggai the prophet, and Zechariah, the son of Iddo, prophesied unto the Jews that were in Judah and Jerusalem in the name of the God of Israel, even unto them" (Ezra 5:1). It was Haggai, however, whose searching words stirred up the renewed enthusiasm that led to the completion of the temple. One of the fine touches in the history of these times is found in Ezra 5:2, which, after stating that not only the people but also Zerubbabel, the governor and prince of Judah, and Joshua the priest personally joined in the work, goes on to say, "And with them were the prophets of God helping them." Surely this picture of the elderly Haggai working shoulder

---

†As a matter of fact, Sheshbazzar, the prince of Judah, is first mentioned (Ezra 1:8, 11) as civil head. Some scholars attempt to identify him with Zerubbabel, but it seems more probable that Sheshbazzar was the first governor of Judah, and Zerubbabel his successor. Cf. Robert Dick Wilson, *International Bible Encyclopaedia*, 4:2766.

to shoulder with his young coprophet in practicing what he
preached is quite in character with the blunt sincerity of his
messages.

DATE AND STYLE.

It was from September through December of the year 520 B.C.
in the reign of Darius Hystaspes, who had given permission for
the work to continue, that Haggai uttered his messages. They
were four in number,‡ and the response to them was immediate.
The people, deeply stirred, took up their implements and went
to work. In the practical results of the prophetic message, Haggai
is without parallel. No prophet was ever more successful. His
simple words produced action. If, as Dr. Jowett insisted,
preaching must be "for a verdict," Haggai was by this token a
great preacher.

In respect to our prophet there is a refreshing lack of critical
disagreement. Although a few scholars§ have attempted to deny
the unity and authenticity of the book, their theories are va-
garies which the weight of critical opinion, both liberal and
conservative, rejects. The fact is that the integrity of Haggai's
book with his four messages is beyond question. Nor is there
doubt about the date. What is, in the study of certain other
prophets, an intricate problem is for Haggai perfectly simple.
With a precision found nowhere else in the prophetic writings,
he set down not only the year but also the month and very day
of the month in which he delivered his messages.|| The first time
the word of the Lord came by him was, he says, "in the second year of Darius, the king, in the sixth month [August-
September] and in the first day of the month." Now every
historian of this period knows that the second year of Darius was
520 B.C. Again Haggai spoke on the twenty-first day of the
seventh month (corresponding to our September-October). And

---

‡Some commentators consider 1:13 a message in itself and strictly speaking it is. But it is closely allied to Haggai's first message and is so brief that
it seems reasonable to treat it as subsidiary to the first message.

§E.g., W. Böhme and M. Tony André.

||Hag 1:1; 2:1; 2:10; 2:20. Hag 1:15 may relate to the response to the
first message rather than to 1:13.

finally he prophesied twice on the twenty-fourth of the ninth month in the Hebrew calendar (November-December), his last two messages being delivered on the same day.

As to literary style, Haggai has been criticized severely and, considering the nature of his mission, unjustly. A typical view is that "the style of Haggai is prosaic and labors under an uncommon tameness and poverty of expression."[4] Dinsmore discusses him, with Zechariah, Malachi, Joel, and Obadiah, under the caption "Prophecy at a Lower Level" and remarks, "The tone of this prophet is that of a 'secretary raising a budget.' "[5] Certainly Haggai was no poet. He wrote plainly and directly. He had neither the soaring genius of an Isaiah nor the sublime expression of a Habakkuk. But such talents were not required for the work before him. Actually his gifts fitted the needs of his day. So the lack of ornamentation and literary finish in his diction is irrelevant. God makes no mistakes in choosing men to speak for Him. The success of Haggai is an inspiring lesson in the marvelous results that can be accomplished through the simple words of a plain man. Therefore, instead of representing "a marked decline" in "prophetic inspiration," Haggai exemplifies the wonderful variety of biblical inspiration.

THE OUTLINE OF THE BOOK

The structure of Haggai's prophecy is self-evident, being determined by the four messages. Each is introduced by the express claim of divine inspiration, "came the word of the LORD by Haggai the prophet."

One of the impressive features of the book is that no less than twenty-five times in its thirty-eight verses Haggai, in one way or another, claims divine authority for his message. Apparently this supposedly matter-of-fact writer had no doubt that his messages were given him by the Lord. A key phrase, five times repeated, is the terse and searching exhortation, "Consider your ways."

The contents of the prophecy may be set forth under this outline:

I. The first message: The sin of putting off the Lord's work (1:1-15)

A. The date (1:1)
B. The message (1:2-11)
   1. The people's procrastination (1:2-4)
   2. Its consequences (1:5-11)
C. The people's response (1:12-15)
   1. Obedience and fear of the Lord (1:12)
   2. The word of encouragement (1:13)
   3. The work begun (1:14)
   4. The date (1:15)

II. The second message: The two temples (2:1-9)
A. The date (2:1)
B. The message (2:2-9)
   1. The temples compared (2:2-3)
   2. The antidote to discouragement (2:4-5)
   3. The universal shaking and the latter glory of the temple (2:6-9)

III. The third message: The contagiousness of sin (2:10-19)
A. The date (2:10)
B. The message (2:11-19)
   1. The priests questioned (2:11-13)
   2. The application (2:14-19)

IV. The fourth message: Zerubbabel the signet (2:20-23)
A. The date (2:20)
B. The message (2:21-23)
   1. The overthrow of earthly power (2:21-22)
   2. Zerubbabel the signet (2:23)

1

THE SIN OF PROCRASTINATION
AND ITS CONSEQUENCES

HAGGAI'S FIRST MESSAGE (1:1-15)

THE DATE (1:1)

> In the second year of Darius the king, in the sixth month, in the first day of the month, came the word of the LORD by Haggai the prophet unto Zerubbabel the son of Shealtiel, governor of Judah, and to Joshua the son of Josedech, the high priest saying (Hag 1:1).

This verse, the first of four similar statements whereby the prophet introduces his messages, is packed with historical data. As has already been pointed out in the introduction, Haggai is uniquely precise in dating his prophecies. Dealing, as he does, with practical matters, his book reflects the man of affairs who insists upon exactness.

The king mentioned here and elsewhere in the course of the prophecy is unquestionably Darius Hystaspes (522-486 B.C.). A Persian ruler of much fame in secular history, he appears in the writings of Herodotus, the great Greek historian. It was this same Darius Hystaspes who commanded the hosts of Persia which the Greeks repulsed at the battle of Marathon in 490 B.C.

The sixth month (August-September) was known as Elul. Elul, the month of the new moon, came at the time of harvest. In Old Testament times the Jews kept the first day of each month (the day of the new moon) holy;[1] on it they assembled in the sanctuary and marked the day by a special offering (Is 1:13-14; Eze 46:1-3; Num 28:11-15). It was, then, on a day peculiarly set apart to the Lord that Haggai proclaimed his first message from the Lord.

205

To be sure, we Christians do not keep the first day of each month as a holy festival. Jewish feast and fast days are not for us. However, we have our weekly Lord's Day. And there is a sense in which every day should be for us Christians as this holy day on which Haggai first received and proclaimed the Lord's message—one in which we have been alone with God and have received a message from His Word. In this important sense, each day should be like that first of Elul on which Haggai received and proclaimed a message from the Lord.

Each of the prophets four messages is preceded by this authoritative statement: "Came the word of the LORD by Haggai the prophet." This reminds us that practically everything God does for men He accomplishes through other men.[2] Think of the untold good the world has gained through the ministry of the prophets and the apostles. Think also of the early leaders of the church, such as Athanasius, Jerome, Augustine, or the reformers like Huss and Luther, Calvin and Knox. Or recall the great missionary leaders and distinguished preachers and teachers down to the present day. But there is a danger in calling attention to great names; these men are so far above the rank and file that we may feel our efforts to be of little use. The fact, however, is that there *is* a specific work for every Christian to do. Whether his place be high or low, each believer is obligated to work for his Lord. Only heaven will reveal what God has done through obscure Christians who, though never acclaimed by the world, were yet dedicated to the task before them.

We are next told in this introductory sentence that the prophet aimed his message directly at the civil and ecclesiastical leaders of Judah. The former, called by Haggai "the governor* of Judah," was Zerubbabel, who was so named because of his birth in Babylon. Shealtiel was the son of Jehoiachin (otherwise called Jeconiah or Coniah) whom Nebuchadnezzar took captive (2 Ki 24:15). It is plain, therefore, that Zerubbabel was in the royal

---

*The word in the original text is the Persian *pechah* (like our English *pasha*). It was retained in the Hebrew much as the Hindu word *rajah* was used in India under British rule (T. T. Perowne, The Cambridge Bible for Schools and Colleges, Haggai and Zechariah, p. 26).

line of David, a fact of importance in relation to the Messianic implications of Haggai's fourth message (2:20-23). It was this same Zerubbabel who led the first group of colonists back from Persia to Jerusalem, as told in the first portion of Ezra.

Following his reference to Zerubbabel, Haggai mentions Joshua, the son of Josedech. The first high priest after the return to Jerusalem, Joshua was the ecclesiastical head of the remnant. In Ezra and Nehemiah he is called "Jeshua," a late form of the name Joshua. His father was Jehozadak (spelled "Josedech" in Hag 1:1, KJV), the high priest transported to Babylon by Nebuchadnezzar (1 Ch 6:15); his grandfather was the high priest Seraiah, put to death by Nebuchadnezzar after the capture of Jerusalem in 587 B.C. (2 Ki 25:18-21).[3]

Not only here but also at the beginning of his other three messages, the prophet addresses himself first of all to the two leaders of the colonists. Thus he reminds us of a principle of administrative responsibility—that anyone who occupies a place of authority over others is specially accountable for those under him. That this in no way absolved the people under Zerubbabel and Joshua from their responsibility is, however, plain from the next verse. So today, Christians who are in positions of authority, whether in government, education, the home or church, in business or profession—wherever human relationships are involved— have a real measure of personal responsibility under God for the welfare of those with whom they work or are related and who at the same time are themselves accountable to God.

THE MESSAGE (1:2-11)

> Thus speaketh the LORD of hosts, saying, This people say, The time is not come, the time that the LORD's house should be built (Hag 1:2).

The lesser known prophets such as Haggai (men who did not have the outstanding ability of a Moses, Isaiah, or Paul) are sometimes relegated to the second or third rank on the ground that their words are mere human utterances of inferior quality. That different portions of the Bible have varying uses (cf. 2 Ti. 3:16-17) and that there are diverse levels of revelation is undeniable. But they are all part of God's inspired Word. There-fore, we do well to give full weight to Haggai's consciousness of the divine origin of his messages. He asserted (v. 1) that it was nothing less than the word of the Lord which came through him. And he went on to introduce a direct quotation with the declar-ation that it was not just he who was speaking, but the Lord of hosts Himself. "Thus speaketh the LORD of hosts." When any man claims *that* for his message, even though he be a minor prophet who wrote nearly two and a half millennia ago, his words command attention.

"The LORD of hosts" refers to Jehovah as the "Almighty" or "All-Ruler." This designation is characteristic of the postexilic prophets, Haggai, Zechariah, and Malachi, where it occurs more than eighty times. The Septuagint translates this name of God *Kurios pantokratōr,* or "All-Powerful." This double name is par-ticularly suitable in Haggai and Zechariah, "books which teach that God's good providence bends the nations to do His good will for Judah."[4]

Now it must be remembered that Haggai dealt with practical matters. His primary emphasis was not so much upon the predic-tive element of prophecy as it was upon the present, corrective ministry of the prophet. In a sense, the heart of his appeal is summed up in the single word *duty.* While God inspired the lofty eloquence of the greater prophets and the profound teaching of the apostles, He also inspired the unassuming Haggai to stress, and stress urgently, the essential theme of duty in the life and service of God's people. Such a principle is timeless. In our own day it applies just as pertinently as it applied to the remnant so recently returned from Persia to Jerusalem. For if God can be depended upon, *and He can,* to strengthen us by His Spirit for the task of proclaiming the gospel, He can also be trusted to enable us faithfully to do our everyday duty to His glory.

But what was it that the Lord was telling the colonists? The very way in which they were addressed is significant. *"This* people say. . . ." He did not call them "My people." Instead there is an undertone of impatience and even of contempt in the demonstrative pronoun *this.* It is as if the Lord, disgusted at the

failure of the remnant to whom He had given such high privileges, was standing aside and looking at them as a notorious
example of disobedience.

The people's procrastination

After this brief but cutting word, we have the reason why the
Lord regarded the remnant with a holy contempt. Observe that
He laid no specific charge against them beyond quoting their
own statement. And what was "this people" saying? Simply this:
"The time is not come, the time that the LORD's house should be
built." It is always true that what men say about the Lord and
His claims upon them opens a window into their spiritual state.
Here was a people, chosen to be the Lord's, who had been
punished for unfaithfulness and who, having learned that idolatry does not pay, had been granted the privilege of returning to
their beloved Jerusalem for the definite purpose of rebuilding
the sanctuary for their worship of the Lord. Yet all the time they
were delinquent in the one task to which above all others they
were committed! Instead of doing their plain duty, they were
making excuses. Therefore the Lord, speaking through Haggai,
exposed the hypocrisy of shirking their divinely commissioned
work.

This first of the prophet's messages focuses attention upon an
ever present problem of spiritual living—the universal human
tendency to put off doing what God requires. The remnant were
by no means unique in their procrastination. Too often, Christians follow their pattern. A particular call comes to serve in
some way—but we put it off, deluded by the error that to wait
for a more convenient set of circumstances justifies procrastination. It is all too easy to take refuge from duty in saying that
"the psychological moment" to do what God wants us to do has
not come.

Such was the sin of the remnant. Allowed to return to
Jerusalem for the specific purpose of rebuilding the temple, they
had soon become occupied with building their own luxurious
dwellings.

> Then came the word of the LORD by Haggai the prophet,
> saying, Is it time for you, O ye, to dwell in your cieled houses,
> and this house lie waste? (Hag 1:3-4).

These words challenge the excuse of the people. While insisting that it was not the right time to continue rebuilding the
temple, they had been finding plenty of time to work for themselves. While remaining idle in respect to the temple, they had
been spending great effort upon their own houses. Again the
note of divine scorn is heard, this time in the emphatic beginning of the rhetorical question, as the prophet asks, "Is it time
for you, O ye, to dwell in your cieled houses?"

But what were these "cieled houses"? In the Hebrew sentence
the word translated "cieled" receives the emphasis. Derived
from the French word for "heaven," the English "cieled" means
"covered." It is a term relating to a type of construction known
to us as paneling or wainscoting.[5] Haggai used it to refer to an
expensive kind of cedar work like that mentioned in 1 Kings 7:7
and Jeremiah 22:14. So the people had been lavishing labor and
money upon the ornamentation of their own dwellings to the
complete neglect of the temple, for the rebuilding of which God
had permitted their return to Jerusalem.

The situation covered by Haggai in this initial message is rich
in implications of continuing significance. It is not only prediction that causes the prophetic Word to live through the centuries; in a very special sense its ethical and spiritual lessons are
also never outmoded. Each age of interpreters has found it so.
An illustration of this is the sermons preached on Haggai by John
Rainolds† (1549-1607), president of Corpus Christi College,
Oxford. In expounding the verses we are considering (1:2-4)
Rainolds says: "So shall we make our best profit . . . if we
compare our church with theirs [i.e., the Jews']; for as the Jews
were long in bondage in Babylon, but at length were brought
back by Cyrus, . . . so our ancestors were held long under the
spiritual slavery of Rome, which is spiritual Babylon (Rev.
18:2, 21), whence by means of Henry VIII, as they by Cyrus,

---

†Rainolds was one of the prime influences in the making of the Authorized, or King James Version of the Bible.

they were delivered." Such an application was for Rainolds quite valid, though it seems quaint to us. But there is more permanent worth in his comment upon the remnant's excuse. "When Adam," he says, "after he had broken the commandment of the Lord, heard His voice in the garden, he hid himself and feared; the cause thereof he says was, for that he was naked.... The cause was not his nakedness, but his wickedness, in that he had eaten of the forbidden fruit. Since which time it has been a custom among the sons of Adam to cover iniquity with hypocrisy, and cloak their offenses with excuses."[6]

But God unmasks the hypocrite. The man who tries to cover up under an excuse the neglect of his plain duty to God may expect to have the wrappings torn from his subterfuge. God is the great Questioner. Whenever our hearts are not right with Him, He asks us some very pointed questions that search the depths of our being. The remnant in Jerusalem had been putting off their plain responsibility for restoring the temple. With a single question God stripped them of their hypocrisy. "Is it time for you, O ye, to dwell in your cieled houses, and this house lie waste?" (v. 4). They might succeed in covering the walls of their homes with precious cedar paneling, but while doing so they could neither cover their consciences nor hide from God their neglected duty.

Its consequences

> Now therefore thus saith the LORD of hosts; Consider your ways. Ye have sown much, and bring in little; ye eat, but ye have not enough; ye drink, but ye are not filled with drink; ye clothe you, but there is none warm; and he that earneth wages earneth wages to put it into a bag with holes. Thus saith the LORD of hosts; Consider your ways. Go up to the mountain, and bring wood, and build the house; and I will take pleasure in it, and I will be glorified, saith the LORD. Ye looked for much, and, lo, it came to little; and when ye brought it home, I did blow upon it. Why? saith the LORD of hosts. Because of mine house that is waste, and ye run every man unto his own house. Therefore the heaven over you is stayed from dew, and the

earth is stayed from her fruit. And I called for a drought upon the land, and upon the mountains, and upon the corn, and upon the new wine, and upon the oil, and upon that which the ground bringeth forth, and upon men, and upon cattle, and upon all the labour of the hands (Hag 1:5-11).

Most of us know the old saying that procrastination is the thief of time. But Haggai shows us that procrastination, indulged in by God's people, robs them of much more than time. In this passage, he summons the colonists to face the results of their selfish evasion of the task for which they had been allowed to return from Babylon. Using the searching phrase "Consider your ways," he reveals procrastination as the thief of blessing as well as of time.

"Consider your ways." The phrase is peculiar to Haggai and has the force of "set your heart upon your ways." Orelli renders it, "Lay to heart your ways."[7] Haggai uses the expression twice in this first chapter, and in the second chapter uses the verb *consider* three more times. His summons to the remnant is, then, one to self-examination, and he supports it by showing the drastic consequences of this neglect of duty.

"Ye have sown much, and bring in little; ye eat, but ye have not enough; ye drink, but ye are not filled with drink; ye clothe you, but there is none warm; and he that earneth wages earneth wages to put it into a bag with holes" (Hag 1:6). Here, in several factual statements, is the result of putting off the Lord's work. Some of the older commentators have seen in this verse a double curse. Calvin points out that God punishes men in two ways: He withdraws His blessing, so that the earth is parched and no rain falls; and He also, even when the earth is productive, prevents men from enjoying its fruit.[8] Both judgments had fallen upon the colonists. Instead of bountiful harvests they had had smaller ones. The seed which they had sowed produced a meager harvest. Their food and drink had not satisfied them, their clothes were inadequate, and all in all it seemed as though their wages had melted away. The last of the series has a modern ring. In a time of rising prices and heavy taxes it seems that purses and bank accounts have holes through which salaries and savings disappear.

"Thus saith the LORD of hosts; Consider your ways" (Hag 1:7). Again the prophet calls the people to search their lives. He has vividly portrayed the result of reversing the principle stated by our Lord in the familiar words: "But seek ye first the kingdom of God, and his righteousness; and all these things shall be added unto you" (Mt 6:33). Now he invites them to look ahead.

"Go up to the mountain, and bring wood, and build the house; and I will take pleasure in it, and I will be glorified, saith the LORD" (Hag 1:8). The mountain referred to is probably not Mount Lebanon, but rather some nearer hills upon which wood for the temple might be found. Although today these hills are denuded, doubtless in Haggai's time some timber was standing.

Having issued this challenge to activity, the prophet returns to the consequences of disobedience. There is a strong note of contempt in the next verse: "Ye looked for much, and, lo, it came to little; and when ye brought it home, I did blow upon it. Why? saith the LORD of hosts. Because of mine house that is waste, and ye run every man unto his own house" (Hag 1:9). The words *I did blow upon it* have been variously interpreted. Some relate them to a popular Oriental superstition, similar to that found among the Muslims,[9] whereby it is thought unlucky for anyone to breathe on a threshing floor full of grain. The breathing is supposed to cause the rotting and carrying away of the grain by the devil. The general interpretation is that the "blowing" upon the produce is meant in the sense of blowing it away. Orelli adopts the rendering, "I blow it away."[10] The third interpretation is that the words are extremely ironical, indicating strong contempt. In this case, they might be translated, "I sniffed at it." This rendering suggests as do the others to a lesser degree, the Lord's open disparagement of what the people had been doing.

Following the rhetorical "Why?" the reason for the divine disgust is forcefully repeated. The Lord's own house, the temple so essential to His proper worship, was allowed to remain in ruins while all the time the colonists were active in building their own homes.

"Therefore the heaven over you is stayed from dew, and the earth is stayed from her fruit. And I called for a drought upon the land, and upon the mountains, and upon the corn [grain] and upon the new wine, and upon the oil, and upon that which the ground bringeth forth, and upon men, and upon cattle, and upon all the labour of the hands" (Hag 1:10-11). Some commentators have strongly objected to the implications of these verses. It is their contention that no connection can be assumed between events in the physical world and God's punitive action. But the objection is not logical. No man knows enough to say categorically what God will or will not do in inflicting His judgements. Moreover, for the Christian who seriously takes the Word of God as meaning what it says the question is settled. The plain sense of the passage is that the Lord withheld from the region of Jerusalem the copious dew with which the land was normally watered, that He brought a real drought upon it, and that the three staple crops of Palestine—grain, new wine, and oil—as well as the inhabitants and their cattle were adversely affected. Instead of arguing about whether God will or will not manifest His judgment through natural and physical means, it is better to take adversity as a summons to searching of heart and life.

With these verses, the first message of Haggai concludes. Let us pause to consider its abiding application. The great underlying lesson is one of priority. If we read Haggai's words as the Bible should always be read, that is, not only with regard to its historical setting and with an eye to its literary qualities and doctrinal teaching, but also with an earnest desire to find in it a personal message for us, we soon discover that Haggai's initial message has something to say to us today. And this, briefly, is its import: God's work *must* come first; it *must* come before our own work. No excuse that contrives to subordinate God's work to any other thing is adequate.

Back in the prophet's day, God's specific work was the rebuilding of the temple. For us it may be one of a thousand things. For some at the threshold of life, the call may be to the ministry or to the mission field. For others of us it may be that God is speaking about a more consecrated use of money or of time. Perhaps there is a neighbor or friend who needs to know what Christ means to us. Again, the call may be to greater devotion in the use of the Bible and prayer. Or it may be a summons to Christian action in behalf of the poor and deprived and to the responsibility for doing something about racial and other injustices. Whatever it is, the essential thing is that God's work must have priority over everything else. The things that crowd our lives and prevent prompt obedience to the Word of our Lord may not in themselves be bad. It is the subtle temptation to prefer the good to the best that hinders full Christian effectiveness. In the case of the remnant, what they were doing was in itself honorable. Men have always considered it a good thing to build a home. But God has something better for His people to do than to spend their energies first of all upon providing more luxurious homes for themselves.

So Haggai is telling us that the Lord's work is urgent. And as we think about his forceful words, we are reminded of an infinitely greater prophet. One day that Prophet said to a man, "Follow Me." But the man made an excuse. "Lord," he replied, "suffer me first to go and bury my father." The reply was one of Jesus' more difficult sayings. "Let the dead bury their dead: but go thou and preach the kingdom of God." It was not that He was callous to brokenhearted bereavement; but He was giving that man and, through him, giving us all a lesson in divine priorities. Nothing, He was saying, not even the most sacred of family duties, is good enough to take precedence over obedience to Him. Similar was the case of another who volunteered to follow Him, but asked first of all to go home and say a good-bye that, in accordance with Oriental custom, might take days or weeks. But again there came a drastic word: "No man having put his hand to the plow, and looking back, is fit for the kingdom of God" (Lk 9:59-62).

"But when," someone may ask, "is the time for doing the Lord's work?" One little word contains the answer. *Now* is the time for serving God. Says the apostle Paul, "Behold, now is the accepted time; behold, now is the day of salvation" (2 Co 6:2). And indeed for those who have yet to open their hearts and receive Christ, salvation has priority. But Haggai was talking to the Lord's chosen people, and members of Christ's church who also are His elect people make no mistake in letting his message search us. For we too may well consider our ways. If God has called us to be His own in His Son, He has done so for a purpose.

Every Christian has a work to do. Nowhere is this principle given more authoritative expression than in these words in Christ's upper room discourse: "Ye have not chosen me, but I have chosen you, and ordained you, that you should go and bring forth fruit, and that your fruit should remain" (Jn 15:16). The word *ordain* is not used here in the sense of ecclesiastical ordination; its meaning is similar to that of "predestine," and it applies to all Christians, whether clergy or laity. Nothing our Lord does is ever futile. And when He calls individuals, as He has called believers, to be His own, He calls them for a purpose. Moreover, that purpose is a fruitful one. There is no waste in God's holy plan for our lives. Therefore, it is perilous folly even to think of living the Christian life without being willing to face the fact that, wherever one is, he must be a Christian worker. In peace as well as in war, governments are on guard against those who would undermine them through subversive activity. But the danger of the Christian church lies not just in the subversive activity of a minority but in the subversive inactivity of a majority of its members. As a distinguished missionary put it, it is possible to have a saved soul and a lost life. He meant that, though eternal salvation is assured through faith in the atoning work of Christ, a whole lifetime of opportunity for fruitful service may be lost through indolence and neglect.

THE PEOPLE'S RESPONSE (1:12-15)

> Then Zerubbabel the son of Shealtiel, and Joshua the son of Josedech, the high priest, with all the remnant of the people, obeyed the voice of the LORD their God, and the words of Haggai the prophet, as the LORD their God had sent him, and the people did fear before the LORD. Then spake Haggai the LORD's messenger in the LORD's message unto the people, saying, I am with you, saith the LORD. And the LORD stirred up the spirit of Zerubbabel the son of Shealtiel, governor of Judah, and the spirit of Joshua the son of Josedech, the high priest, and the spirit of all the remnant of the people; and they came and did work in the house of the LORD of hosts, their God (Hag 1:12-14).

Of Haggai's four messages, only this first one is followed by a statement of the people's response. Again Haggai names the two leaders of the people, Zerubbabel and Joshua, and goes on to include with them *"all* the remnant of the people." Evidently his first challenge had been completely successful. How it must have cheered the prophet to realize that his words were received with such full approbation!

Reflection upon this passage brings to light certain principles about the ministry. Observe exactly what Haggai wrote. Zerubbabel and Joshua, together with all the colonists, he declared, "obeyed the voice of the Lord their God and the words of Haggai, the prophet." The phraseology is remarkable. There is, for example, the level of quality upon which "the voice of the Lord" and "the words of Haggai the prophet" are placed. Unquestionably for those returned Jews, the prophet was none other than the mouthpiece of God. That in itself explains much regarding their obedience to his message. Apply the thought to our times, and the responsibility resting upon the Christian ministry is evident. For our day the ministry is the prophetic order. How wonderful if all the Lord's messengers standing in pulpits would speak only the Lord's message! And what a responsibility this would place upon their hearers! No one listening to the Word of God preached today has the privilege of receiving it passively. If the message goes to his heart, he must act upon it.

It requires only brief observation of churches and congregations to show us that Christian people have yet much to learn about listening to God and His messengers. How *do* we listen to preaching? Is it for us a kind of pious entertainment, as we relax in the pews and expect the minister to interest and divert us? Or is it a critical exercise, as we say to ourselves something like this: "He is not so inspirational as Dr. so-and-so"; "His delivery is not so effective as that of the Rev. Mr. ————"; "His illustrations are not so interesting as those of Dr. ————"? There is a better way than these to hear preaching. It is to sit before the speaker with this uppermost thought in mind: "What does this messenger of God have to say to me?"

Acts 10:33 shows us the New Testament pattern of listening to the Lord's messenger, a pattern relevant to this passage in

Haggai. Peter, in response to the Spirit's leading, has gone from
Joppa to the house of Cornelius in Caesarea. When he arrives
there, he finds Cornelius and a considerable group of other Gentiles waiting to hear him. Just before Peter speaks Cornelius says
to him: "Now therefore are we all here present before God, to
hear all things that are commanded thee of God." What a
change there would be, were every church service to be entered
upon by every member of the congregation in such a spirit!

"And the people did fear before the LORD." Such an attitude of
reverence comes from believing reception of the Word of God.
But how foreign it is to many men today. Unbelief has gone to
such an extent that the fear of the Lord is almost forgotten.
Yet the dismissal of this holy awe of the Almighty has not
emancipated men from fear; on the contrary it has enslaved
them. In place of the vertical fear of the transcendent God who
rules heaven and earth, men have but substituted the horizontal
fear of each other. As a result, millions today, despite scientific
progress and intellectual enlightenment, are afraid of what other
men will do to them.

"Then spake Haggai the LORD's messenger in the LORD's message unto the people, saying, I am with you, saith the LORD"
(Hag 1:13). Again there is the identification of the prophet with
the Lord and His message. In his German Bible, Luther translated the word rendered in English "messenger" by "Engel,"
which is like our word *angel*. And it is true that the chief
function of angels, as they appear in the Bible, is to bear God's
messages to men. Haggai, of course, was but a man such as you
and I, and angels are quite another order of beings from men;
nevertheless, it is our high privilege to share their function of
bringing God's help to those in need.

The actual message Haggai gave the people following their
wholehearted response is very brief, consisting of this one sentence: "I am with you, saith the LORD." Brief though it is, it is
wonderfully comprehensive and satisfying. "I am with you, saith
the LORD." What else do we Christians need but that? It is
nothing less than the personal assurance of our Immanuel, who
is truly "God with us," and who gave His disciples that glorious

pledge, "And remember, I am with you always, day by day, until the close of the Age" (Mt 28:20, Weymouth).

How simple it is! Obey the Lord as He speaks to you through His Word and through His messengers. Do His work. Fear Him. Then it will follow, as surely as night follows day, that He will be with you. Just as certainly as Jehovah was with that remnant in Jerusalem once they were at work, so our Lord Jesus says to every faithful and obedient Christian, "I am with you."

Lest this matter of response to the message of the prophet seem to be on the level of mere human effort, we are next told plainly that "the LORD stirred up the spirit of Zerubbabel . . . and the spirit of Joshua . . . and the spirit of all the remnant of the people; and they came and did work in the house of the LORD of hosts, their God." The people had made their choice in response to the divine message. Once they had done that, the Lord met them in a gracious way. He did what He always does for those who listen to His Word and prove their obedience by taking action. He Himself joined with their human spirit and infused into them the enthusiasm they needed for carrying on His work.

> In the four and twentieth day of the sixth month, in the second year of Darius the king (Hag 1:15).

For the second time Haggai dates his prophecy. A little over three weeks after his initial message, the people were back at work. As one man, they were laboring at their great task of restoring the temple; their spirits having been stirred by the Lord Himself, they were again busy. Their own interests had been put in second place. God's business had their full attention. Such satisfaction as was theirs may be ours also. The passing of the years has not changed the spiritual principle; there is no substitute for the satisfaction that comes from giving priority to the Lord's work.

2

THE TWO TEMPLES

THE DATE (2:1)

> In the seventh month, in the one and twentieth day of the month, came the word of the LORD by the prophet Haggai, saying, (Hag 2:1).

About a month after the wholehearted response of the remnant to the prophet's first message, he spoke again to the people The date is given in the same precise formula used in chapter 1. In this case the message came during the seventh month (September-October), called Tishri in the Talmud. The twenty-first day of this month brings to an end the Feast of Tabernacles. The feast began five days after the Day of Atonement and continued seven days, during which all males in Israel were commanded to live in specially built booths. The booth was a thatched structure, adequate for protection against the sun and at the same time open enough to allow the stars to be seen at night. Leviticus 23:42-43 gives the historical meaning[1] of the Feast of Tabernacles: "Ye shall dwell in booths seven days; all that are Israelites born shall dwell in booths: that your generations may know that I made the children of Israel to dwell in booths, when I brought them out of the land of Egypt: I am the LORD your God."

It has been suggested that the close of this feast brought the colonists a deep note of sadness, as they contrasted the mighty deliverance of Israel from Egypt with their state of poverty and

weakness as returned captives.[2] The suggestion is in keeping
with the general tone of this portion of the book, for Haggai's
second message is one of comfort and encouragement for a
discouraged people.

THE MESSAGE (2:2-9)
> Speak now to Zerubbabel the son of Shealtiel, governor of
> Judah, and to Joshua the son of Josedech, the high priest, and
> to the residue of the people, saying, Who is left among you that
> saw this house in her first glory? and how do ye see it now? Is it
> not in your eyes in comparison of it as nothing? (Hag 2:2-3).

The temples compared

The second verse of this chapter is in good part a repetition of
the introduction to the first message. Again the prophet addresses Zerubbabel, the governor, and Joshua, the high priest.
Now, however, another phrase is added, for the prophet is
directed to speak also to "the residue of the people." Not only
are the rulers singled out; the remnant as a whole are specifically included as recipients of the message.

"Who is left among you that saw this house in her first glory?
and how do ye see it now? Is it not in your eyes in comparison
of it as nothing?" (Hag 2:3). The three questions show the
emotions of the people at this time. Ezra had described the
varying feelings when the temple foundations were first laid
sixteen years before: "But many of the priests and Levites and
chief of the fathers, who were ancient men, that had seen the
first house, when the foundation of this house was laid before
their eyes, wept with a loud voice; and many shouted aloud for
joy: so that the people could not discern the noise of the shout of
joy from the noise of the weeping of the people; for the people
shouted with a loud shout, and the noise was heard afar off"
(Ezra 3:12-13). And now that the work was again under way,
the same feelings prevailed. Some sixty years had passed since
the destruction of Solomon's temple by Nebuchadnezzar. But
there were still some of the older people who remembered it in

all its glory. Haggai himself may have been among them.* And the contrast between the temple as it was being rebuilt and the magnificence of the first temple, whether personally remembered or described by those who had seen it, was so great as to lead to discouragement. It is this mood which the questions of verse 3 bring to light. "Who is left among you that saw this house in her first glory?" (An appeal to the aged who could remember Solomon's temple.) "And how do you see it now?" (An invitation to take note of the proportions of the new temple, as it begins to rise.) "Is it not in your eyes in comparison of it as nothing?" (An invitation to make the inevitable comparison between the two structures.) The prophet, discerning the feeling of the people, brings it out into the open with these blunt questions, the better to deal with it through the words of comfort he is about to utter.

According to the Babylonian Talmud, the following, all of which were in Solomon's temple, were lacking in the second temple: the ark of the covenant, the sacred fire, the Shekinah glory, the Holy Spirit, the Urim and Thummin. Haggai 2:3, however, cannot refer to a point-by-point comparison of the two temples, because "the reconstruction of the Temple had just begun. . . . The comparison is more general and based on an evaluation of plans and resources . . . many may well have bewailed the lack of certain items of the Temple furniture."[3]

The antidote to discouragement

> Yet now be strong, O Zerubbabel, saith the LORD; and be strong, O Joshua, son of Josedech, the high priest; and be strong, all ye people of the land, saith the LORD, and work: for I am with you, saith the LORD of hosts: According to the word that I covenanted with you when ye came out of Egypt, so my spirit remaineth among you: fear ye not (Hag 2:4-5).

---

*In opposition to this quite commonly accepted view is the brief notice of Haggai in the ancient but legendary *Lives of the Prophets* (generally dated in the first century A.D.) which says of Haggai: "Probably as a youth he came from Babylon to Jerusalem." See C. C. Torrey, *The Lives of the Prophets*, p. 44.

Before considering these words in detail, let us look at what they imply for us today regarding encouragement through the Bible. Nothing that can happen to the Lord's people is beyond the comfort of the Scriptures. God is able through His Word to bind up the broken hearts of His children. The variety of human trials is great, but there is balm for it all in the consolation of Christ, as the Spirit ministers Him to our hearts through the Bible. For He has said: "Come unto me, all ye that labour and are heavy laden, and I will give you rest. Take my yoke upon you, and learn of me; for I am meek and lowly in heart: and ye shall find rest unto your souls" (Mt 11:28-30).

Returning to the first portion of Haggai's message to the remnant at this time of mingled disappointment and joy, observe the significant succession of phrases. The reader might mark them in his Bible, connecting them with a series of lines in order to show the logical sequence. They are as follows: "Be strong . . . be strong . . . be strong . . . and work . . . I am with you . . . according to the word that I covenanted with you . . . so my Spirit . . . fear ye not." Scholars find in the Hebrew of these verses considerable difficulty. But whatever the grammatical problems, a great message shines through the words. The antidote to discouragement and despair, the prophet is telling the people, is to strengthen oneself in the Lord. Three times he exhorts them to be strong.

Essential as courage and strength are, however, they are of little practical value unless they find active expression. Therefore, the next exhortation is the injunction to work. One of the most effective remedies for a discouraged heart is service for the Lord and for others in His name. When that remedy is taken, then the comforting assurance of the Lord's presence comes.

There is a companionship with the Lord in service and a closeness to Him that those who have never given themselves wholly to His work cannot realize. But God not only stands by His resolute workers; He also channels His blessing to them through His promises. His Spirit is mighty to inspire and empower His believing servants, but the Spirit acts in accordance with the promises of God. The courageous believer, busy despite feelings of discouragement, knowing that the Lord Himself is with him, may assuredly trust the Spirit of the living God to work in his behalf according to the promises. When this chain of spiritual logic is grasped, fear is conquered and anxiety banished. Therefore, the final exhortation of the series is "Fear ye not."

In *The Pilgrim's Progress*, Part I, Bunyan relates how Christian and Hopeful are led off the direct road into By-path Meadow, which brings them to Doubting Castle. There they are set upon by the owner of the castle, Giant Despair, whose wife is named Diffidence. The Giant throws Christian and Hopeful into a "very dark dungeon" where many another pilgrim has perished. Incited by his wife, he goes down to the dungeon and beats his prisoners with his "grievous crab-tree cudgel." There is, however, a strange thing about Giant Despair. Whenever the sun comes out,† he falls into some sort of a fit which renders him powerless. Bemoaning their fate, Christian and Hopeful are ready to give up, when Christian remembers that he has in his bosom the Key of Promise. He applies this key to the door of the dungeon and is delivered. The key opens the other castle doors also, and, just as the lock is turning in the last iron gate, Giant Despair, awakened by the noise, takes after them. But he has one of his fits, the iron gate flies open, and the pilgrims are released.

So it was in Haggai's day; so it is in our time. The key that fits the lock of difficulty is the key of promise. As the believer, committed to the Lord's work, conscious of the Lord's presence, is relying upon the Word, he may trust the Spirit of God to bring victory over the paralysis of despair.

The universal shaking and the latter glory of the temple

> For thus saith the LORD of hosts; Yet once, it is a little while, and I will shake the heavens, and the earth, and the sea, and the dry land; and I will shake all nations, and the desire of all nations shall come: and I will fill this house with glory, saith the LORD of hosts. The silver is mine, and the gold is mine, saith the LORD of hosts. The glory of this latter house shall be greater than of the former, saith the LORD of hosts: and in this place will I give peace, saith the LORD of hosts (Hag 2:6-9).

---

†In Bunyan's allegory the sun has been taken to stand for those gleams of hope Christian has when his heart turns to God.

We now come to a passage glorious in prophetic outreach and difficult in interpretation. A glance at its place in the prophet's logic is first of all in order. As we have just seen, many of the colonists were discouraged at the contrast between Solomon's lavish temple and this smaller house of God. They had fallen prey to what has been called "the snare of comparisons" in Christian work.‡ How prone to the same error we are today! How easy it is to measure spiritual success by a material yardstick! We say, "There are not so many people out for this service as there were a month ago," or, "There were fewer who seemed definitely helped after this message than when I last spoke," or, "The collection is not so large as it was a week ago." The tendency to make judgments of this kind with consequent discouragement may result in loss of joy and power.

For this spiritual malady Haggai has already given a tonic remedy (vv. 4-5). But that is not all, for with the next four verses his prophecy broadens into one of the glorious Messianic utterances of the Old Testament. The logic is something like this. Haggai is, in effect, saying to the people: "This temple, about the modest nature of which you are so sad, will yet come into its own in a way far greater than anything you have ever imagined. God's work centered in His temple has a magnificent future; despite its present vicissitudes, it will surely be crowned with ultimate glory and peace. But associated with this there will be a divine shaking of all things."

"For thus saith the LORD of hosts; Yet once, it is a little while, and I will shake the heavens, and the earth, and the sea, and the dry land" (Hag 2:6). Exactly what is the "shaking" referred to in these words? Interpreters of Haggai are divided. The general view is that it refers to political and governmental upheavals prior to the first advent of the Lord Jesus Christ.§ Now it is true that the birth of our Lord was preceded by such changes in Persia, Greece, and Rome. And it is also true that in them we find a fulfillment of the prophet's words. That it was *the* fulfill-

---

‡Cf. G. Campbell Morgan, *Living Messages of the Books of the Bible*, 1:306 ff., for a discerning application of this point.

§The opening of verse 7, "And I will shake all nations," is, of course, carrying forward the thought of verse 6.

ment, including the exclusive and final event to which these words point, is another matter. If Haggai's words mean what they say, no merely governmental upheavals will suffice for their complete fulfillment. The prophet clearly speaks of a shaking of "the heavens, and the earth, and the sea, and the dry land" as well as of "all nations." Such a universal convulsion has yet to be experienced in human history. Therefore, the conclusion is plain that the ultimate "shaking" is still to come. The future event that most fully answers to it is the final upheaval of all things at the return of Christ in glory. In impressive words the author of Hebrews quotes this prophecy as definitely related to the coming kingdom: "Now he hath promised, saying, Yet once more I shake not the earth only, but also heaven. And this word, Yet once more, signifieth the removing of those things that are shaken, as of things that are made, that those things which cannot be shaken may remain" (Heb 12:26-27). It is significant that some expositors see a relationship between Haggai's prediction of universal upheaval and the remarkable passage in 2 Peter 3:11-13, in which the apostle looks forward to a new heaven and a new earth at the return of the Lord in glory.[4]

The objection may be made, however, that Haggai speaks of these things taking place in "a little while." The answer to this is the well-known fact of the foreshortening of the future in prophecy. The "little while" is not according to man's reckoning. As Orelli puts it, "We should not forget that the history of a temple must be measured by another standard than that of a man: and, moreover, 2 Pet 3:8 ('But, beloved, be not ignorant of this one thing, that one day is with the Lord as a thousand years') applies to the steps in the growth of God's kingdom."||,[5]

"And I will shake all nations, and the desire of all nations shall come: and I will fill this house with glory, saith the LORD of hosts" (Hag 2:7). The beautiful phrase of the King James Version, "the desire of all nations," has long been suspect on the ground of inaccuracy. And there is reason to question it. It goes back to the Septuagint and to Jerome's Vulgate; in the latter we

---

|| Though Orelli has in mind the period of five hundred years between Haggai's time and the first coming of Christ, the principle applies also to the much longer period up to the second coming.

find, *"Et veniet desideratus cunctis Gentibus."* Beautiful as this
is, many feel it to be, with its English equivalent, "the desire of
all nations shall come," only a splendid mistranslation. The difficulty is as follows: The Hebrew for "desire" (*chemdah*) is singular, but the verb translated "shall come" is plural. Therefore, many Hebrew scholars have insisted that the meaning
cannot be "the desire of all nations," but rather that it must be
"the desire of all things" or "the precious things of all nations." It
is these "precious things," they say, that are to be thought of as
coming to Christ. So the American Standard Version reads, "and
the precious things of all nations shall come," and the Revised
Standard Version has "the treasures of all nations shall come in."
It is in some such way that most modern translations render the
words.

Two questions now arise. The first is whether any interpretation retaining the word *desire* in its full Messianic sense as
applying personally to Christ is linguistically possible. The second is whether the translation along the line of the precious
things of all nations coming as tribute to the temple rules out the
general Messianic import of the passage.

In answering the first question, we cannot be dogmatic. However, there is a translation that retains the full Messianic sense of
chemdah as "desire" and at the same time offers a solution of the
grammatical problem. Dr. Young, the compiler of the *Analytical
Concordance,* in his literal translation of the Bible, renders the
verse as follows: "And I have shaken all the nations, and they
have come to the desire of all the nations."

This solution, as advanced by Cocceius, Mark, and others, is
discussed by Keil[6] and rejected, not so much for grammatical
reasons as on the ground that the thought of the coming of the
nations to the Messiah would be completely foreign to the
context. But if we see in this portion of Haggai's prophecy
ultimate reference to the glorious second coming of Christ, the
objection loses its force.

Leaving now the details of the passage, we come to the
wider Messianic import of the statement. From ancient times
this word of Haggai has been accepted as pointing to the Messiah. Even some of the rabbinical interpreters saw it as such.

Among them was R. Akiba, a disciple of Gamaliel, whose para-
phrase is as follows: "Yet a little of the kingdom, lo! I will shake
heaven and after that will come Messiah." Down to the present
day, the Messianic bearing of the passage has been recognized.
As A. C. Gaebelein puts it, "Christ is the object of the desire of
all nations. This does not necessarily mean that He is subjectively
the desire of the nations. But He is objectively, for through Him
alone the nations can be blessed and receive the righteousness
and peace which they need."[7] Raymond Calkins in a more recent
study of the minor prophets says: "From the earliest times, the
passage in verse 7, 'the desire of nations,' has been interpreted to
refer to Christ. The word 'desire' has been personified by the early
church fathers and even by Luther himself. Correctly translated
in the plural, 'the desirable or costly things of the nations,' it
loses little of its Messianic meaning. One is reminded of the
glorious passage in Isaiah 60:9-11."[8] And Feinberg declares,
"From earliest days the majority of Christian interpreters followed the Jewish tradition in referring the passage to the coming
of Israel's Messiah. It seems clear to these interpreters that the
longing all nations have in common must be their yearning for
the Deliverer. . . . Moreover, in Hebrew an abstract noun is often
used instead of a concrete; thus a reference to the Messiah is not
automatically ruled out on the basis of language considerations.
The use of a plural verb does not militate against the Messianic
interpretation, for there are instances in which the verb agrees
with the second of the two nouns."[9]

"And I will fill this house with glory saith the LORD of hosts"
(Hag 2:7b). Again there is much variety of interpretation. Some
explain the glory here spoken of as the Shekinah glory. A general view is that the prophecy points to our Lord's coming to the
temple at His first advent. And that is surely within the scope of
the words. But once more the larger meaning must be included;
as in the case of verse 6, for the final fulfillment we must look
forward to the second coming and the establishment of the
kingdom.

The designation of the temple as "this house" is not to be
applied merely to the temple the colonists were rebuilding.
God's house in Jerusalem was built and destroyed, then rebuilt

and destroyed; and it will, according to prophecy, be rebuilt once more during the kingdom. The last eight chapters of Ezekiel are mostly occupied with this millennial temple and its services. But whatever the outward form of the house, it is in the Lord's sight the one temple and the one earthly center of His worship. "The true glory of the temple lay in what it was—'My house'—not in what it was like."[10]

"The silver is mine, and the gold is mine, saith the LORD of hosts" (Hag 2:8). Here Haggai injects into his splendid Messianic prediction a comforting word of assurance, a word the remnant could seize upon as their very own. He reminds them that the Lord is the possessor of all riches. Therefore, He to whom the silver and the gold ultimately belong is able fully to take care of the needs of His work. It is foolish, then, to let concern for material things trouble us, when we have a God of such infinite resources.

"The glory of this latter house shall be greater than of the former, saith the LORD of hosts: and in this place will I give peace, saith the LORD of hosts" (Hag 2:9). The correct reading is not "the glory of this latter house" but "the latter glory of this house shall be greater than the former." The verse does not relate to the splendor of the different temples but rather to the glory that Messiah (Christ) would bring to the temple (for the various temples are, as we have seen, one before God) at His first and second advents.

How beautifully the final thought of Haggai's Messianic prediction fits our troubled age! "And in this place will I give peace, saith the LORD of hosts." We are indeed living in a time when nations are being shaken and world events are taking on an apocalyptic aspect. The Holy Land and Jerusalem itself continue to be the scene of strife and bloodshed. Peace seems far distant. But the Word of God assures us that the wrath of man is not everlasting. It tells us that, although God does not measure time as does man, "the little while" will one day be over. The King will return to His temple, troubled humanity will at last experience worldwide, universal peace—not through any dictator or balance of power maintained by human might but through the reign of the Prince of Peace Himself.

3

THE CONTAGIOUSNESS OF SIN

THE DATE

> In the four and twentieth day of the ninth month, in the
> second year of Darius, came the word of the LORD by Haggai
> the prophet, saying (Hag 2:10).

Exactly three months from the time when the colonists had
resumed the construction of the temple (1:15) and approximately two months after the second message (2:1), Haggai
spoke again. The date was the twenty-fourth of the ninth month,
called "Chislev" by the Hebrews. This month covers the latter
half of November and the first half of December. It was the time
"when the sowing of the winter crops that commenced after the
feast of the tabernacles was finished and the autumnal (early)
rain had set in, so that in the abundant fall of this rain they
might discern a trace of the divine blessing."[1]

THE MESSAGE

> Thus saith the LORD of hosts; Ask now the priests concerning
> the law, saying, If one bear holy flesh in the skirt of his garment,
> and with his skirt do touch bread, or pottage, or wine, or oil, or
> any meat, shall it be holy? And the priests answered and said,
> No. Then said Haggai, If one that is unclean by a dead body
> touch any of these, shall it be unclean? And the priests answered
> and said, It shall be unclean (Hag 2:11-13).

The third message of the prophet is different from his other
utterances. In fact, its form is highly original. Rather than continuing in the hortatory mood of his first two messages, Haggai
turns to a unique illustration based on asking questions of the

priests. In a time when the asking and answering of questions is a popular diversion, we can understand the method Haggai now uses. Radio and television quizzes, public forums, panel discussions, and also public opinion polls are an accepted part of modern life. And Haggai conducts, as it were, a quiz or a panel discussion with the priests at Jerusalem. In this there is a fine sense of realism,* as the prophet draws out a vital spiritual principle from the ceremonial law.

The priests questioned

"Thus saith the LORD of hosts: Ask now the priests concerning the law, saying, If one bear holy flesh in the skirt of his garment, and with his skirt do touch bread, or pottage, or wine, or oil, or any meat, shall it be holy? And the priests answered and said, No" (Hag 2:11-12). It is actually a *torah* for which Haggai is asking the priests. This Hebrew word means an "*oral direction* given by the priests to the laity, in accordance with the traditional body of principles and usages on (principally) points of ceremonial duty: in process of time the term came further to denote *a body of technical direction* (or 'law') on a given subject. . . ."[2] It is plain, therefore, that Haggai is requesting an authoritative deliverance regarding a point of the Mosaic law. What this particular point was is clear from the twelfth verse. It had to do with the transfer of sanctity. The relevant Old Testament passages are Leviticus 22:4-6; Numbers 19:11. Putting Haggai's question in contemporary language, we have something like this: "Suppose a man carries in a fold of his clothing a portion of an animal used in sacrifice to the Lord and suppose the fold of clothing brushes against bread, or cooked cereal, or wine, oil, or any other food stuff, shall the food touched by the clothing that is in direct contact with meat sacrificed to the Lord be therefore made holy?" To this question the priests answered no. That was undoubtedly the right answer. The Mosaic law definitely teaches that holiness is not so easily transferred. While

---

*Cf. Gordon Pratt Baker, *The Witness of the Prophets*, pp. 106-7, for a good comment on Haggai's realism in this respect.

the garment in which the sanctified meat was held might be considered as holy, it had no power to transfer its sanctified character to everything it touched. In other words, *Holiness is not transferable from person to person; it is an individual matter.*

But Haggai is not finished with the priests. He immediately follows this question with another. "If one that is unclean by a dead body touch any of these," he continues, "shall it be unclean?" The underlying query is the same as for the first question the prophet asked. Only now it is the opposite principle that is in view. According to Old Testament law, contact with a dead body incurred a high degree of contamination. So the prophet was really asking about the contagiousness of evil. Again the answer of the priests came promptly, as they said, "It shall be unclean." And again they were perfectly right. The law was very explicit about defilement by a dead body. Whereas holy food, even that which had been sacrificed to the Lord, could not communicate sanctity, defilement had a much wider outreach. That is to say, *Evil is more catching than good.*

Putting the two questions together, we begin to see what the prophet was aiming at. The truth he had drawn out of the priests was undeniable. In setting forth this second principle, Haggai performed the great service of bringing into focus a misunderstood yet vital moral law. For it is a fact of the moral order that human nature is so constituted that goodness is far less communicable than wickedness.

There are educators and parents who overlook this fact. "Just put youth," they say, "in a good atmosphere and the influence of good associations will make them good." So they fall back on the adage, "Religion is caught, not taught." True, a good example is by no means devoid of power, nor would any sensible person deny the essentiality of good influences. But these are not enough. Silent influence and unspoken example are not sufficient to pass on the salvation that alone frees from sin. It takes some kind of specific communication of the gospel, backed, to be sure, by example, to do that,† and the proclamation of the

---

†This, of course, is the norm. But the power of the Holy Spirit to bring men to the knowledge of Christ in exceptional circumstances without human communication should not be forgotten.

gospel that leads to salvation must be empowered by the Holy
Spirit. Far different is it with evil. Doubtless because of the old
fallen nature, evil is highly contagious. Therefore, while one
man's good example cannot save another, one man's evil influence can lead to the damnation of his brother. Somewhere in his
writings Samuel Taylor Coleridge speaks of the terrible repro-
ductive power of sin. Evil is not only contaminating but also
highly contagious. Moreover, to be realistic, we must recognize
that Christians are no exception to this rule. It is possible for a
believer to do great harm by the force of a bad example.

The application

> Then answered Haggai, and said, So is this people, and so is
> this nation before me, saith the LORD; and so is every work of
> their hands; and that which they offer there is unclean. And
> now, I pray you, consider from this day and upward, from
> before a stone was laid upon a stone in the temple of the LORD.
> Since those days were, when one came to a heap of twenty
> measures, there were but ten; when one came to the pressfat for
> to draw out fifty vessels of the press, there were but twenty. I
> smote you with blasting and with mildew and with hail in all
> the labours of your hands; yet ye turned not to me, saith the
> LORD. Consider now from this day and upward, from the four
> and twentieth day of the ninth month, even from the day that
> the foundation of the LORD's temple was laid, consider it. Is the
> seed yet in the barn? Yea, as yet the vine, and the fig tree, and
> the pomegranate, and olive tree hath not brought forth; from
> this day will I bless you (Hag 2:14-19).

The prophet now turns to the immediate application of the
strange dialogue with the priests, as he gives the people the
Lord's word regarding it: "So is this people, and so is this nation
before me, saith the LORD; and so is every work of their hands;
and that which they offer there is unclean" (Hag 2:14). Once
more there is the undertone of divine contempt ("this people,"
cf. 1:2). In the case of the remnant, there had been a dead thing
among them. Their procrastination had contaminated them.
Years of failure to put God first, years of devotion to selfish
interests, were not easily set aside. Even though the remnant

were now at work rebuilding the temple, the consequences of the years when they had allowed high purpose to die within them and selfishness to reign were being felt. Therefore, the prophet challenges them to look back ("upward" in v. 15 has the meaning of "backward"). He shows that, over the months between the resumption of the building and his present message, lack of blessing in harvest through destructive weather and poor crops was persisting. The colonists were still paying the price for their procrastination.

What had happened was that the people were confusing their work on the temple with the sanctification that comes only from the Lord. They had yet to learn that righteousness is not communicated by what men do but that it is a thing of the heart and that God desires for His work those who are clean in heart. As Calvin says in relation to this passage in Haggai: "As soon as any very wicked person has performed one or another of the duties of the law, he does not doubt that it will be accounted to him as righteousness; but the Lord proclaims that no sanctification can be acquired from this action unless the heart has first been well cleansed."[3] So the remnant, although doing a good thing in resuming their building, are to understand that full blessing comes only to those whose hearts are right.

Yet the passage ends on a note of hope. "Is the seed yet in the barn? Yea, as yet the vine, and the fig tree, and the pomegranate, and the olive tree, hath not brought forth: from this day will I bless you" (Hag 2:19). Although destructive weather and scanty crops had accompanied the resumption of building the temple, these judgments were not to persist indefinitely. Now that the people were showing renewed obedience to Him, the Lord encouraged them with a special promise: "From this day will I bless you." With this hopeful word the prophet ends his third message, so penetrating in its analysis of good and evil.

4

ZERUBBABEL THE SIGNET

The Fourth Message: Zerubbabel the Signet (2:20-23)

THE DATE

> And again the word of the LORD came unto Haggai in the four and twentieth day of the month, saying (Hag 2:20).

On the same day in which the prophet had questioned the priests, God spoke to him a second time. As the introduction to this last discourse reads, "Again the word of the LORD came unto Haggai."

It was a notable day, that twenty-fourth of Chislev (November-December) in the second year of Darius, because in it Haggai delivered to the remnant two memorable communications. If the first of these, contrasting the transfer of good with the contagiousness of evil is unique, the second brings the whole prophecy to a climax.

THE MESSAGE

> Speak to Zerubbabel, governor of Judah, saying, I will shake the heavens and the earth; and I will overthrow the throne of kingdoms, and I will destroy the strength of the kingdoms of the [nations] and I will overthrow the chariots, and those that ride in them; and the horses and their riders shall come down, every one by the sword of his brother. In that day, saith the LORD of hosts, will I take thee, O Zerubbabel, my servant, the son of Shealtiel, saith the LORD, and will make thee as a signet: for I have chosen thee, saith the LORD of hosts (Hag 2:21-23).

Here the prophet is reverting to a thought he has already expressed. The declaration "I will shake the heavens and the

earth" recalls the prediction recorded earlier in this chapter: "Yet
once, it is a little while, and I will shake the heavens, and the
earth, and the sea, and the dry land; and I will shake all nations,
and the desire of all nations shall come" (Hag 2:6-7). Now,
however, the great upheaval is linked not just to the temple, as
in the second message, but to the overthrow of human power
prior to the manifestation of the Messiah.

Unlike the first two messages, which are addressed both to
Zerubbabel the governor of Judah and to Joshua the high priest,
this one is directed to Zerubbabel alone. As the text puts it,
"Speak to Zerubbabel, governor of Judah" (2:21), and, "In that
day, saith the LORD of hosts, will I take thee, O Zerubbabel, my
servant" (2:23). What, then, is the prophet telling Zerubbabel?
The answer is that, few though the words of the message are,
they convey two great ideas. In the first place, they announce
divine judgment of such irresistible force as not only to shake the
physical world but also to overthrow human governments and
their material might. This time of universal judgment is set
forth in verses 21 and 22. In the second place, a great mission is
assigned Zerubbabel, for he is to be nothing less than the "signet" of the Lord of hosts. And he is to be such because he has
been expressly chosen for this office (v. 23).

The interpretation of Bible prophecy is not an easy task.
There is, for example, the hazard of unimaginative literalism.
This is not peculiar to fundamentalists, as some would insist; on
the contrary, a certain type of interpretation is so preoccupied
with the historical background of the text (which must indeed
be taken seriously) that it fails to see the wider outreach of
Scripture. Now the passage before us illustrates the need for
combining a proper historical sense with insight that looks further
than the textual meaning, essential though that is. Addressed to
the governor of the small and (as measured against the world
powers of 520 B.C.) weak colonists of Judah, it sees the strength
of earthly kingdoms in terms of chariots, riders, horses, and
swords. And it uses as the climactic symbol of the book the
figure of the "signet," a symbol hardly familiar to the modern
mind.

Some scholars, of whom Wellhausen is representative, have

interpreted this last message to mean that Zerubbabel is designated as the Messiah promised by the former prophets.[1] But such undiscerning literalism will not do. It discredits Haggai by making him predict a false Deliverer, and it overlooks the great river of Messianic prophecy into which this final discourse flows. While the Bible is not properly interpreted merely by marshaling authorities, it must be admitted that the weight of exegesis is overwhelmingly on the side of the full Messianic meaning of this passage. Whether it is a rabbinical scholar like Abarbanel, as quoted by Pusey, or a conservative Anglican scholar such as Pusey himself,[2] a critical one like Driver,[*] a Plymouth Brother like Kelly,[†] or such contemporary writers on the minor prophets as Calkins[3] and Wolff,[4] most expositors agree regarding the clear Messianic import of Haggai's closing words.

The overthrow of earthly power

The end of verse 21 and the whole of verse 22 ring with power. In these sentences, Haggai sounds with stirring conviction a note becoming ever more audible amid the confusion of world affairs today. It is the note of impending judgment, signaling the fall of human might under divine judgment.

"But by what right may we expect," someone asks, "the actual realization of this universal shaking and destruction?" Well, there was a time when man fancied that, as Peter wrote in answering the scoffers of his time, "all things continue as they were from the beginning of the creation" (2 Pe 3:4). For in that time, and it continued until this century, the indestructibility of matter and the immutability of all things were seldom questioned. Moreover, great confidence was placed in the might of nations and their armaments. It is not surprising that, with such presuppositions, many found it difficult to take seriously the portions of

---

[*]"The Messianic aspirations which attached formerly to the Davidic king are transferred by Haggai to Zerubbabel, who becomes, in virtue of the position thus assigned to him, a type of Christ" (S. R. Driver, cited in E. P. Pusey, *The Minor Prophets*, 2:169).

[†]"The throne of David should be established by the gracious power of Jehovah on the judgment of the Gentile Kingdoms. . . . Zerubbabel, though but Governor, is clearly the type of Christ as King" (W. Kelly, *Lectures Introductory to the Minor Prophets*, p. 430).

Scripture that so plainly teach that all human power, and even this physical earth, is to be overthrown. But the time of such implicit reliance upon either the uniformity of the physical world or upon human power has passed. If man, by his own misuse of atomic fission, may destroy civilization, then how can the actual fulfillment of Haggai's word about the shaking of the physical world and the overturning of human government be thought incredible?

Granted that the predicament of the world is such as to ultimately demand divine intervention, there are apparently two possibilities. Either God will destroy the present order and bring out of it a new creation, or He will work through gradual improvement. The present moral and spiritual state of the world makes the former alternative seem the more probable. But those for whom Scripture is authoritative need not depend upon probabilities. The Bible clearly says that God is going to intervene drastically and even catastrophically in this world order. Not only the Old Testament prophets, both major and minor, but also Christ and the apostolic writers unite in declaring that judgment is in store for mankind. This judgment, beginning with the overthrow of human power, will culminate in the purging of the earth by fire to be followed by the new heavens and the new earth (2 Pe 3:10-13).

It is the initial part of this protracted time of judgment spoken of in both Old and New Testaments as "the day of the Lord" that is in view in Haggai's final message: "I will shake . . . I will overthrow . . . I will destroy . . . I will overthrow" (2:21-22). Clearly these are the declarations of a divine ruler whose judgment is certain and whose power irresistible.

As always when the future aspect of prophecy comes to the fore, the question arises, "When?" Apparently the prophet himself thought of the "shaking" of which he was speaking as being near. And, in a preliminary sense, significant political changes were at hand back there in the sixth century before Christ. Nor can anyone tell the extent to which Haggai felt Zerubbabel to be the fulfillment of this prophecy. Looking back, we can see that it was only in his representative position as a scion of the house of David that Zerubbabel typified the Messiah. Actually, we are still looking forward to the full realization of the prediction. But as to the definite time of the ultimate fulfillment, it is not only futile but absolutely wrong to manipulate the study of prophecy so as to set a date for the day of the Lord.

Consider an illustration. In preparing a bibliography for publication, a writer takes pains to ascertain the publication date of the books on his list. Occasionally, however, a book is published without bearing a date. In a scholarly bibliography, such volumes are listed with the two letters *n.d.* (no date) in place of the year of publication. The abbreviation applies also to the fulfillment of prophecy. Scripture speaks definitely about the future. But it encourages no one to set dates. Quite the contrary, our Lord Himself warned against this in the familiar words: "But of that day and hour knoweth no man, no, not the angels of heaven, but my Father only" (Mt 24:36). Again, just before He ascended, He said to the disciples who were with Him, "It is not for you to know the time or the seasons which the Father hath put in his own power" (Ac 1:7).

Now if it is true that no man can fully accept the authority of Scripture without believing that Christ is coming again according to the many prophecies of His return, it is equally true that no man can set dates for that coming without calling in question the authority of Scripture, which expressly forbids such a practice. Moreover, we are warned against attempting to narrow down the future to "times and seasons" (Ac 1:7). Yet it must be admitted that some Bible teachers, while repudiating any actual date-setting, have come perilously close to it by speaking of certain years or groups of years as the probable season of the Lord's return. More than one Christian magazine has carried articles inferring that a particular year might be of decisive prophetic significance. But when it comes to our Lord's return and the last things, *n.d.* remains the only safe principle. Far better to leave speculation and occupy oneself with prayerful and holy living. As Matthew Henry said at the close of a sermon preached in 1703 on a national fast day for England's victory in the war with Spain, "Let rumors of wars drive us to our knees. Pray, pray, and do not prophesy. Spread the matter before God. . . . Patiently wait the issue with a humble submission to the will of God."[5]

Zerubbabel the Signet

> In that day, saith the Lᴏʀᴅ of hosts, will I take thee, O
> Zerubbabel, my servant, the son of Shealtiel, saith the Lᴏʀᴅ,
> and will make thee as a signet: for I have chosen thee, saith the
> Lᴏʀᴅ of hosts (Hag 2:23).

Turning from the destruction of thrones and kingdoms, the
prophet ends by focusing attention upon Zerubbabel. The promise is that Jehovah will make him "as a signet." Here is a great
Messianic symbol. In the ancient world the signet ring had a
wealth of meaning. Monarchs considered their personal seal as
conferring their own authority. Therefore, the possessor of the
king's signet had at his disposal, as it were, the power of the
king himself. As Orelli puts it, "A signet ring . . . is more intimate-
ly associated with the person of the possessor than any other
ornament; it bears his initial and is the token attesting the
genuineness of his utterance."[6] Likewise Pusey says, "The signet
was very precious to its owner, never parted with, or only to
those to whom authority was delegated (as by Paraoh to Joseph,
or by Ahasuerus to Haman and then to Mordecai); through it his
will was expressed."[7] So great is the significance of the signet
that it becomes clear that Zerubbabel could not in himself fulfil
the type. But if we understand that Zerubbabel stands for the
Davidic line, culminating in the Messiah, just as David is spoken
of in prophecy in the larger relationship of His divine Descend-
ant, then the difficulty is resolved.

In Hebrews 1:3 the Son through whom God has spoken "in
these last days" is called "the express image of God." The Greek
word translated "express image" is *charaktēr*, from which we
derive our English word "character." The Greek means "an
impress, reproduction, representation"[8] and the thought of the
writer of Hebrews is that Christ is the exact representation or, to
use Haggai's term, "the signet" or "seal"‡ of the Father. On this
passage Pusey quotes the beautiful comment of St. Cyprian:
"The Son is the Image of God the Father, having His entire and
exact likeness and in His own beauty beaming forth the nature of

---

‡*Charaktér* occurs in the Greek New Testament only in Heb 1:3; the

the Father. In Him too God seals us also to His own likeness, since, being conformed to Christ, we gain the image of God." He follows this with À Lapide's rich exposition of the same truth: "Christ, as the Apostle says, is *the image of the invisible God, the brightness of His Glory and the express Image of His Person*, Who, as the Word and Seal and express Image, seals it on others. Christ is here called a *signet*, as Man, not as God. For it was His Manhood which He took of the flesh and race of Zerubbabel. He is then, in His Manhood, the signet of God; (1) as being hypostatically united with the Son of God; (2) because the Word impressed on His Humanity the likeness of Himself, His knowledge, virtue, holiness, thoughts, words, acts and conversation; (3) because the Man Christ was the seal, i.e., the most evident sign and witness of the attributes of God, His power, justice, wisdom, and especially His exceeding love for man. For, that God might shew this, He willed that His Son should be Incarnate. Christ thus Incarnate is as a seal, in which we see expressed and depicted the love, power, justice, wisdom, etc., of God; (4) because Christ as a seal, attested and certified to us the will of God, His doctrine, law, commands, i.e., those which He promulgated and taught in the Gospel. *No one, St. John saith, hath seen God at any time: the Only-Begotten Son Who is the Image of the Father, He hath declared Him.* Hence God gave to Christ the power of working miracles, that He might confirm His words as by a seal, and demonstrate that they were revealed and enjoined to Him by God, as it is in St. John, *Him hath the Father sealed.*"[9]

Many expositors have noted the reversal in Zerubbabel of the judgment announced to his grandfather, Jehoiachin (Coniah, or Jeconiah), "As I live, saith the LORD, though Coniah the son of Jehoiakim king of Judah were the signet upon my right hand, yet would I pluck thee thence" (Jer 22:24-30); for the judgment was turned about and Zerubbabel and his descendants became the line through which the Messianic promise to David was carried on.[10] That Zerubbabel is named in both New Testament

regular Greek word for "seal" or "signet" is *sphragis* (used in the Septuagint of Hag 2:23). But it is *charaktēr* that affords the fuller insight into the Messianic implications of the mention of Zerubbabel "as a signet."

genealogies of Christ (Mt 1:12; Lk 3:27) proves his place in the royal line that guaranteed our Lord's title to the Davidic throne. Although Zerubbabel was in his day "the honored and trusted vicegerent of Jehovah"[11] the promise of his being the signet awaits complete fulfillment in Christ's return as God's divine Vicegerent, King of kings and Lord of lords.

"For I have chosen thee, saith the LORD of hosts." Great as is the honor ascribed to Zerubbabel, he is finally reminded that it is not of himself but only through God's election that he has been designated a type of the Messiah.

No Christian has the princely distinction of standing in the line of the coming Deliverer. Nevertheless, we too are chosen. We are chosen by God as recipients of the gracious salvation purchased by the Lord Jesus Christ. Again, we are chosen to make Him known and to point others to the cross and resurrection by which He accomplished mankind's redemption and thence to point them to His coming reign. In all this, as in every blessing He has given us, the initiating cause is not our merit, nor human choice, nor our faith; it is solely God's sovereign election. Humility and thanksgiving, therefore, should mark the attitude of all who have been redeemed by the Lord, to whom, through Zerubbabel as the signet, Haggai has directed our thoughts.

What, finally, is the relation of this fourth discourse, so strongly Messianic in its import, to the book as a whole? Though that relation is not specifically indicated, it is implicit in the logical progress of Haggai's messages. It may be stated like this: In pointing toward the day of the Lord and to the coming Messiah, the prophet is relating God's work in his own day as well as in everyday life to the great consummation of all things. For the service of God is never an isolated event; whenever and wherever done, it always stands in relation to something else. It is part of the stream of history. As it flows through the lives of God's children, this stream takes on eternal significance. Though the end of all things is distant from what we do, let alone from what the colonists did in Jerusalem long ago, the use we make of our lives is related to it. Thus every Christian has his part in preparation for Him who is "the Signet"—"the express image"—of the Father.

5

PRINCIPLES FOR SERVING GOD

That the Bible must be read in the light of its historical setting is a basic principle of interpretation. But it has an important corollary. Because the Bible differs from all other writings in that it is the inspired Word of God and thus a living book, to read and study it in the light of its historical setting, though necessary, is not enough. God's Word speaks to every generation and to every age.

This aspect of our prophet's message is well expressed by Calkins, who calls attention to "the singular relevancy of Haggai's teaching to the problems of our modern world" and points out that he "speaks to us as well as to his own countrymen in stern rebuke for neglecting to build religion into the structure of society, a neglect which is the cause of all our woes. His message, word for word, can be spoken to men today. . . . How modern it all sounds! Is there nothing in this stinging indictment for us in this day to think over? Haggai's preaching may have been in prose, but it was inspired prose."[1]

Outwardly and locally, the ministry of Haggai centered around a single theme, the temple and its rebuilding. Inwardly and universally, the implications of his message find their lasting value in their application to the Lord's work—anywhere, anytime. Each of his four messages, dealing so realistically with the problems of the remnant in their task of rebuilding the razed temple, encompasses principles of permanent worth in doing the work of the Lord. Let us look at them once more. To bring them together in restatement may serve the double purpose of fixing them more firmly in mind and renewing commitment to the work God has given us to do.

What, then, is Haggai saying to Christians today? These four things constitute the basis of his message; these are his principles for serving the Lord:

1. *The Lord's work takes priority over every other obligation.* God's call is urgent; procrastination in responding may mean loss of blessing and even judgment. The Lord's work must come first, and the time to do it is the present. For God speaks through the everyday duties of life.

2. *Those who obey God and work, trusting in His abiding presence, are kept from discouragement.* Measuring spiritual progress by material standards is dangerous; but courageous persistence in service, relying upon the divine promises, brings the encouragement of the Lord's own presence.

3. *The Lord's work demands clean instruments, separated from sin.* Evil is more contagious than good. But when men, repenting of their sin and forsaking it, once more set their hands to the Lord's work, former failure will cease to hinder and blessing will follow.

4. *The Lord's work, believingly carried on, is linked to His sovereign plan for men and nations.* The faithful servants of God have before them a glorious future. Despite the failure of men, universal victory through Christ and His kingdom is certain.

These are some enduring lessons from this most practical of the prophets. Nor does the fact that Haggai deals with such a bricks-and-mortar matter as getting people to finish a building program mean that his message is not important. As George Adam Smith put it, "The meagreness of his words and their crabbed style, his occupation with the construction of the Temple, his unfulfilled hope in Zerubbabel, his silence on the inheritance of truth delivered by his predecessors, and the absence from his prophesying of visions of God's character and of emphasis upon the ethical elements of religion, have moved some to depress his value as a prophet almost to the vanishing point. Nothing could be more unjust. In his opening message Haggai evinced the first indispensable power of the prophet: to speak to the situation of the moment, and to succeed in getting men to take up the duty at their feet; in another message he announced a great ethical principle; in his last he conserved the Messianic traditions of his religion."[2]

Those who doubt the relevance of Haggai's exhortations to our times are undiscerning indeed. After all, the predicament in which modern civilization now finds itself results in good part from preoccupation with secular things to the forgetfulness of God and His Christ. Proud in their technological and scientific advance, men have lavished labor upon their "cieled houses" of material progress, but have neglected the up-building of that spiritual house which is the church of the living God. And Haggai, from his vantage point of exhortation nearly twenty-five hundred years ago, calls us back to an older and higher scale of values.

"Consider," he insists, "consider your ways." Not once, nor twice, but five times in his little book he urges his readers to do this essential thing. As has already been pointed out (cf. comment on Hag 1:5), the Hebrew for "consider" has the meaning of "set your heart to." For a suggestion about how to do this, we may look* at our English word *consider*. Coming from the Latin *con* meaning "with," and *sidus* meaning "star,"[3] it points to a lofty attitude of self-examination.

The creative arts like music, literature, architecture, and painting have an important place in Christian life. But the most creative art of all is the art of living, and to live a true and loving Christian life is an accomplishment of lasting worth. Such an accomplishment demands the foundation of one's life upon Christ the Rock and its self-judgment in the light of His perfect standard. Therefore, the believer is obligated to "set his heart" to his ways under "the true light, which lighteth every man that cometh into the world" (Jn 1:9). So the author of Hebrews writes, "Wherefore, holy brethren, partakers of the heavenly calling, consider the Apostle and High Priest of our profession, Christ Jesus" (Heb 3:1). And in the last chapter of the Bible we

---

*Not by way of exegesis of the original, which is not done at second hand, but as a sidelight upon our obligation to view our lives as in the sight of the Lord.

read the words of the risen Lord, "I am the root and offspring of David, and the bright and morning star" (Rev 22:16).

The people of God today have no central place of worship such as that which Haggai encouraged the remnant to complete. The temple in Jerusalem, destroyed by Titus in A.D. 70, has never been rebuilt, although prophecy promises its future restoration (Eze 40—48). To be sure, we have our church buildings and, on occasion, ours is the privilege of contributing to their erection. But in a higher and wider sense every Christian without exception takes part in building a spiritual house. In his first epistle, Peter says, "Ye also, as living stones, are built up a spiritual house" (1 Pe 2:5). That spiritual house is the church of our Lord Jesus Christ. It is His body and bride, made up of all the regenerated throughout the ages, and it is built upon the "chief corner stone, elect, precious," that stone which, though "disallowed" by the builders, is now "made the head of the corner" (1 Pe 2:6-7). To it every Christian has his contribution to make. Into its ever enduring structure each of us builds one stone— ourselves and the lives we live for Christ.

It is the great merit of Haggai that his plain and practical message sets forth the essential principles for this kind of temple building. Let each of us, then, make sure that he is a "living stone," a possessor of eternal life through personal faith in the Saviour. "For other foundation can no man lay than that is laid, which is Jesus Christ" (1 Co 3:11).

NOTES

Introduction

1. E. B. Pusey, *The Minor Prophets*, 2:295.
2. W. Drake, cited in *The Bible Commentary*, 6:693. Cf. also *The International Standard Bible Encyclopaedia*, s.v. "Haggai."
3. Pusey, p. 295.
4. *The New International Encyclopaedia*, s.v. "Haggai."
5. C. A. Dinsmore, *The English Bible as Literature*, p. 235.

Chapter 1

1. Cf. *The New Bible Dictionary*, s.v. "Calendar," "Moon."
2. E. B. Pusey, *The Minor Prophets*, 2:299.
3. S. R. Driver, The Century Bible, *The Minor Prophets*, 2:154.
4. W. Emery Barnes, The Cambridge Bible for Schools and Colleges, *Haggai and Zechariah*, p. 4.
5. Cf. Charles L. Feinberg, The Major Messages of the Minor Prophets, *Habakkuk, Zephaniah, Haggai and Malachi*, p. 78.
6. John Rainolds, *The Prophecy of Haggai, Interpreted and Applied in Sermons*, pp. 7, 12.
7. H. K. von Orelli, *The Twelve Minor Prophets*, p. 285.
8. John Calvin, cited in Carl F. Keil, Bible Commentary on the Old Testament, *The Minor Prophets*, p. 179.
9. Samuel R. Driver, The Century Bible, *The Minor Prophets*, 2:156.
10. Orelli, p. 286.

Chapter 2

1. Cf. Aaron Judah Kligerman, *Feasts and Fasts of Israel*, pp. 55-60.
2. E. B. Pusey, *The Minor Prophets*, p. 307.
3. Richard Wolff, *The Book of Haggai*, p. 44.
4. Cf. Carl F. Keil, Bible Commentary on the Old Testament, *The Minor Prophets*, 2:197-98.
5. H. K. von Orelli, *The Twelve Minor Prophets*, p. 294.
6. Keil, p. 193.
7. A. C. Gaebelein, *The Annotated Bible*, 5:257-58.
8. Raymond Calkins, *The Modern Message of the Minor Prophets*, p. 105.
9. C. L. Feinberg in *The Wycliffe Bible Commentary*, p. 893.
10. J. McIlmoyle in *The New Bible Commentary*, p. 746.

CHAPTER 3

1. Carl F. Keil, Bible Commentary on the Old Testament, *The Minor Prophets*, pp. 202-3.
2. S. R. Driver, The Century Bible, *The Minor Prophets*, 2:163.
3. John Calvin, *Institutes of the Christian Religion*, III, xiv. 8.

CHAPTER 4

1. Cf. George L. Robinson, *The Twelve Minor Prophets*, p. 145.
2. E. B. Pusey, *The Minor Prophets*, 2:321.
3. Raymond Calkins, *The Modern Messages of the Minor Prophets*, p. 106.
4. Richard Wolff, *The Book of Haggai*, p. 80.
5. Matthew Henry, cited in Wilbur M. Smith, *This Atomic Age and the Word of God*, p. 264.
6. H. K. von Orelli, *Old Testament Prophecy*, p. 425.
7. Pusey, p. 320.
8. William F. Arndt and F. Wilbur Gingrich, *A Greek-English Lexicon of the New Testament*, p. 884.
9. À. Lapide, cited in Pusey, p. 320.
10. Cf. Wolff, p. 80.
11. Robinson, p. 145.

CHAPTER 5

1. Raymond Calkins, *The Modern Message of the Minor Prophets*, pp. 107-8.
2. George Adam Smith, *The Book of the Twelve Prophets*, 2:147.
3. *A New English Dictionary*, s.v. "Star."

BIBLIOGRAPHY

Albright, William Foxwell. "The Psalm of Habakkuk" in *Studies in Old Testament Prophecy* (Presented to T. H. Robinson). Rowley, H. H., ed. New York: Scribner's, 1950.

Allen, Roy M. *Three Days in the Grave.* New York: Bible Truth Depot, 1942.

Anderson, Sir Robert. "Three Days and Three Nights." *Our Hope,* July, 1932.

Archer, Gleason L., Jr. *A Survey of Old Testament Introduction.* Chicago: Moody, 1964.

Baker, G. P. *The Witness of the Prophets.* New York: Abingdon Cokesbury, 1948.

Banks, William L. *Jonah, The Reluctant Prophet.* Chicago: Moody, 1966.

Barnes, W. Emery. *Haggai.* Cambridge Bible for Schools and Colleges. Cambridge: University Press, 1883.

Baron, David. *Types, Psalms, and Prophecies.* London: Hodder & Stoughton, 1907.

Bewer, Julius A. *Obadiah.* The International Critical Commentary. New York: Scribner's, 1911.

Blanchard, Charles A. *An Old Testament Gospel.* Chicago: Bible Institute Colportage Association, 1918.

Burn, Samuel Clift. *The Prophet Jonah.* London: Hodder & Stoughton, 1880.

Caldecott, W. Shaw. "Jeroboam II." In *The International Standard Bible Encyclopaedia,* vol. 3. Chicago: Howard-Severance, 1930.

Calkins, Raymond. *The Modern Message of the Minor Prophets.* New York: Harper, 1947.

Calvin, John. *Institutes of the Christian Religion.* 2 vols. Translated by Ford Lewis Battles. Edited by John T. McNeill. Philadelphia: Westminster, 1960.

Carlisle, Thomas John. *You! Jonah!* Grand Rapids: Eerdmans, 1968.

Chase, Mary Ellen. *The Bible for the Common Reader.* New York: Macmillan, 1944.

Cheyne, T. K. "Jonah." In *The Encyclopaedia Britannica*, 14th ed. Chicago: Encyclopaedia Britannica, 1932–1938.

Cornill, Carl Heinrich. *The Prophets of Israel*. Translated by Sutton H. Corkran. Chicago: Open Court, 1895.

Davidson, A. B. "Obadiah." In *The Imperial Bible Dictionary*.

Deere, D. W. *The Twelve Speak*. 2 vols. New York: American Press, 1958.

Dinsmore, Charles A. *The English Bible as Literature*. New York: Houghton Mifflin, 1931.

Doughty, Charles M. *Travels in Arabia Deserta*. New York: Random House, n.d.

Douglas, George C. M. *The Six Intermediate Minor Prophets*. Edinburgh: T. & T. Clarke, n.d.

Drake, W. S.v. "Haggai." In *The Bible Commentary*. Edited by F. C. Cook. New York: Scribner's, 1899.

Driver, Samuel R. *Habakkuk and Haggai*. The Century Bible, vol. 2. New York: Oxford, n.d.

Eiselen, F. C. S.v. "Habakkuk." In *The International Standard Bible Encyclopaedia*, vol. 2. Chicago: Howard-Severance, 1930.

Ellison, H. L. *The Prophets of Israel*. Grand Rapids: Eerdmans, 1969.

Farley, C. L. *The Progress of Prophecy*. London: Religious Tract Society, 1925.

Feinberg, C. L. *Habakkuk, Zephaniah, Haggai, and Malachi*. The Major Messages of the Minor Prophets. New York: Am. Bd. of Missions to Jews, 1951.

———. *Joel, Amos, and Obadiah*. The Major Messages of the Minor Prophets. New York: Am. Bd. of Missions to Jews, 1948.

———. *Jonah, Micah, and Nahum*. The Major Messages of the Minor Prophets. New York: Am. Bd. of Missions to Jews, 1951.

———. "Haggai." In *The Wycliffe Bible Commentary*. Chicago: Moody, 1962.

Fosdick, Harry Emerson. *The Modern Use of the Bible*. New York: Macmillan, 1924.

Fowler, A. B. "Haggai." In *Zondervan Pictorial Bible Dictionary*. Grand Rapids: Zondervan, 1963.

Freeman, H. E. *An Introduction to the Old Testament Prophets*. Chicago: Moody, 1968.

Fuerbringer, L. *The Eternal Why*. St. Louis: Concordia, 1957.

Gaebelein, A. C. *The Annotated Bible*, vol. 5. New York: Our Hope, 1916.

Hamilton, Floyd E. *The Basis of Christian Faith.* 3d rev. ed. New York: Harper, 1946.

Herodotus. *Clio.* Translated by H. C. and G. Rawlinson.

Hart-Davies, D. E. *Jonah: Prophet and Patriot.* London: Thynne & Jarvis, 1931.

Heschel, Abraham. *The Prophets.* New York: Harper, 1962.

Heyerdahl, Thor. *Kon-Tiki.* New York: Rand McNally, 1950.

Hill, J. G. *The Prophets in the Light of Today.* New York: Abingdon, 1919.

Horton, R. F. *Obadiah and Jonah.* The Century Bible. New York: Oxford, n.d.

Hutton, John A. *The Persistent Word of God.*

Huxtable, E. *Jonah.* The Bible Commentary. New York: Scribner's, 1899.

Josephus, Flavius. *Antiquities.* New York: Armstrong, 1897.

———. *The Wars of the Jews.* New York: Armstrong, 1897.

Keil, Carl F. *The Minor Prophets.* Bible Commentary on the Old Testament. Edinburgh: Clark, 1873.

Kelly, William. *Lectures Introductory to the Minor Prophets.* London: Rouse, 1906.

Kennedy, John. *On the Book of Jonah.* London: Alexander & Shepheard, 1895.

Kerr, David W. "Haggai." In *The Wycliffe Bible Commentary.* Chicago: Moody, 1962.

Kligerman, A. J. *Feasts and Fasts of Israel.* Baltimore: Immanuel Neighborhood House, 1931.

König, Eduard. "Jonah." In *Hastings Bible Dictionary,* vol. 2. New York: Scribner's, 1907.

Layard, Sir Austen H. *Nineveh and Its Remains.* New York: Putnam, 1849.

———. *Nineveh and Babylon.* London: Murray, 1874.

Livingstone, G. Herbert. "Obadiah and Jonah." In *The Wycliffe Bible Commentary.* Chicago: Moody, 1962.

McIlmoyle, J. "Haggai." In *The New Bible Commentary.* Grand Rapids: Eerdmans, 1953.

Martin, Hugh. *The Prophet Jonah.* London: Strahan, 1866.

Meyrick, F. "Obadiah." In *The Bible Commentary.* New York: Scribner's, 1899.

Miller, Earl A. *Was Jesus Crucified on Good Friday?* Grand Rapids: Miller, 1931.

Mitchell, Stuart. *Jonah the Self-Willed Prophet.* Philadelphia: Claxton, Remsen, & Hoffelfinger, 1875.

Morgan, G. Campbell. *Living Messages of the Books of the Bible,*
vol. 1. New York: Revell, 1911.

———. *The Minor Prophets.* New York: Revell, 1960.

Orelli, H. K. von. *The Twelve Minor Prophets.* Translated by J. S.
Banks. Edinburgh: Clark, 1893.

Ottman, Ford C. *God's Oath.* New York: Our Hope, n.d.

Perowne, T. T. *Obadiah and Jonah.* The Cambridge Bible for Schools
and Colleges. Cambridge: University Press, 1883.

Pike, James A. with Kennedy, Diane. *The Other Side.* Garden City:
Doubleday, 1968.

Pinches, J. A. "Nineveh." In *The International Standard Bible
Encyclopaedia,* vol. 4. Chicago: Howard-Severance, 1930.

Pusey, E. B. *The Minor Prophets,* vol. 2. New York: Funk & Wag-
nalls, 1886.

Rainolds, John. *The Prophecy of Haggai, Interpreted and Applied in
Sermons.* Edinburgh: James Nichol, 1864.

Raleigh, Alexander. *The Story of Jonah.* Edinburgh: Black, 1886.

Redford, R. A. *Studies in the Book of Jonah.* London: publisher 1883.

Robinson, D. W. B. "Jonah." In *The New Bible Commentary.* Grand
Rapids: Eerdmans, 1953.

———. "Obadiah." In *The New Bible Commentary.* Grand Rapids:
Eerdmans, 1953.

Robinson, George L. *The Twelve Minor Prophets.* New York: Doran,
1926.

———. *The Sarcophagus of an Ancient Civilization.* New York: Macmillan, 1930.

Ryrie, C. C. "Perspective on Palestine." *Christianity Today,* May 23,
1969.

Sampey, J. R. "Jonah." In *The International Standard Bible Encyclopaedia,* vol. 4. Chicago: Howard-Severance, 1930.

Scarlett, William. "Jonah" (exposition). In *The Interpreter's Bible,*
vol. 6. New York: Abingdon, 1956.

Schultz, Samuel J. *The Prophets Speak.* New York: Harper & Row,
1968.

Scott, R. B. Y. *The Relevance of the Prophets.* New York: Macmillan,
1968.

Smart, James D. "Jonah" (introduction and exegesis). In *The Interpreter's Bible,* vol. 6. New York: Abingdon, 1956.

Smith, George Adam. *The Twelve Prophets Commonly Called Minor.*
2 vols. Rev. ed. Garden City, N.Y.: Doubleday-Doran, 1929.

Smith, Wilbur M. *This Atomic Age and the Word of God*. Boston: Wilde, 1948.

Speer, Robert E. *The Finality of Jesus Christ*. Grand Rapids: Zondervan, 1968.

Stephens-Hodge, L. E. H. "Habakkuk." In *The New Bible Commentary*. Grand Rapids: Eerdmans, 1953.

Thompson, J. A. "Obadiah." In *The New Bible Dictionary*. Grand Rapids: Eerdmans, 1962.

Torrey, C. C., ed. *Lives of the Prophets*. Philadelphia: Society of Biblical Literature and Exegesis, 1946.

Torrey, R. A. *Difficulties and Alleged Contradictions in the Bible*. New York: Revell, 1907.

Trumbull, H. Clay. "Jonah In Nineveh." In *Journal of Biblical Literature*, 1892.

Unger, Merrill F. S.v. "Habakkuk." In *Unger's Bible Dictionary*. Chicago: Moody, 1957.

———. "Haggai." In *Unger's Bible Dictionary*. Chicago: Moody, 1957.

———. "Jonah." In *Unger's Bible Dictionary*. Chicago: Moody, 1957.

———. "Obadiah." In *Unger's Bible Dictionary*. Chicago: Moody, 1957.

Wade, G. W. *Habakkuk*. Westminster Commentaries. London: Methuen, 1929.

Ward, W. H. *Habakkuk*. The International Critical Commentary. New York: Scribner's, 1911.

Wilson, R. D. S.v. "Zerubbabel." In *The New International Bible Encyclopaedia*, vol. 4. Chicago: Howard-Severance, 1930.

Wiseman, D. J. "Assyria." In *The New Bible Dictionary*. Grand Rapids: Eerdmans, 1962.

Wolff, Richard. *The Book of Haggai*. Grand Rapids: Baker, 1967.

Wurmbrand, Richard and Foley, Charles. *Christ in the Communist Prisons*. Coward-McCann, 1968.

Young, Edward J. *Introduction to the Old Testament*. Grand Rapids: Eerdmans, 1958.